OUR BODIES, OUR DATA

HOW COMPANIES MAKE BILLIONS SELLING OUR MEDICAL RECORDS

ADAM TANNER

Beacon Press
Boston

Beacon Press
Boston, Massachusetts
www.beacon.org

Beacon Press books
are published under the auspices of
the Unitarian Universalist Association of Congregations.

20 19 18 17   8 7 6 5 4 3 2 1

This book is printed on acid-free paper that meets the uncoated paper
ANSI/NISO specifications for permanence as revised in 1992.

Text design and composition by Kim Arney

Library of Congress Cataloging-in-Publication Data
Names: Tanner, Adam, author.
Title: Our bodies, our data : how companies make billions
selling our medical records / Adam Tanner.
Description: Boston : Beacon Press, [2016] |
Includes bibliographical references and index.
Identifiers: LCCN 2016016233 (print) | LCCN 2016017139 (ebook) |
ISBN 9780807033340 (hardcover : alk. paper) | ISBN 9780807033357 (ebook)
Subjects: | MESH: Electronic Health Records | Confidentiality | Data Mining
Classification: LCC R858 (print) | LCC R858 (ebook) | NLM WX 175 |
DDC 610.285—dc23
LC record available at https://lccn.loc.gov/2016016233

To my parents, who, each in their own way,
inspired me to become a writer and to explore
the world's unanswered questions

□   □   □   □   □

CONTENTS

INTRODUCTION

S OON AFTER YOU tell your doctor about an intimate medical problem, data about your condition are sold commercially to companies that have nothing to do with your treatment or billing. The electronic medical record company may sell information about your embarrassing problem that the physician logs into the computer. The lab performing the blood test often sells a copy of the results. The pharmacy receives money for sharing the details of your prescribed medications, as does the insurer covering the cost of your treatment. Middlemen companies connecting pharmacies, doctors, hospitals, and insurance providers receive cash for sharing details about your health conditions. Such digitized details may only be worth a few pennies per transaction, but when repeated billions of times, they become not only big data, but also big business.

For-profit health care data mining companies buy information from all of these sources to assemble a detailed history about you and hundreds of millions of others. Their dossiers omit your name and contact details but list age, gender, and partial ZIP code. Those trafficking in anonymized medical records say their activities will fuel new, important research on vast populations of patients. Privacy advocates say this hidden trade will undermine trust in the health-care system and lead to discrimination and embarrassment.

Paradoxically, the digitization of medical data may not help when we need it most. Imagine that a man collapses during an out-of-town trip. The ambulance team arrives, opens his wallet, and finds a link to his electronic medical records. They call the health record bank and verify that he has authorized the emergency release of information. The team reviews the details and sends a copy to the emergency room physician. The file warns about potential clashes with existing medications and offers insights into the patient's condition. In an era when a few mouse clicks can retrieve obscure documents, such easy access to medical records might seem unexceptional. Yet, for the most part, this scenario remains a hope for the future rather than a present-day reality. Even half a century after pioneers started digitizing health records, a hodgepodge of different systems and providers vexes an individual's ability to assemble a complete medical dossier.

Many people realize that companies we interact with every day, whether that company is Google, Facebook, or Amazon, gather details as we go about our lives. They note what we buy, where we go, what we eat, how we search the Internet, and what we read and watch. Few people realize that a sophisticated system of medical data gathering has evolved into a multibillion-dollar business, constructed from details few of us would share willingly with outside companies. It's not only ordinary folks who remain in the dark about these practices. I've met deans of top US medical schools and public health programs, doctors, pharmacists, and nurses who have no idea how vast this trade has become. A 2014 White House report explained the business in rather understated language: "Personal health information of various kinds is shared with an array of firms, and even sold by state governments, in ways that might not accord with consumer expectations of the privacy of their medical data."[1]

Imagine if priests and pastors, accountants and lawyers all sold anonymized notes about their confidential conversations with parishioners and clients. The aggregated results might provide fascinating insights about what type of people are most likely to sin, cheat on their taxes, or proclaim innocence when guilty of a crime. The insights could prove valuable to moral leaders, tax collectors, and law enforcement. It's easy to imagine the outcry that might ensue if such sales actually took place, for such sharing would undermine the trust essential to those professions. But similar sharing—which US law allows for anonymized medical data—occurs millions of times of day across our health-care system.

In recent years, businesses and researchers have heralded the great promise of *big data*, the staggering quantity of complex, digitalized information that unprecedented computing power can store and analyze. Yet for all the hype, a surge of health-care breakthroughs has yet to arrive. Asked to name the most dramatic discovery resulting from aggregating hundreds of millions of patient histories known as longitudinal data, company executives who trade such information often speak of efficiencies and interesting insights rather than bold breakthroughs. "The reality is that data-driven benefits for health care have still not materially showed up," said Kris Joshi, executive vice president at health-data company Emdeon. "Health care is generating a very, very pitifully small amount of value, given the amount of data there."[2]

The evidence so far suggests that companies I refer to as *medical data miners* have oversold the scientific benefits of their for-profit trade, at least in terms of what has emerged to date.[3] Joshi emphasized that for all of big data's scientific promise, companies typically use this vast trove of information for mundane commercial purposes: "It is being used to market drugs, for example, and it is being used to figure out which doctors prescribe what drugs." Such results raise the question of whether there might be a better way to harness the promise of big data in medicine.

I have spent years researching the dramatic increase in corporate data gathering that takes place without our knowledge or active consent. My previous book, *What Stays in Vegas: The World of Personal Data—Lifeblood of Big Business—and the End of Privacy as We Know It*, recounts how smart, well-intentioned executives across many industries have made the continuous acquisition of information about all of us a central focus of their businesses.[4] Sometimes such practices benefit consumers; often they do not. As in other sectors of the growing data economy, many good, idealistic people are involved in the trade of medical information. Yet nowhere is the potential for negative consequences greater, from the denial of life insurance to medical identity theft, from job rejection to blackmail. Actor Charlie Sheen illustrated the power of medical data to do harm when in 2015 he revealed that he had paid millions of dollars in blackmail money to keep his HIV-positive status secret. As computing grows more powerful, ordinary folks also face greater risks as commercial patient dossiers become increasingly vulnerable to re-identification. This means that even after a name, an address, and other direct links to a person's identity are removed—a process called *de-identification*—outsiders may still be able to puzzle out the real identity of the patient from other clues—a reverse process known as *re-identification*—creating a potential target for theft or exploitation.

To unravel the behind-the-scenes evolution of this system, I have interviewed hundreds of industry insiders to weave together the human stories of the entrepreneurs and their impact on patient lives. I traveled across North America, Europe, and Asia to peel back layers of the inner workings of an industry that fiercely resists revealing itself. The trade involves our most intimate information, yet companies fear that openness about their practices could disrupt the lucrative enterprise. This is a world of visionary executives and idealistic doctors, data scientists, clever salespeople, and beleaguered patients whose intimate medical data are ever more vital to commerce and science—and potentially dangerous to our well-being at the same time. What follows is the story that many in the health-data-mining industry would rather keep to themselves.

CHAPTER 1

□ □ □ □ □

WHAT THE PHARMACY KNOWS

Deborah Peel at the Pharmacy

As she handed her prescription to the pharmacist, Deborah Peel peered over the counter and saw something that instantly raised her hackles. By the late 1990s, few customers would have paid much notice to the blinking lights of a new computer. But Peel, a Freudian psychiatrist sworn to protect her patients' secrets, sensed trouble. She demanded to see the owner.

The Tarrytown Pharmacy in Austin, Texas, seemed like the kind of place that would resist disruptive change. The drugstore, founded in 1941, preserved a sense of community long gone from chain stores, with pharmacists cheerily greeting customers by name and asking about the family.

Throughout her career, Peel has preferred therapy to pills for her patients, but she sometimes prescribes medication for bipolar disorder, depression, withdrawal from addictive substances, or psychosis. She knows that her diagnosis of a mental health problem or substance abuse requiring medication can create discrimination against a patient, even fear or hatred, if others beyond the pharmacy or the doctor's office find out. That's why Peel was upset that day in the pharmacy. A passionate believer in the Hippocratic oath dating back to the fifth-century BC, she worried that computers would facilitate easy sharing without patient consent.

"I don't want my family's records entered into this!" she told Brian Newberry, who had succeeded his father and uncle as owner of the pharmacy.

She demanded to know why they had installed a computer. The question surprised Newberry. A technological revolution was sweeping across health care. Prescriptions and insurance claims required a lot of processing that computers greatly simplified. Plus, a major drug wholesaler, McKesson, had offered him the software for free.

"Our geese are cooked," Peel thought.

She resolved to battle the proliferation of patient data.[1] The strong-willed Texan would take on big pharma and the medical establishment in defending patient privacy in the era of big data.

An Outsider in Psychiatry

A child of the 1950s, Peel grew up in an academic family. Her father, Abraham Charnes, was a prominent expert in applying mathematics to management science. Mother Kathryn, who worked for a time as a home economics teacher, encouraged her daughter to live her life independently. As her professor father changed university jobs, Peel moved from her birthplace in Pittsburgh to West Lafayette, Indiana, then Evanston, Illinois, and finally, in 1968, to Austin, where she lives today.

Exceptionally bright, Peel sped ahead at school. In 1968, after her high school junior year, she enrolled in college at the University of Texas at Austin. From Chicago's 1960s atmosphere of jeans and counterculture, she felt transported back a decade to an alien world of fraternities and sororities, where women wore formal dresses, pantyhose, and gloves to parties. The campus buzzed about the beauty queen who had just dropped out after her junior year to make her mark on Hollywood. Soon the rest of America would be talking about Farah Fawcett as well.

Peel continued to excel academically. Technically dropping out of college as she had from high school, she enrolled in medical school at age eighteen at the University of Texas Medical Branch at Galveston. She was one of just 10 women in her class of 124; eventually she focused on psychiatry. Some fellow students and professors did not welcome female intrusion into their male bastion, long a profession of bearded or mustached men such as Sigmund Freud or Carl Jung. Within medicine, many saw psychiatry as a lesser discipline, an attitude that made her a double outsider.

Working with Freudian psychoanalysts after her residency, Peel learned about the need for absolute privacy when treating repressed, painful conditions; patients would only open up if they felt confident that nothing they told a psychiatrist would go beyond the office walls. Peel started her practice in 1977. Given her training, it came as a surprise when some of her very first patients asked, "If I pay you cash, will you keep my medical records private?"

She began to wonder, How far and wide do medical records and insurance claims travel? Who can access such information, and what do they do with it? Such questions are fundamental to a psychiatrist, who listens to people's innermost feelings: fears about bodies and minds, desperate loneliness, suicidal thoughts, buried rage and hatred, crippling insecurities and envy. The deep bonds forged during as many as five visits a week for years or even decades can turn the psychiatrist into the patient's most trusted confidant.

The lure of a psychiatrist's secrets have inspired Hollywood plots and real-life cloak-and-dagger crime, the most infamous of which occurred when Peel was in medical school. One notorious episode started to take shape over the summer of 1971 as President Richard Nixon and his aides sought to identify who had leaked a damaging secret history of the Vietnam War to the *New York Times* and *Washington Post*. After determining that a former RAND Corporation military analyst, Daniel Ellsberg, gave journalists access to what came to be known as the Pentagon Papers, some of Nixon's aides and loyalists gathered for a secret meeting in a small basement office of the Old Executive Office Building across from the White House. They were angry and they wanted revenge.

With the resources of the world's greatest superpower at their disposal, these men could have recommended an extensive tax audit, a plant of incriminating evidence, or perhaps a public charge that Ellsberg harbored Communist sympathies. Instead, they decided that stealing files from his psychiatrist's office would most damage him. On September 3, 1971, several burglars, acting on the direct authority of the White House, broke into the Beverly Hills office of Lewis Fielding, Ellsberg's psychoanalyst. The plumbers (so called to deter media leaks), led by former CIA agent E. Howard Hunt, went straight for the doctor's gray metal filing cabinet in search of Ellsberg's intimate medical and personal secrets.

They searched the medical records for evidence of drugs or deviant sexual practices, anything to tar the man. "We've got to get this son of a bitch," the president told his attorney general. A Vietnam veteran, Ellsberg had experienced depression and some troubled relationships.[2] Yet the plumbers turned up nothing. The mission failed, marking the start of the downward spiral to the Watergate scandal, which culminated in Nixon's 1974 resignation.

Surveying Pharmacies

Prescriptions written by a psychiatrist can provide significant insights into someone's mental health, which is why the new computer at Deborah

Peel's pharmacy alarmed her. What she did not know, however, was that outsiders had already long been mining patient scripts for commercial insights. As with much about the business of medical data, few people, even health experts, know the story of these pioneering efforts.

In 1947, Ray Gosselin, a graduate pharmacy student researching his thesis, asked Massachusetts drugstores to let him copy their prescription records. The World War II navy combat veteran wanted to estimate the average cost of drugs, determine their most common ingredients, and calculate other statistics.[3] Gosselin enlisted a dozen juniors and seniors at his Massachusetts College of Pharmacy to help. These volunteers fanned off to 92 of the state's 2,142 pharmacies to assemble a representative sample from towns of various sizes and locations. Each volunteer copied details from forty-eight prescriptions at each store, twelve from each of the year's four seasons. Drugstore owners and managers gladly participated and allowed the students to record anything they wished. The researchers could see patient names too, but did not record them.

Gosselin's thesis produced a plethora of numbers and charts, everything from the average prescription cost in 1947 ($1.42) to the percentage of ingredients written in Latin (2.67 percent). He noted frequent misspellings in prescriptions and other errors, including two dangerous overdoses that pharmacists had noticed and corrected before they dispensed the medication.

Pharmaceutical companies learned about Gosselin's study with considerable interest. Until that point, firms struggled to obtain precise sales data on how well their companies stacked up against the competition. They relied on crude proxies, such as sending salespeople to peruse the files of willing pharmacies. Such efforts took a lot of time and were impressionistic at best. A statistical sample of pharmacies from across the state promised far more precise insights. One drugmaker offered Gosselin $2,000—a considerable sum for a graduate student at the time—to detail his data insights in a report.

Gosselin repeated the Massachusetts survey in 1948 and 1950, expanding to ninety-five drugstores, 5 percent of the state's total. In 1952, he started a business to conduct bimonthly nationwide pharmacy surveys he called the National Prescription Audit. Borrowing $4,000 from his mother-in-law, Gosselin and his wife, Chris, set up in a basement office in Boston. Initially, he focused on fifteen cities and two hundred pharmacies; over the years, he expanded to four hundred, then eight hundred, and eventually even more.[4]

For some years, the firm relied on eager university students in different parts of the country to visit pharmacies and record data by hand. Gosselin eventually started compensating workers five cents for each prescription they had gathered; later he paid drugstores a nominal amount to mail in their data directly. In 1959, Gosselin expanded his information gathering to doctors' offices as well. He asked physicians to share details about their prescription writing so he could generalize which specialties generated what drug sales, according to a physician's age, university degree, and other categories.

Many years later, the pharmacy computer that incensed Peel allowed outsiders to expand and automate the collection of health information in ways pioneers such as Gosselin never anticipated. Peel's instinct that day in her local pharmacy was spot-on. Computers were facilitating a commercial scramble for medical data, with considerable rewards for those who could figure out how to best mine the system. This burgeoning trade fueled a drive for even more information and eventually turned a patient's most intimate secrets into a commodity for sale.

□ □ □ □ □

CHAPTER 2

DATA BONANZA FOR PHARMACIES AND MIDDLEMEN

The Eureka Moment

The rapid sweep of computerization in the 1980s and 1990s represented a great commercial opportunity for health-care companies. Government regulations and insurance claims required a staggering amount of paperwork, but digitization greatly simplified the process. What's more, logging all this information onto machines produced a valuable by-product that others would buy. Just like lumber mills selling wood chips to particle-board manufacturers, pharmacies and various health-care middlemen could now profit from data they were producing anyway. If they were lucky, they might sell their by-product multiple times to different companies.

The new health-data merchants that created a market in such information did not seek to disrupt medicine or undermine patient privacy. They just wanted to seize new profit opportunities by helping drug companies market their medications. It was all very exciting to executives who saw big dollar signs in the zeros and ones of digitized data.

"Holy shit, we are getting tons of data in real time!" Fritz Krieger thought, after Cardinal Health, one of the nation's largest drug wholesalers, hired him in 1998 to create a business to profit from all the information the company processed.

Little known to the public, Cardinal stood at an important crossroads of health care and was a major American business in its own right. In the late 1990s, it sat 145th on the *Fortune* 500 list, with more than $11 billion in annual sales. In addition to supplying pharmacies with drugs, Cardinal could also monitor drugstore transitions through its service that helped pharmacists receive the maximum reimbursement when customers used insurance cards to pay for prescriptions.[1] In the split second it takes to process the data, Cardinal's ScriptLINE received a digital copy of every transaction. The company could read the pulse of the pharmacy business every minute of the day.

Cardinal executives soon decided that Krieger should not only start a new data business, but also run ScriptLINE, which had lost $3 million in the year since its formation. One Thursday, his boss gave him until the end of 1998 to make ScriptLINE profitable or shut it down. As Krieger drove home on his three-and-a half-hour weekly commute back to his family in Detroit the following evening, he pondered what to do next.

A flash of inspiration hit him. He became so excited that he pulled his Ford Expedition to the side of the four-lane highway to think clearly. A company founded in the mid-1950s, IMS Health, had long dominated medical data mining after acquiring many of its rivals, taking into the fold top experts such as pharmacy survey pioneer Ray Gosselin. Yet IMS—which billed itself as the "world's leading provider of information solutions to the pharmaceutical and healthcare industries"—took too long to compile its reports, which detailed how well different drugs sold. Krieger thought this delay of many weeks could represent an Achilles' heel. He would build a new company—soon to be christened ArcLight— offering drugmakers up-to-the-minute market-share data. Not only would he use ScriptLINE information, but he would also seek to convince pharmacy chains—with which Cardinal had close ties as a major wholesale supplier—to sell information about their transactions.

Challenging IMS in health-care data was akin to taking on Coke by introducing a new cola. But Krieger felt energized by the possibility of a David-and-Goliath fight. He started his search for more data by approaching two executives at CVS. The pharmacy chain was already selling information to IMS, but Krieger told it that the market leader was "screwing" the chain by not paying enough. The executives were impressed by his vision but responded that CVS received $4 million a year and that as part of the agreement, CVS agreed not to sell data to anyone else for less. Although Cardinal Health enjoyed a profit of $181 million in 1997, an expenditure of $4 million just for data from one drugstore chain, albeit a major one, was too risky and expensive. Krieger visited Cardinal's CEO, Bob Walter, to seek his advice.

"Why don't we just make them partners?" Walter suggested. He was talking about the big pharmacy chains.

That simple idea could represent a substantial threat to IMS. Clever tactics and aggressive pricing made it hard for newcomers to challenge the largest data miner, but if drugstores had a stake in ArcLight, they might decide to withhold data from IMS and undermine its dominance. Lured by the promise of an ownership stake, CVS signed up, as did Kmart and others. Walmart had stopped sharing data with IMS in the late 1990s because it had learned that competitors could deduce individual store revenue numbers from IMS reports. The retailer liked ArcLight's upstart approach and signed up as well.

Soon, ArcLight was gathering information on 60 percent of all pharmacy sales in the United States. Capable, motivated executives were doing exactly what their companies wanted them to do, expanding the new, potentially very profitable trade in data. Few pondered the impact on the source of all this information—individual patients—as businesses continued to expand the collection of ever more personal data.

Digitizing Pharmacies

ArcLight, IMS, and other data miners could easily obtain copies of a significant percentage of US prescriptions because of pioneering work dating back to the early 1970s. That's when people such as Denny Briley, a University of Kentucky Medical Center doctoral student, started programming computers for hospital pharmacies. His hospital invested around $500,000 dollars—worth five times as much in today's inflation-adjusted dollars—in a program to prevent patients from getting multiple prescriptions for the same drug and to alert pharmacists against filling prescriptions that might cause adverse interaction with other medications. "It transformed pharmacy," Briley said. "The big thing that computerization of the pharmacy system did was it changed the whole realm of checking for patient safety."

In these early days of computers, the hope was to improve patient outcomes, not to bolster anyone's bottom line. Yet businesses quickly realized that storehouses of patient information could give them a competitive edge, so commercial drugstores followed the early efforts by Briley and others. In 1981, the same year IBM introduced its home PC, five branches of the Walgreens chain in Des Moines, Iowa, installed satellite-linked computers. The connectivity allowed patients to get refills at any of the five branches. By 1997, Walgreens had connected all of its stores nationwide.[2] "It's the system of the future caring for you today," Walgreens advertised in newspapers. One late 1980s TV spot showed smiling, linked cartoon computers. "Walgreens has a network of friendly computers," the narrator declared.

Digitization also enabled data miners to follow pharmacy sales much more precisely than ever before, one prescription at a time. "What we were trying to do in the 1970s," said Dennis Turner, a former president of IMS America, "is get the industry data on medical practices. But we could only do it in a very crude way by actually collecting information from pharmacies and wholesalers on sales, not on prescriptions."

By 1986, about two-thirds of pharmacies had started using some form of computers to manage dispensing and patient records, Turner said. The digitization gives data miners an easy way to buy copies of prescriptions and gives marketers important insights not only about what the drugstores are stocking, but about what they actually dispense and at what pace. Jeremy Allen, the CEO of IMS America from 1987 to 1991, explained that such information was especially important to understand whether new drugs would become big sellers: "For a new product launch, for example, everyone purchases it to get it in stock. But unless you know what is leaving the pharmacy, it is not of much value to you."

Early technology adopters such as Thomas Menighan were among the first to cash in on the new secondary market in pharmacy data. In 1978, he opened a Medicine Shoppe franchise in Huntington, West Virginia. Shortly thereafter, he was growing frustrated by all the time he spent manually filling out insurance claims on customer orders. He installed a computer the following year. Soon he was surprised to hear from a company he had not heard of before. IMS Health offered to pay him fifty dollars a month to copy his prescription files onto an eight-inch floppy disk and send it in by mail. IMS software removed the patient's name but left the patient's age, the doctor's name, and the details about the medication and dose. "I would load it," Menighan recalled. "I'd mail it back to them, and I got fifty dollars a pop for that. And I thought I was making out like a bandit!"

Over time, data miners focused on chains such as CVS and Walgreens rather than mom-and-pop operations. In this way, the miners could scoop up millions of records from thousands of stores in a single transaction. Selling data seemed as easy as printing money, since stores were gathering it anyway; most pharmacy chains participated enthusiastically. Mail-order pharmacies such as CVS Caremark and Express Scripts, the largest US pharmacy benefit manager, which handles prescription orders for many companies, also participated in this new market.

(Mostly) No Comment from Pharmacies

Nowadays, pharmacy chains are happy to make money selling anonymized copies of patient prescriptions—the companies just don't like talking about it. Ernie Boyd has worked in the pharmacy business for four decades and today heads the Ohio Pharmacist Association. "The closer you get to the truth," he said, "the tougher your fight is going to be because these guys don't want their model exposed. They don't want everybody to know how it works. The less they want to talk, the more there is something there."

I contacted chains large and small, turning to both executives and customer service representatives to hear what they had to say about their data sales. Their evasions and double-talk seemed almost comical. For example, a customer representative at Rite-Aid (the fourth-largest US chain before its 2015 sale to Walgreens) answered my questions about data sales this way: "Rite Aid does not sell any customer information as we value our customers [sic] privacy."[3] Andrew Palmer, vice president of compliance monitoring, told me the opposite: "Rite Aid Corporation does sell to IMS information in much the same way as others do."[4] Twenty minutes after I received an e-mail from Palmer, I heard back from the assistant for Dan Miller, senior vice president of pharmacy operations. He declined to answer the very same question.

Publix, which operates supermarkets with pharmacies throughout the American Southeast, gave a variety of responses. "Publix pharmacy does not sell any of your private health information," said Jon Pybus, a pharmacy supervisor.[5] David Kirkus, the director of pharmacy administration, took a different tack, suggesting that to protect patient privacy, he could not reveal if Publix sells prescription information to data miners. "In consistency with our policy to protect and respect our customers' privacy, we do not participate in studies of this nature," he said.[6]

How about Walgreens, the nation's largest drugstore chain? "We won't be able to provide you with the information you're looking for, but I'd suggest that you may want to reach out to the National Association of Chain Drug Stores for some insight from an industry perspective," wrote Michael Polzin, the divisional vice president overseeing communications.[7]

Cindy Davis, Walmart's executive vice president of global customer insights and analytics, said, "We do not share this kind of information externally."

Other retailers that declined to comment included Costco, Loblaw (Canada's largest food and pharmacy retailer), Sears, and Safeway. Such reticence is likely to stem from the financial benefit to pharmacies, middlemen, and data miners when medical data are shared. All the participants in data sharing have an interest in preserving the status quo. Some former and current industry officials told me that too much discussion of these practices could upset the public and perhaps spur demands for a different approach.

Two companies I contacted, CVS (the second-largest pharmacy chain) and the supermarket chain Kroger, stood apart by clearly confirming that they do indeed sell anonymized data. "Pretty much everyone who is in the business has some sort of supply arrangement for de-identified prescription data," said Per Lofberg, executive vice president of CVS Health. "CVS Caremark is one of the providers of data into that marketplace. On the retail side of the business, they also have pretty extensive data collection ranging from loyalty cards and that sort of thing to track people's shopping patterns. Also on the retail pharmacy side, like most retailers, they will sell certain types of data to market research companies and so on."

Traditionally, pharmacies received about a penny per script, which added up to millions or tens of millions of dollars annually for big chains. "With some exceptions, there is no reason not to do it," Lofberg said. He called the revenue akin to a "rounding error" for a company as large as CVS, which recorded revenues of nearly $140 billion in 2014, with profits of $4.6 billion. Still, $50 million or so from selling data would add 1 percent to the company's bottom line.

As for the customer's role in determining the fate of the prescription data, he said, "The patient is not really a component of this, because their name and connection to the prescription have been stripped off."

The Data Crossroads

The prescription represents just the tip of the informational iceberg in the health-data bazaar. When former West Virginia pharmacist Thomas Menighan, today the CEO of the 62,000-member American Pharmacists Association, first sold his drugstore's data to IMS, no one else could access that information: It was stored only on his computer. A few years later, he started transmitting pharmacy claims electronically, giving pharmacy software companies access to valuable medical insights.

As more insurance plans covered prescription drugs, a layer of data processors called clearinghouses, or switches, emerged. These companies route claims from the pharmacy or doctor's office to those paying the bills such as the insurance company or government entity like Medicare. Like a railroad switch, the data switch routes medical information in a multitude of directions. Entrepreneurs running switches and pharmacy software programs learned that they could make extra cash by selling their expertise to the secondary market.

"At first," said Stephen Schondelmeyer, head of the Department of Pharmaceutical Care and Health Systems at the University of Minnesota, "the software companies started collecting that data as it went through their switch so they had a bigger aggregate, not just a pharmacy at a time, or a chain at a time, but everything that went through these switches. And they started selling to IMS and others."

Doug Long, the IMS vice president of industry relations, confirmed that middlemen processing data from thousands of independent pharmacies allow data miners access to their information. "We would get their information through their software vendors," he said, referring to pharmacies. With independents, "in terms of having an information relationship, it's harder to do."

Early in the evolution of digitized health data, some middlemen sold data passing through their hands without informing pharmacies, even in the fine print of contracts. "Some central source was selling the data, but the individual pharmacist was not aware," said Roger Korman, a former president of IMS Canada and Latin America. "The computer vendors eventually realized that they had to inform their clients because they were kind of ripping off their assets."

Tery Baskin, who owned two drugstores in Little Rock, Arkansas, was one of many pharmacists surprised to learn that others were selling data related to an individual store's sales. One day, another Arkansas pharmacist told him a customer had received a letter from a drug manufacturer saying one of its products had been recalled. "How did this drug company know that my patient was taking their drug?" the colleague wondered.

As Baskin investigated, he learned about the mushrooming array of middlemen, from pharmacy software companies to switches and pharmacy benefit managers.[8] "The pharmacist, for the most part, didn't even know this was going on," Baskin said. "It was very much of an annoyance. It was, 'So you are making money off of my prescriptions? Those patients came to my pharmacy. Now you are taking that data and you are profiting from it, and I'm not even in the know.'"

In 2003, IMS Health and about sixty software vendors were sued in Illinois on allegations that they had stolen trade secrets by selling prescription data from thousands of drugstores starting in the 1990s. IMS settled the case and a related lawsuit for $10.6 million.[9] To this day, some drugstore owners do not know where their customers' data may end up after the information passes through the hands of so many brokers. "I'm a nine-store chain," said Morley Cohn, owner of Kopp Drug in Pennsylvania, a few months before he closed his business in 2014. "So if my Rx data is being sold, I'd venture that it's by a PBM [pharmacy benefit manager]."

Nowadays, the fine print of long contracts typically sets out who can sell in the big medical-data bazaar.[10] Owners of independent pharmacies such as Tarrytown Pharmacy in Austin, Texas, where privacy activist Deborah Peel once confronted the owner over the data-sharing implications of the pharmacy's new computer, sometimes lament that they do not profit from these lucrative sales. "It's unfortunately one of the pitfalls of being the small guy, because you don't get to take advantage of that data mining," said owner Mark Newberry, whose father Peel had confronted years ago. "We all know that there is a ton of value in all of that stuff, all the way to insurers from drug manufacturers to planned sponsors. We have zero access to that."

Newberry said that even as the owner, he does not know where the data from his pharmacy end up: "Even if I did, there is nothing I can do about it."

HIPAA

The United States allows all of this data trading behind the scenes under the Health Insurance Privacy and Accountability Act (HIPAA), which passed in 1996 and came into force in stages by the early 2000s. It provides for the protection of health data with identifiable information such as name, Social Security number, home address, or telephone number. Data anonymized by one of two methods no longer enjoy this protection and, in fact, get none at all.

In another twist, many entities that handle health information are not required to follow HIPAA. Only health-care providers such as doctors, pharmacists, health plans such as insurance companies and government health programs, and health-care clearinghouses (a fancy way of saying middlemen) cannot collect, use, or disclose personal health information without a patient's authorization (with some legal exceptions, further confusing the issue). These are *covered entities*. Other parties are allowed to trade such information freely, a loophole I'll discuss more in chapter 12.

Before HIPAA, data miners such as IMS did occasionally receive identified patient data. In 1995, the *New York Times* quoted Robert Merold, the IMS vice president of marketing, who said that data suppliers such as pharmacies sometimes are "not sophisticated enough to separate out the patient names, and they just get passed along in commerce."[11] Times have changed. Nowadays, data suppliers strip out names and other identifiers before selling information to third parties. HIPAA "started to force everybody to get their act together," Merold told me when I asked what had happened since then. "Any responsible organization, they cleaned up their act, because the liability is too enormous."

HIPAA became law as ArcLight and its competitors began in the 1990s to capitalize on the flood of digitized medical information. By then, the dominant data miner, IMS Health, seemed to have already been around forever, an unshakable rock that towered above the others. However, few knew very much about the company, which had long shunned public attention. To better understand the evolution of the big health-data bazaar, I investigated the history of IMS, which in mid-2016 renamed itself Quintiles IMS Holdings, following a mega merger of health-care data companies.[12] I uncovered secrets the company and its founder had long tried to suppress.

CHAPTER 3

□ □ □ □ □

THE COVERT ALLIANCE

Secretive Company

A mother gazes upon her daughter in a hospital bed, a computer monitor placed between them. In the background, a new age soundtrack plays a fast series of minor arpeggios. A male actor playing a doctor in a white coat, stethoscope perfectly balanced over his shoulders, walks toward the young patient and scans the UPC code on her plastic bracelet. "When health care works, it seems to perform miracles," an announcer says as a flash of blue light cascades over the girl. "But health care only works at its best when everyone has access to the right information at the right time."

IMS Health, the company sponsoring the ad, had prospered for decades behind the scenes of health care, invisible to patients. But in 2014, ahead of an initial public offering (IPO), it produced several polished commercials to introduce its services to investors. "Physicians need to know what medicines are effective for their patients. Researchers need to identify treatment gaps to develop more targeted novel medicines," the narrator in the three-minute video intones. "Biopharmaceutical companies want to better pinpoint the patient groups that will benefit most from specific therapies. And hospitals must understand the total patient experience to improve the efficiency and quality of care."

Highly pixelated doctors, researchers, and patients interact ghost-like against color backgrounds. "With reliable, connected information, and real-world insights, health care runs smarter for all of us," it continues. "IMS Health links information from more than a hundred thousand data suppliers around the world and across health care. We deliver a comprehensive view of treatments, costs, and outcomes."

Then a slogan appears: IMS Health. INTELLIGENCE APPLIED.[1]

At the end of the video, the highly pixelated hospitalized girl reappears, her ghostly image reviving into full-resolution color. She sits up and smiles as her mother and doctor beam back at her. The commercial creates a good feeling about the benefits of medical data but offers little insight on how the business really operates.

IMS is one of America's thousand largest companies, with $2.9 billion in revenue in 2015. It gathers anonymized medical dossiers on hundreds of millions of patients, very few of whom know anything about the company. After researching my first book on the world of nonmedical customer data, I knew very well that companies that focus on gathering data about people are reluctant to reveal themselves. Yet even by those standards, IMS stands apart, showing an especially strong aversion to public exposure. Current executives declined to speak with me, over several years of requests.[2] Robert Hooper, the former IMS North America CEO, told me that the reticence stems from fear: "People have that in the back of their minds: Am I going to get fired? Am I going to get sued? Am I going to get generally in trouble?"

Struck by the irony that a company can buy and sell our medical data and be so unknown, I set out to learn more. The origin of IMS presents a compelling story because it illustrates an inclination toward secrecy even before computerization dramatically expanded the use of intimate patient data. And the story is full of intrigue. The company's past history set the tone for the entire big health-data bazaar today.

The corporate timeline on the IMS website starts with an entry from 1954: "Bill Frohlich, an advertising executive, and David Dubow, a visionary, form IMS, a market research company that enables organizations to make informed, strategic decisions about the marketplace."[3] When I asked around, I learned that Frohlich was the true founder, but a former employee told me it would be hard to unravel the truth about his old boss. "When you dig into Frohlich's life, it is a screen of deceit," said Bill Castagnoli, a retired ad industry executive and author of a history of medical advertising. "He lived in a world of a screen to protect himself. . . . Who knows what else he was pretending about his life. It was all hidden under rocks all over the place."

Frenemies

Ludwig Wolfgang Frohlich emigrated from his native Germany to the United States in 1935, a turbulent time when the Nazis were building the Third Reich.[4] By 1943, he had set up a Madison Avenue medical advertising agency, L. W. Frohlich & Co., which helped publicize the many new drugs coming to market in that era. Soon after his arrival in New York, Frohlich befriended Arthur Sackler, who would have a profound influence on Frohlich's professional life. The two men prospered in medical advertising after World War II, a period of creative innovation. Although one hailed from Germany and the other from Brooklyn, they had much in common. Born within a few weeks of each other in 1913, each embraced self-reliance and hard work. Sackler's family also had recent emigrant roots—his Jewish father emigrated from Galicia (now part of Ukraine); his mother, from Poland.

When the two men first met, Sackler worked in the advertising department of Schering, a German company whose US assets were seized during World War II. Sackler subcontracted jobs to the type shop where Frohlich was first employed; the relationship expanded after Frohlich set up his advertising agency.[5] Also in 1943—the timing was no coincidence, it emerged many years later—Sackler joined the William Douglas McAdams advertising agency, which focused on drugs and vitamins. He rose quickly from medical and creative director to vice president, and by 1947, he owned most of the company.

Sackler, Frohlich, and other "med men" brought Madison Avenue sophistication to medical advertising as an era of "miracle drugs," including penicillin, began curing people of previously untreatable diseases. Many experts credit Sackler in particular for revolutionizing promotion to doctors, the gateway to sales, since it is doctors who write the prescriptions. In one high-profile 1952 campaign, Sackler's agency convinced Pfizer to send telegrams to wholesalers to announce the imminent arrival of a new antibiotic called Terramycin, the first branded drug from Pfizer (until then, Pfizer had been a chemical and mining company). It inserted a mini-brochure into the prestigious *Journal of the American Medical Association* and sent out direct mail to doctors, wholesalers, hospitals, and others. Some ads relied on clever graphics. One resembled an optometrist's reading chart with letters growing ever smaller from the top, with the name of the new drug given only in tiny print at the bottom:

O
C U
L A R
I N F E C
T I O N S
R E S P O N D
T O B R O A D
S P E C T R U M
T E R R A M Y C I N

The campaign was a huge success, reaching many thousands of doctors—and earning admiration from Sackler's advertising rivals. Medical advertising became increasingly creative and widespread. Drug companies supplemented their promotions by sending out small armies of detail men (and, later, women as well) to tell doctors about the latest medications. Yet advertising continued to command a far greater reach.

The television show *Mad Men* portrayed rival firms fighting aggressively to win accounts, with executives wining and dining potential clients and drafting elaborate campaigns over sleepless nights to outdo competitors. By all logic, Frohlich and Sackler would also have clashed as millions of dollars were at stake. In public, Frohlich spoke of "competitive zeal in the pharmaceutical industry which would have warmed Adam Smith's heart."[6] Yet instead of elbowing out each other to win accounts from leading drug companies, Frohlich and Sackler regularly met behind the scenes to divvy up business and to share information about potential clients.

It was an arrangement to their mutual advantage that insiders would discuss publicly only half a century later. "It was very, very important at that time to divide up business to make sure you could get as much business as possible because you could not have competing products," Sackler's attorney Michael Sonnenreich told me.

An agency could not advertise two competing drugs, Sonnenreich explained, but two secretly cooperative agencies could:

> If you make a drug and [someone else makes] a drug and they are the same drug, if I am an agency and I go and I win you, I then can't go and get [the other manufacturer], because there is a conflict of interest. So what they did was they set up two agencies. I could get one tranquilizer. I couldn't get another one, but Frohlich could get another one, so that's what happened.
>
> It was not illegal. Two separate agencies, two separate reporting entities. If we are friends, if I say to you, "I have Valium but I don't have chlorpromazine. Why don't you go over and get the chlorpromazine?" What's wrong with that? What's collusion? I already have Valium. I can't get chlorpromazine, but if I help you, I am being your buddy.

Richard Leather, who served as Frohlich's attorney starting in 1960, broadly confirmed this arrangement: "Those two agencies very much helped one another. They were very cooperative."

Sonnenreich also said that Sackler had a financial stake in the L. W. Frohlich agency, something several former Frohlich agency executives suspected but which Sackler denied during his lifetime.[7]

Studying the Market

To win new business, these agencies highlighted their artwork, clever messaging, and attention-grabbing advertisements. It remained difficult, however, to prove how any campaign affected the client's bottom line. To address this issue and boost his advertising business, Frohlich created a market research company, Intercontinental Marketing Services, which over time became abbreviated as IMS.[8] Ad clients paid for research to see how well they were doing against competitors. If the data showed that a company enjoyed a large market share, the ad agency might suggest that the client protect its lead with more advertising. If the company's market share was small, it needed more ads to boost its profile.

One influential developer of twentieth-century American market research methods was Arthur Charles Nielsen, who started the A. C. Nielsen Company in 1923. A decade later, at the height of the Great Depression, he launched the Nielsen Drug Index. He paid 750 pharmacies to share their wholesale invoices every two months, a practice that allowed him to project overall US sales. Nielsen staffers also visited stores to count products such as Alka-Seltzer on shelves to monitor how fast they sold. The research helped firms target advertising and sales more effectively, such as according to specific times of year, or particular geographic areas.[9] Other market research companies built on Nielsen's innovations. One such company was Davee, Koehnlein and Keating (DK&K), a Chicago firm founded in 1936 that became known for its estimates of the total size of the pharmaceutical market by category, based on receipts from US pharmacies and manufacturers.

IMS Starts in Germany

Throughout his career, Frohlich was never shy about adopting someone else's good ideas. He replicated DK&K's model with Intercontinental Marketing Services in Germany. With a tradition in pharmacies dating to the thirteen century, Germany was a backbone of the worldwide pharmaceutical industry.[10] Frohlich dispatched ad executive David Dubow to Germany to set up the new company known locally as the Institut für Medizinische Statistik. IMS published its first national estimates of the German market through the acquisition of purchase data from wholesale pharmacies in 1957.[11] This first audit was a commercial success, and in the following years, the new company expanded to several other Western European countries.

Frohlich had ample personal reasons for wariness before starting a venture in his former homeland. But if he had qualms about doing business there, he did not display any such sentiments to his staff, who knew almost nothing about his early life or how he came to the United States. The topic remained a mystery, something he did not discuss, even as many speculated about his background.

Some who knew Frohlich thought that his rigid temperament, authoritarian leadership, German accent, and demand for neatness suggested a hidden Nazi past. The possibility was real enough that in 1943, at the height of World War II, the FBI investigated his background for links to the Third Reich.[12] Others speculated that he must have been Jewish. Frohlich did not disabuse people of either impression. He just did not discuss his youth or private life, even with his top executives. They knew only that he had emigrated from Germany. When, why, and how remained a mystery, which is how Frohlich preferred it.

Thanks to meticulous German archival records and interviews, I uncovered many clues about Frohlich's secretive life in my research. He was born in Giessen, thirty-two miles north of Frankfurt, a year before the outbreak of World War I. In early 1933, very soon after Adolf Hitler came to power, Frohlich joined the Reichsarbeitsdienst (RAD), a youth work brigade whose members wore red swastika armbands and swastika pins on their caps. He had just completed high school and was sent to East Prussia, Germany's easternmost region. In 1934, Frohlich enrolled at the Goethe University's economic and social science division in Frankfurt. He dropped out a year later and moved to New York City to work at a company that designed typefaces. He stayed in the city for the rest of his life.

Frohlich had good reasons to leave Germany. Religion, as well as fear of anti-Jewish persecution, was not one of them—or at least that's what his closest business associates and even subsequent ancestors believed. "Having known him and known his sister and at one point met his mother—I would not have said that any of them is Jewish," Frohlich's attorney Richard Leather told me decades later. Lars Ericson, a distant relative who socialized with Frohlich and served for a time as president of IMS, also told me that Frohlich was not Jewish.

Both men were mistaken. Frohlich was indeed Jewish, a heritage confirmed in many official papers, including US emigration filings, birth certificates, and passenger ship logs. Documents for his sister, mother, and grandmother confirm this heritage as well.

Frohlich remained circumspect about both his Jewish heritage and his sexual orientation (he was gay) throughout his life amid continued anti-Semitism in the United States. "You would sit at meetings where they would tell Jewish jokes, anti-Jewish jokes, and you had to sit there and swallow it, and laugh along with the boys," Sackler's attorney Sonnenreich said. "That's what you needed to do if you were going to make the business."

Expanding Horizons

From its initial focus on overall pharmaceutical sales trends, IMS took its first steps closer to patient data by asking doctors to share the details about which medications they were prescribing for which illnesses. In these early days of medical data mining, some physicians found such a request intrusive. "I have received a request from an organization called Intercontinental Medical Statistics," Kenneth Inman wrote to the *British Medical Journal* in 1963, "asking me to complete a large folder with information about my methods of treatment. In appreciation I am offered a gramophone record. It seems to me an impertinence that these folders should be sent to add to the bulk of my mail, without any previous inquiry as to my willingness to co-operate." He suggested that other doctors reject such solicitations.[13]

Whenever possible, IMS tried to get the raw data for its reports for free, telling pharmacists or doctors that sharing information would help science. Then the company gave doctors Kennedy half-dollar coins to thank them for sharing copies of their prescribing data, a reward that eventually increased to about $50 a month. Handel Evans, who headed up IMS' later expansion into the United States, explained: "We tried to convince the doctor that he was doing something good, that he was doing it for the benefit of medicine, and that a pen would be fine. It's really about . . . what can you get away with."

Eventually IMS paid pharmacies as well, offering about a penny per prescription to send in copies of the drugs they dispensed to patients or to allow IMS reps to microfilm these records. The payments might total $25 to $150 a month for a pharmacy.[14]

In those early years, IMS and the L. W. Frohlich advertising agency worked close together, sometimes sharing the same office. Such cooperation could represent an ethical tangle, because market data from IMS might be presented to win business for the ad agency. Dubow's personal

assistant Maureen Gahan said that "things weren't quite right" in the relationship between the two halves of the Frohlich empire in the early
years. Eventually she was troubled enough by these conflicts of interest
to march into Dubow's office.

"I am going to leave," the nineteen-year-old said.

"Why are you going, Maureen?" Dubow asked.

"I don't believe in the ethics of this company!"

Dubow assured her that he intended to create greater separation between IMS and the advertising business. Gahan stayed, and over time,
IMS flourished independent of the L. W. Frohlich agency.

The Passing of the Founders

Frohlich regularly visited IMS worldwide offices but focused mostly on his
medical advertising agency, which continued to grow and prosper. By the
mid-1960s, one thousand people worked for L. W. Frohlich/Intercon, an
agency name expanded to reflect its international expansion to New York,
London, Paris, Frankfurt, Milan, Madrid, and Tokyo.[15] It earned $37 mil-
lion in 1970 and $43.8 million in worldwide billing revenue in 1971, but the
expansion ultimately ended because of Frohlich's health troubles.[16]

In early 1971, the boss returned from a Caribbean holiday, and his
executives expected to see him rested and focused when they gathered
for a meeting of senior staff. Yet he started babbling incomprehensively
and, to the shock of the senior staff, passed out. When he regained consciousness, he admitted having experienced other such spells. Frohlich
checked into a hospital for tests and was diagnosed with a brain tumor.
He never returned to work after the diagnosis, and in September of that
year, Frohlich died. He was fifty-eight.

The obituary in the *New York Times*, like much of what Frohlich presented about himself to the public, contained omissions and inventions.
The article incorrectly listed his middle name as William (not the more
German Wolfgang) and said he graduated from Goethe University in
Frankfurt in 1931 at age eighteen (he dropped out after his freshman year
in 1934–1935); it mentioned that he came to the United States in 1931, two
years before Hitler's rise to power (he first visited the United States in
1935 and immigrated permanently in 1936).

The story highlighted his advertising agency work, with only one of
eighteen paragraphs mentioning IMS, what turned out to be his greatest
enduring legacy.[17] Even in death, Frohlich did not acknowledge his Jewish
heritage. His funeral service took place at a prominent Episcopal church
in Manhattan, St. Bartholomew's. Pharmaceutical executives filed into

the cavernous church at 51st Street and Park Avenue to pay their last respects. His death delivered a fatal blow to the L. W. Frohlich ad agency: several top executives quickly left, and the company closed in 1972.[18] By contrast, IMS prospered. Much as he had tried to insert himself into day-to-day operations, Frohlich was not essential to the company's survival. From the very beginning, David Dubow had run the company in Frankfurt and then London, far enough from Frohlich in New York to build his own power base.

Frohlich's biggest secret came to light a year after his death as IMS executives completed the due-diligence work to take the company public. The IMS team learned that Frohlich had a secret agreement, called a tontine, in which Arthur Sackler's brothers Raymond and Mortimer inherited the overwhelming majority of IMS upon Frohlich's death. Some had already suspected that Frohlich and Sackler, the two great "Medicine Avenue" rivals, shared information and divided up advertising clients. But their pas de deux was far more elaborate: Arthur Sackler was the secret power behind the IMS throne.[19]

When the Sackler brothers finally allowed the IPO to go forward, the fine print of the share offer revealed that Frohlich's sister, her family, and a charitable trust he had set up received $6.25 million, a fraction of Raymond and Mortimer Sackler's haul of nearly $37 million.[20] I wondered how Arthur's younger brothers rather than Arthur himself ended up with the lion's share of the proceeds, so I called Raymond Sackler, who was born in 1920 and was the last surviving brother, at his Connecticut home. His wife said she remembered Frohlich well. But Raymond Sackler said he had nothing to do with running IMS and did not remember the details of the transaction that brought many millions of dollars his way. "I knew very little if anything about that business," he told me.

Arthur Sackler's lawyer explained that Arthur made Raymond and Mortimer the tontine beneficiaries to distance the deal from his McAdams advertising agency. "He couldn't possibly have been one of [Frohlich's beneficiaries]," Sonnenreich said, "because he was running McAdams and it would have been a conflict. So he put his brothers into it. Arthur was running it. The brothers weren't running IMS—they had nothing to do with it."

Sonnenreich, who later also represented IMS CEO David Dubow for some of his legal work, had one more surprising revelation when I met him: Before joining the L. W. Frohlich agency, Dubow had worked for Arthur Sackler at the McAdams agency. In other words, the day-to-day head of IMS was Sackler's man before he was Frohlich's man. The lawyer said

Sackler came up with the idea for IMS and thought Frohlich would be a better public face because the German immigrant and his ad agency had a less prominent public profile.[21] "Obviously if you want to have impartial figures and facts coming out, you don't want the advertising agency to swing them in favor of their clients," Sonnenreich said. "You couldn't have an IMS attached to an advertising agency. I think it would be a conflict of interest."

In early 1980, Dubow, who preferred to work behind the scenes, granted a rare interview to *Forbes*. The magazine described IMS as "hyperprofitable" and expressed admiration for the company's growing revenues, up 20 percent every year over the past decade. IMS operated in forty-two countries. It described the CEO as still "young and energetic at 60."

In reality, however, he looked older in the story's accompanying photo.[22] Dubow had serious heart problems and needed coronary bypass surgery, at the time a relatively new procedure whose effectiveness was still being debated. Doctors told him he could quit his job and live longer—or stay at IMS. Dubow chose work and did not get the surgery. In September of the following year, while he was in New York, Dubow had a heart attack and died at age sixty-two.

Dubow built a company that continues to dominate the business of medical data. The Christmas before he died, he had sent a warm letter to his deputy Lars Ericson. "I think each year gives added strength and substance to the IMS business," he wrote. "I think it is solid with a very, very promising future." He was spot-on. Dubow died just weeks after the introduction of the IBM PC heralded an era of small computers that could record data in any pharmacy or doctor's office.

Dubow's most enduring success was his decision to expand into the United States in 1969 by buying Davee, Koehnlein and Keating (DK&K), the pioneering pharmaceutical research firm whose model IMS had copied in Germany. His legacy endures in all the commercial medical-data collection that takes place today.

Around the same time that IMS was plotting its expansion into the United States, some pioneering doctors sought to use early computers not for commercial gain, but to revolutionize how their profession delivers health care. They achieved some early successes, but they soon found that helping patients through digitizing their medical data was far more difficult than creating a business profiting from it.

CHAPTER 4

□ □ □ □ □

PATIENT POWER

Weeding Out Bad Medical Practices

The instructor walked down the hospital hallway and stopped to look at a resident's patient notes. Even though Lawrence Weed was just a few years older than the Yale School of Medicine students he was supervising, he looked rather intimidating. He wore his hair short, nearly a crew cut on the side, and had a balding dome. Thick eyebrows gave his eyes particular intensity as he fixed on the harried medical student.

"You just have these impressions scribbled down? There's no discipline around here," he lamented. "Oh my God, the patient's record is your scientific notebook!"

In the late 1940s and early 1950s—the same years Ludwig Frohlich built his advertising agency—Weed concluded that medical schools did a terrible job of training physicians. He became convinced the system fostered inexactitude that hobbled patient care. Born in 1923, Weed was a product of the very system he condemned. A graduate of Columbia University's College of Physicians and Surgeons, Weed possessed an especially sharp mind, analytical clarity, and the confidence that he could envision a better future unseen by others.

"When I come by tomorrow, I want a list of the patients' problems stated at the level for which you have evidence," Weed told the resident. "Then we will work from there and we will turn this patient's record into a scientific notebook. And we'll see if you want to get a PhD or not!"

Real patients with real ailments lay in the hospital training ward, and Weed felt they were not getting proper treatment. He summoned his medical residents and interns and set down the rules: Revise all of their records, making them as detailed as a submission to a medical journal.

It was the late 1950s, and the students thought twice before questioning the teacher. But a few cautiously resisted, suggesting Weed was asking for too much.

"I can't get them all done," one said.

"Do you want them all done?" another pleaded, suggesting that the students could revise the notes for just a few patients initially.

"These patients think you are taking care of them!" Weed bellowed. "You are not taking care of part of them. You'd better get the whole list of problems, and I want to see what's going on."[1]

Though he may not always have displayed the most delicate bedside manner, Weed cared passionately about improving patient care. Such exchanges and other experiences in medical schools inspired him to develop a more systematic way of recording patient symptoms, an approach he called the *problem-oriented medical record*. Doctors should not scribble down random impressions and thoughts. They would follow a logical sequence when recording data. By the 1960s, Weed became convinced that computers offered the best way to organize and record such information and to tap the vast wealth of medical knowledge that no doctor could remember.

In 1966, when he was in his early forties, Weed, and some colleagues at Western Reserve School of Medicine in Cleveland (known today as Case Western) started working with early touch-screen computers to enable patients and doctors to enter their histories directly at the time of treatment. The era of computerized medicine was under way. Patients would gain more control over their records; doctors would have access to better, more detailed information; and health care would improve.

The straight-laced Weed did not write computer code, so he recruited a long-haired, thickly mustachioed mathematician, Jan Schultz, to transform computers into storehouses of medical knowledge. A few researchers had already dabbled in transcribing doctors' notes into computers before Weed's team tried, but the group had much bigger ambitions.[2]

The First Patient Record Computers

The group's initial system at Cleveland Metropolitan General Hospital in 1968 relied on a remote computer transmitting data via telephone lines to twenty-five touch-screen monitors worth $20,000 each (about $134,000 in 2015 inflation-adjusted dollars). It allowed patients, assisted by a nurse, to input data directly. "You will now be asked a series of questions about your past medical history," the computer asked. "To answer each question, touch the box next to your answer on the TV screen."

The patient profile sought standard demographic information but also asked patients to rate sensitive statements such as "I am satisfied with my present job"; "I have financial problems that I would like to discuss with someone"; "I have electric light in my home"; "I find intercourse or marital relations satisfactory"; "There are times when I feel very lonely so that I cannot go on living"; and "I sometimes take a drink in the morning."

Despite the high costs, the results were so promising that the University of Vermont hired Weed, Schultz, and several others on their team to implement their vision there. It was July 1969, and technology seemed both limitless and inevitable. Replacing the illegible scribbles of a doctor's handwriting with the order of computers seemed like child's play compared with landing a man on the moon, which had happened earlier that month.

The digitization of medical records by these pioneers ruffled lots of feathers. To start with, Weed showed little patience for those who disagreed with him. In addition, using computers to record patient data and recall medical knowledge made doctors uneasy. The concept threatened to demystify those whom Weed mocked as MDieties, physicians who supposedly possessed unique knowledge that others could neither access nor understand. Computers would spread the knowledge to other doctors, nurses, and even the patients themselves. On top of that, Weed's system suggested how the doctor should treat a patient reporting a certain set of problems. Presuming no one could know everything, the computer led physicians down the path to figure out, for example, the source of any one of seventy different causes of stomach pain.

"You shouldn't have every Tom, Dick, and Harry working up abdominal pain in his own way. There should be a consistent way to get histories," Weed said.

Perhaps the biggest problem was that although calling up information instantaneously has become commonplace today, half a century ago Weed's idea far outstripped the primitive capabilities of that era's computers.

Around the same time that Weed demanded higher standards from his students in the early 1950s, Warner Slack was becoming intrigued by the potential of computing machines. As a Princeton University undergraduate, he had heard a lot of talk and excitement about what these new machines might do. In 1959, Slack finished his MD at Weed's alma mater, Columbia University's College of Physicians and Surgeons. The same year, an article by Robert Ledley and Lee Lusted in *Science* magazine excited him about the future of computers in medical diagnostics: "Computers are especially suited to help the physician collect and process clinical information and remind him of diagnoses which he may have overlooked."[3] Slack won a fellowship at the University of Wisconsin–Madison to explore the possibility of using computers in medicine. Several years later, working five hundred miles to the west of Weed in Cleveland, Slack developed a similar system for computers to record patient data.

"I was disturbed by the way in which we were keeping our data, writing illegibly in a chart," Slack recalled years later. "What I wanted to do with the medical history was to model the doctor as an interviewer. The problem with the self-administered questionnaires was that there was no detail. If the patient said, 'Yes, I have a headache,' there was no way to find out when it started or how serious it was. I did have the thought that the computer might deliver this."

His approach, which he inaugurated in the mid-1960s, drew on 450 computerized questions, presented according to how a patient responded. Users sat at an elevated keyboard, as tall as a box of tissues, and looked at a tiny screen—really a cathode-ray oscilloscope—a few inches wide and surrounded by rectangular slats to reduce glare. Reel-to-reel magnetic tapes, a sign of high-tech brains in that era, spun above in front of a wall of machinery.

One of the first patients to use Slack's program on LINC (the Laboratory Instrument Computer) was an elderly man recovering from a heart attack. He diligently worked through the questions, laughing out loud at some of the humorously phrased items Slack had inserted to lighten up the process. "You know, I really like your computer better than some of those doctors over in the hospital," he told Slack afterward. "For one thing, I'm sort of deaf and have trouble hearing them."[4]

If someone who may have been born in the nineteenth century could embrace the technology, its future looked bright. Slack's work attracted national attention, including a television documentary called *LINC with Tomorrow*.[5] "There is a human traffic jam in the doctor's office today," narrator David Prowitt says. Waving a binder in his hands, he highlights the importance of getting patients to describe their health issues: "The medical chart. Hallowed in theory. Often disappointing in practice. Mistakes here can lead to serious trouble later on. Faulty diagnosis, incorrect treatment, possibly death. We're at the University of Wisconsin Medical Center, where researchers have developed an exciting new weapon to attack this problem."

The camera pans across the computer, and the announcer approaches Slack, who is wearing a crumpled, oversized jacket and sporting a crew cut. He is seated to the side of the machine.

"Warner," says Prowitt, "you seem pretty comfortable talking to a machine. How does the average patient take to it?"

"Well, it's really no problem. Actually, the LINC is quite sociable as far as computers go," Slack says with a smile.

Prowitt puts LINC to the test and answers his own medical questionnaire, pondering a few seconds at each screen. The well-groomed announcer works his way through screen after screen of black-and-white flickering sentences in ALL CAPS, generating a click with every response.

"FOR ABOUT HOW MANY YEARS HAVE YOU SMOKED AND INHALED?" the machine asks.

Prowitt, who is in his early thirties, types in two digits, 1 and 5.

Slack adds some additional information from his own observations such as how well Prowitt responded to his reflex test. The doctor then takes out a needle and draws blood. After a teletype printer noisily punches out a summary of the results, including his cholesterol reading, Slack reviews its findings.

"I've been looking at your record and it's normal except for one thing," Slack says. "I must agree with LINC on one point here."

The television announcer arches his brow as he awaits the doctor's assessment.

"You smoke too much."

"Agreed. No arguments at all."

After the diagnosis, Slack predicts a future of small, cheaper standalone computers in doctors' offices and terminals linked to online central computers to give the professionals unprecedented expertise.

Computers seemed as far out as the Magical Mystery Tour the Beatles sang about that year. But Slack was confident that a health-care revolution was under way. If patients could access their health histories and their other medical records, they could be more involved and better informed in making decisions for themselves. In the language of the 1960s, Slack promoted what he called "patient power."

Slack's innovations and the mantra that patients should be encouraged to be more involved not only attracted wide attention, but also fomented misunderstanding and dissent. Some doctors scoffed at the idea of giving patients more say in matters that laypeople knew little about. The *New England Journal of Medicine* rejected an article Slack submitted some years later titled "The Patient's Right to Decide" (the *Lancet* did publish it).[6] Other doctors thought patients would be forced to make complicated medical decisions, whether they wanted to or not. "That wasn't what I was saying," Slack said, "that the patients should be doctors. I was saying that we, as doctors, should be providing the patient with as much information as we can, but the patient should be, if she or he wanted to be, in charge of her value systems and decide, 'Maybe I'll wait. Maybe I'll do it.'"

The Elusive Future

A few years ago, Garry Harper, a state prison tower guard from Hutchinson, Kansas, experienced firsthand how electronic medical records still fall short of the vision of Weed and Slack, with dangerous and potentially fatal consequences. The words of the documentary narrator describing old paper records could aptly apply to the current state of digitized medical record keeping: "Hallowed in theory. Often disappointing in practice."

A veteran of the armed forces from 1972 to 1993, Harper typically drives to a clinic at an air force base about an hour away in Wichita to monitor his irregular heartbeat, high blood pressure, and prediabetes condition. In 2012, Harper and his wife visited their son in Topeka. After the three-hour drive, he felt unusually fatigued and feverish. Then sixty-one, Harper checked into St. Francis Hospital with a temperature of 106.7 degrees Fahrenheit. Unless doctors could bring down his temperature, he would die. Doctors ascertained that he had some heart-related issues, but knew little about his medical history or the exact names of his medications, which neither he nor his wife could remember.[7] The hospital did not obtain his past medical records; the frequent change of duty doctors and nurses on the wards of St. Francis required new teams to puzzle out his condition from scratch every day.

Three days later, Harper's son Chris visited from the Kansas City area. Chris worked at the insurance company UnitedHealth studying medical data for insights from many millions of people's records. In his job, he merged the insurer's claims data with outside marketing and demographic information to gain a better understanding of patients employed at companies such as GM and IBM and those on Medicare. All of this information could, for example, help spot health trends or weed out insurance fraud. Yet such sophisticated data analysis definitely did not benefit his father when he needed it the most. There was no quick and simple way for Garry Harper's new doctors to obtain his medical records.

"He's on twelve different medications. Did you call his cardiologist?" Chris asked the duty doctors.

They had not, and they never did call. The Topeka hospital team never learned the details of Harper's medical past. Garry Harper recovered after a week, although what had hit him remained a mystery to the hospital. It might have been a strain of methicillin-resistant Staphylococcus aureus bacteria (MRSA), which is resistant to ordinary antibiotics and often spreads in the prison system where he worked. But without full access to his medical history to supplement their knowledge, the medical personnel were not sure.

"It doesn't seem like it was done right," Harper said later. "Yeah, they kept me alive and everything, but there is no record of it or anything. Everybody talks about how great the computer is and everything, but all I ever see is people doing things on paper."

Harper left the hospital with a $20,000 bill, which his insurance covered. "It was the most expensive holiday I ever had," he joked.

Overall, Harper experienced the data paradox in American medicine. Our health-care system gives us a little of what we want and need—easy access to our comprehensive medical records to help professionals with our treatment. But it has also given us much of what we fear—others trafficking in our records. With big money harnessing big medical data for sales and marketing, entrepreneurs have made far greater progress on the commercial rather than the treatment side.

CHAPTER 5

THE DOSSIER ON YOUR DOCTOR

A New Innovation in Doctor Data

Soon after graduating from college in 1969, New Jersey native Shel Silverberg landed a job at Lea Associates, an early company gathering medical data for marketing. Lea asked doctors to fill out questionnaires on their diagnoses and prescriptions over a two-day period and sold those aggregated insights to pharmaceutical companies. Silverberg ended up at IMS after it bought Lea in 1972, and he eventually became vice president for international marketing.

In 1978, McKesson Corporation, the largest US drug wholesaler, hired Silverberg away from IMS to run Pharmaceutical Data Services (PDS), a new subsidiary aggregating millions of claims processed by its pharmacy benefit manager business. McKesson was ready to challenge IMS and felt that many professionals could welcome a choice in the world of medical data. "Everyone wanted a competitor for IMS because they did not want to deal with a monopoly," Silverberg said.

Not only did PDS project how well individual medications sold, but by 1982 or 1983, it also started ranking individual doctors into tiers according to which physicians prescribed certain drugs the most. To get this information, PDS sent out hundreds of thousands of surveys in which doctors, paid anywhere from $2 to $10, indicated how many prescriptions they wrote out per week and their preferred medications. Rankings based on this information allowed drug companies to target key doctors and pay sales reps according to the sales they generated.

Such information added new tools to an old game in which drug companies dispatch salespeople, called *detailers* or *reps*, to convince doctors to prescribe their drugs. The focus is easy to understand: Patients and their insurers pay for drugs, but doctors serve as the gatekeepers.

Since the 1850s, pharmaceutical firms have dispatched salespeople, who are armed with information and small gifts, to convince doctors about the comparative merits of their pills.[1] The job of detailing flourished in the mid-twentieth century amid the introduction of many new wonder drugs.

To target sales pitches, detailers have always sought to learn as much as possible about a doctor's prescribing habits ahead of a visit. Before computers, the reps sweet-talked pharmacists, hoping that the druggists would share details about local doctors.

"How is Dr. Watanabe doing with amphetamine X?" Henry Marini, a detail man for Smith, Kline in Hawaii in the mid-1960s, would ask.

"Well, he's prescribing pretty regularly," the pharmacist would answer. "He's pretty much consistent."

Around that same time, Reed Maurer worked for Eli Lilly in Wilmington, North Carolina. Since Eli Lilly provided data and advice to pharmacies, the druggists would even let Maurer and other reps peak at their files. "A Lilly man could go behind the counter and look at the scripts that were written by the doctor," he recalled half a century later.

Pharmacists shared insights about doctors' prescribing outside the United States as well. Handel Evans, who later became a top IMS official, began his career as a detail man in Scotland in the late 1950s. "You could only go to the pharmacy and ask the pharmacist whether the doctor was prescribing your products and which doctors were prescribing your products," he recalled. "Some were kind enough to tell."

Yet such efforts had obvious limitations, as any single pharmacist could only give an incomplete picture, and looking through the files took a lot of time. Maurer remembers spending at least an hour a week on the task.

Silverberg's rankings of leading prescribers based on doctor surveys gave greater insights than did chatting up the pharmacist, but even this data mining advance had shortcomings. Not all physicians accurately log their prescribing, and even if they do, some patients fail to buy the medications doctors prescribe for them. Such information could come only from scripts that patients actually filled. So in the early 1980s, PDS started purchasing doctor-identified prescriptions from 150 to 200 drugstores, a tiny fraction of total US pharmacies. In buying such records, PDS could see the doctor's name, but not that of the patient. To get real insights on individual doctors, it needed information from many thousands of pharmacies—an expensive proposition—so it asked drug companies to back the effort. Merck, Pfizer, and Key Pharmaceuticals all committed a few million dollars a year.[2] Paying about a penny per script, PDS gathered prescriptions from eight thousand US pharmacies by 1988, about 35 percent of all prescriptions, Silverberg said.

Two former IMS executives, Evans and Dennis Turner, saw the great potential of mining prescriptions and convinced outside investors to buy PDS in 1988. As cofounders of the acquiring parent company, Walsh International, they pressed Silverberg to do more than just broadly rank doctors in relative terms. They wanted dossiers that detailed exactly what every doctor prescribed, enough detail to show that, say, Dr. Jones wrote forty-one scripts for drug A and seven for rival drug B that month. And by buying details directly from pharmacies, data miners could tally just the prescriptions that actually resulted in sales (a sizable percentage—perhaps as many as a third—of all prescriptions are never filled, according to one study).[3]

IMS Health had already developed a popular service called Drug Distribution Data (DDD), which merged information from drug wholesalers and pharmaceutical companies to determine total sales broken down into individual salesperson territories. DDD, however, did not take into account *traveling prescriptions*, which occur when a script is written in one sales territory but is filled in another, thus crediting the sale to the wrong detailer (for example, a patient who sees a doctor near work in New York City but who fills the prescription near home in New Jersey).

Generating physician profiles by counting filled prescriptions overcame this problem and made it easier for drug companies to accurately reward their reps according to actual sales performance. With aspirations to spread this service worldwide, PDS was renamed Source International.

To avoid alienating the doctors, Silverberg had not previously published individual doctor dossiers. He thought that his three main pharmaceutical company backers would be cautious, lest they attract negative publicity and criticism from physicians. Never a man to take no for an answer, however, Evans held a series of meetings with the American Medical Association to explain why it was vital for the pharmaceutical industry to gather profiles on individual doctors by assembling copies of millions of pharmacy prescriptions. The AMA eventually acquiesced, which also benefitted the group financially.[4] That's because the AMA sold (and still sells) details from its Physician Masterfile about doctors and their backgrounds to data miners, companies that add the information into what came to be known as *doctor-identified information*, or *prescriber-identified information*. The three big drug companies that had been supporting PDS went along as well, and soon pharmaceutical companies paid millions of dollars annually for these insights.[5] Pharma embraced doctor-identified data with little internal debate. The companies believed in their medications, so if more information could help them sell more of their products, they were all for it.

"We felt it was for a greater good," said Mark Degatano, who worked at Merck for twenty-four years and was part of its decision to buy Source International's doctor-identified data. "I don't know if it was arrogance. I am a believer in the pharmaceutical industry. If there are new products coming out that better help the people, why shouldn't it be out to physicians as fast as possible?"

For all the enthusiasm about doctor-identified data, only pharmaceutical companies and drugstore executives knew about it; doctors had no clue that a company they had never heard of was collecting data on them. "We weren't going around telling anybody," Silverberg said years later. "We had nothing to gain by letting them know. If they know they are being tracked, it might alter their behavior. That's kind of a basic of market research. And the reality is that the drug companies did not want their reps telling the doctors they were watching. That's a bad scenario when that happens."

Drug companies told their salespeople to stay mum about the dossiers they had at their disposal. "We always told our reps, 'You are not supposed to say, 'Hey, Doc, you are lying to me, Doc. You didn't sell anything. You say you love me, but you are not selling anything,' because that is never a good conversation," said Degatano, who oversaw Merck's use of physician-level and other data.

While doctor-identified dossiers caught on in the United States, regions such as Europe and Japan, with stronger privacy traditions, resisted the trend. "In the US at the time when I was in charge, we had individual information on every damn physician you could find," said Tommy Boman, a Swede who served as IMS North America CEO from 1993 to 1998. "But that you never do in Europe. That was so offensive for the Europeans."

The secrecy in the United States set the seeds for what would eventually become a huge court fight over the proper boundaries in the business of medical data. But it would still be a decade before enough doctors realized what was going on for protests to grow. Patients, at the center of all the data collecting, would remain in the dark far longer.

IMS Enters the Game

The industry's dominant data miner, IMS Health, was slow in following Source in compiling exactly how many scripts each doctor wrote for each medication, partly because it did not want to erode sales of its wildly profitable Drug Distribution Data service. The success of DDD and IMS' other offerings prompted Dun & Bradstreet to buy IMS for nearly $1.7 billion in 1988, bringing the data miner under the same corporate ownership that held market research pioneer A. C. Nielsen.

In 1993, IMS joined the bandwagon and started profiling individual doctors in its new Xponent service. It told pharmaceutical companies that these data would dramatically boost sales: "Research has shown that winning just one more prescription per week from each prescriber, yields an annual gain of $52 million in sales. So, if you're not targeting with the utmost precision, you could be throwing away a fortune. . . . A sales person can use this model to target doctors who have switched from the drug they are selling and to devise a specific message to counter that switching behavior."[6]

To gain even more insights on US physicians, IMS and its rivals raced to buy as many prescriptions as possible from different vendors, engaging in what insiders called "store wars." Obtaining all these prescription data was costly, and for the first five years, IMS never made a profit from its doctor-identified data, according to former IMS North America CEO Tommy Boman. The investment certainly paid off on the longer term, however. The introduction of many new drugs in the 1990s, combined with the new doctor-prescribing profiles, prompted drug companies to double their sales forces. In the United States, the number of detailers soared to 87,892 in 2001, up from 41,855 just five years before.[7] Drug companies increased their total promotional spending—80 percent of which is related to free samples and detailing—from $9.1 billion in 1996 to $15.7 billion in 2000.[8] By 2005, IMS "sales force effectiveness" products generated 48 percent of its worldwide revenue.[9]

The Education of a Sales Rep

Doctor-identified data do indeed empower reps with a secret weapon as potent as a comic book superhero's X-ray vision. Before each visit, the salesperson studies extensive reports that track exactly how many prescriptions a doctor writes for each drug. Much as a baseball manager analyzes past averages to plot strategy, the rep uses the prescribing profiles to refine the next sales pitch. Yet the data collection does not take place in public, where everyone knows the score. For many years, doctors did not realize outsiders were tallying statistics on how they treat patients in the privacy of their own offices.

These reports were so secret that reps did not bring laptops, which also contained personal observations about physicians, into the office as they made the rounds. If somehow a doctor suspected the reps knew his or her exact prescribing trends and asked about it, reps would change the subject or deny the allegation. "It was super-top-classified," said Shahram Ahari, who started working for Eli Lilly in 1998. "It was taboo. It was forbidden to ever mention that topic."[10]

Ahari joined Lilly straight out of college, imagining that detailers alleviated patient suffering by enlightening busy medical professionals about the latest medications. When Lilly offered him a job paying about $75,000 a year, with stock options, a car, and other perks, he felt he had hit the jackpot. His work turned out to be rather different from what he had expected. Over several weeks of training, he realized that an engaging personality, attractiveness, and enthusiasm, rather than knowledge of science, would make or break his success.

Sure, Lilly and its rivals taught its sales reps about the virtues of its drugs and the shortcomings of rival products. Yet the key to thriving involved adjusting each office visit according to the doctor's personality. Ahari learned the importance of sizing up and categorizing each doctor. Some physicians warmly welcome and banter with reps, but others remain aloof. Gifts and pampering influence mercenary physicians to change what they prescribe; other doctors pretend willingness to convert while they continue to write scripts for rival drugs. No-shows avoid the pharma rep altogether.[11]

Lilly assigned Ahari to cover a territory of several hundred psychiatrists in Brooklyn and Staten Island. Paired with an attractive woman in her mid-twenties, Ahari made solo visits, as did his partner, but they shared detailed notes about who might get along best with each physician. As in many businesses, knowing the product often proved less valuable than establishing a trusted relationship with the doctor.

Ahari developed an anthropologist's eye for detail in seeking to understand a doc's personality. Family photos on the desk provided an opening to talk about spouses, children, and schools. Books might reveal a passion for French or Russian literature; a religious object, clues about faith; sports equipment, a love for golf or tennis. The rep recorded all these details into a laptop after each visit. "Just saw Dr. Cohen," Ahari might jot down. "She went to Yale." Ahari did not attend the school, but another Eli Lilly rep might be a fellow Yalie who could use the alumni bond to build a seemingly real friendship.

Ahari and his partner had different interests and talents and deployed them accordingly. He was keen on politics, culture, and travel. She loved haute cuisine and fine arts and played classical guitar music. Flirtation can come into play, and romantic relationships sometimes develop. Ahari never became intimate with a doctor, but he thought two Russian psychiatrists in Staten Island were trying to set him up one night when their daughter joined them for dinner.

Using IMS data, the reps fussed over the biggest prescribers of Eli Lilly drugs. Of 450 doctors in the territory, Ahari and his partner actively targeted about 200, with the 50 biggest prescribers receiving lavish attention such as invitations to fancy Manhattan restaurants. Perhaps the good doctor fancies a meal at Il Mulino for baby arugula with shaved parmesan, scallops over squid-ink pasta, and fine wine? If not, how about Nobu, for some black cod miso, yellowtail sashimi, and free-flowing sake? Even getting a reservation in such places can prove difficult—but not for free-spending, repeat visitors from big drug companies.

As the wine flows freely, reps joke and banter, all the while avoiding sales talk. Pharmaceutical firms want doctors to consider the rep a real friend, a great guy or gal who happens to work as a salesperson. But as friendly and relaxed as the evening might get, Ahari always remembered his training mantra: "The doctor is sitting with a friend; you are sitting with a client." All the good cheer had a clear goal: When Ahari next visited the office to promote a drug such as Zyprexa to treat schizophrenia or bipolar disorder, the doctor should increase prescriptions of the drug.

Officially, company guidelines limited Ahari to $100 per doctor per meal. But with drinks, a top Manhattan restaurant might charge $250 per head. Fortunately, his managers gave him ample latitude, which meant writing out paperwork indicating that two or three doctors had attended. A top prescribing doctor might even merit a $1,000 meal. The generosity did not end with the meals. Reps regularly delivered breakfast or lunch to the doctor's office, ensuring a friendly front office staff. Bringing a rich spread of fresh bagels, lox, and orange juice every week helped make certain that the receptionist would find the rep a few minutes on the doctor's schedule. A cake might arrive noting the birthday of the doctor's kid or staff member. Over the course of the year, Ahari spent $60,000 to $80,000 catering and dining out at restaurants three or four times a week.

If doctors receiving all the generosity did not prescribe more Eli Lilly drugs, the largess would taper off. "We didn't get you the bagels and lox, but here are some doughnuts with coffee," Ahari might say in explaining the box of doughnuts rather than gourmet lox. "I felt bad I have not been able to do this—it's out of my own pocket—but I like you guys." Naturally, he was hoping that the staff would prod the doctor about prescriptions. "It is uncomfortable for the physician to lose those gifts," Ahari reasoned, "but it's a whole different thing when they have to deal with a veritable rebellion on their hands when the staff has accustomed themselves to all those free bagels."

Sometimes he might honestly explain why the gourmet spread had turned into a motel-quality breakfast. "My boss said docs who are prescribing at least the average amount of Prozac should get the gifts, should get the lunches. Since you are prescribing less than average, I can't bring lunch anymore. I am really sorry," he might say.

By Ahari's second year, drug companies spent nearly $5 billion promoting their medications through detail men and women. The investment made sense because they could precisely measure the impact of detailing on each doctor's prescribing. Within two or four weeks of wining and dining, Ahari received a report indicating whether a psychiatrist was writing more prescriptions for Prozac or other Eli Lilly drugs than before.

Why Detailing Works

In theory, physicians can learn about new treatments by reading the latest medical journals. A long-standing reality is that such diligence after long days of treating patients rarely happens. "Unfortunately most M.D.s do not have the time to study such literature as would acquaint them with drugs in their respective fields; consequently they rely on the advice given them by the detail man," one doctor explained in a 1955 survey.[12] "Many of them are not too happy about this, but have no choice in the matter."

Former Merck executive Mark Degatano added this observation: "Some people will counter with, 'Shouldn't the physicians read all the journals?' You know what? Yeah. And everybody should eat a good meal and exercise four times a week, and use their safety belt every time they get into a car, and never smoke, and put a helmet on whenever they ride a bike."

Some physicians have always avoided detailers. In a 1963 memoir about his forty years in the detailing profession, R. L. McQuillan tells of a New York City doctor who met a pharma rep in the waiting room, escorted him down a long hallway, opened a door, and then pushed him into a back alley. On another occasion, a detail man asked if he could wait to see a pharmacy owner. "Go ahead," a clerk said. "Wait as long as you want to." Only half an hour later did the rep learn that the owner was on holiday in Florida.[13]

Some medical practitioners feel the same way today. "I think most physicians find most pharmaceutical reps annoying because it is kind of like dealing with a used-car salesman or an insurance guy," said David Johnson, a Wisconsin anesthesiologist. "The attitude toward them was, 'They only sell the drug to me that is good for them, or they only promote the drug that is good to them.'"

Yet many doctors still see the pharma reps, even if just for a few minutes. Detailers make the encounters more pleasant with free meals, sample medications, pens, pads, hats, and souvenirs. Many offer good company as well. "Many reps are so friendly, so easygoing, so much fun to flirt with that it is virtually impossible to demonize them," Carl Elliott writes in *White Coat, Black Hat*. "How can you demonize someone who brings you lunch and touches your arm and remembers your birthday and knows the names of all your children?"[14]

Pharma rep Norman Cohen easily fits that description. He was a great friend to doctors in the Philadelphia area. He tells amusing stories, is fun to be around, and knows the best local restaurants. His embrace would extend beyond the dinner table. He would gladly go shopping with you and would even help negotiate the contract to the house you were buying. "I was their pal," he told me years after his retirement. "I was very close to a lot of them, and they would write for my products. I never felt that the patients suffered."

At Cohen's firm, only the top prescribers merited such close attention, namely, the thirty or so who generated 60 percent of sales in his region for statins, the ubiquitous class of anticholesterol medications. Cohen would closely monitor to see if his friendships led to additional prescriptions for his company's drugs. "All of this was based on IMS data," Cohen said. "I would know if I was successful within two weeks."

Clearly, human interactions have long influenced how even well-trained, serious professionals approach their work. "I imagine one of the things that affects me indirectly in the drugs I buy is the personality of the detail man, especially when it comes to antibiotics, which all do the same thing," one doctor told the 1955 survey.[15]

Sometimes, baser instincts prompt doctors to embrace detailers. When I asked one retired doctor why he saw pharma reps throughout his career, he grinned and answered, "Because they gave free samples and because they had big tits."

Critics have long argued that armies of detail people distort rather than advance knowledge. A. Dale Console, former medical director at pharmaceutical company E. R. Squibb & Sons, testified to this effect before a congressional committee in 1960: "There is a simple maxim, I learned from detail men, which is known to most if not all in the pharmaceutical industry. If you can't convince them, confuse them. With the enormous resources at its command, it has usurped the place of the medical educator and has successfully substituted propaganda for education." He added that detailing was a "numbers' racket with its never-ending barrage of new products, confusing names, conflicting dosage schedules and indications, claims and counterclaims."[16]

Love-Hate Relationship

By the 2000s, the pharmaceutical industry concluded that its spending on doctors had become a bit unseemly and that the industry should show some self-restraint. In 2002, its Pharmaceutical Research and Manufacturers of America (PhRMA) trade group deemed that members should not pay for golf games, sports tickets, or dine-and-dash takeout meals in which doctors received free takeout if they were willing to hear a brief spiel or take some brochures as they picked up the food. Variants included a free car wash, flowers, even Christmas trees. Gifts should not exceed $100 and should be limited to medically related items such as anatomical models or stethoscopes (a 2009 update refined the guidelines to say stethoscopes were out, as they did not have an educational function).

The lavish drug company spending on physician meals and gifts has slowed since then, but doctor-identified data remains a vital component of the US drug business. In 2014, I asked Doug Long, the IMS Health vice president for industry relations, what the public should know about his company. He spoke of doctor-identified data: "We make health care more efficient by identifying the doctors worth calling on and those that aren't for a particular manufacturer." The data allow drug companies both to ignore some physicians unlikely to generate large sales and to concentrate on those most likely to prescribe more of their medications.

If anything, the explosion of information flowing from pharmacies, insurance claims, and various middlemen has made IMS reports even more essential. Drug companies have to have them, whatever the cost— and the price is certainly high. Big pharma companies pay $10 million to $40 million a year for a full package of IMS data, consulting, and other services.[17] Such information is so vital that IMS executives receive rock star treatment at industry conferences. Robert Hooper remembered how he viewed IMS when he was the president of Abbott Laboratories Canada. "I fought to get into hear IMS because they were Yoda," he said.

Hooper assumed the mantle of the Star Wars Jedi master when he became president of IMS Americas in 1997. At one major industry conference, the first speaker, the chairman of Glaxo Wellcome, told the audience that Glaxo was the second-largest drug company, according to IMS data. The second speaker, Merck's chairman, proclaimed that Merck was the world's biggest drug company, citing IMS. Then Hooper took the podium and announced he *was* IMS. The audience laughed and cheered. "I could not have won a better setup for how important we were to the industry," he reflected years later.

Still, as much as pharmaceutical companies, Wall Street, and others crave IMS data, many resent the company's high prices and arrogant attitude. "It was kind of a love-hate relationship, Hooper said. "You needed their data, you loved their data, but you were paying too much for it. If a customer would call with a complaint, nobody would get back to them. I mean, they just wouldn't. Like, 'Screw you. What are you going to do? I'm the only game in town.'" Things haven't really changed, current IMS CEO Ari Bousbib acknowledged in late 2015: "Our clients love us or hate us but they cannot do without the IMS data."[18]

Sometimes, however, those whose information IMS gathers resist and fight back. Such was the case when physicians realized they had been subject to unwelcome surveillance by IMS in reports detailing their prescribing. That fight would go all the way to the Supreme Court.

CHAPTER 6

□ □ □ □ □

SUPREME COURT BATTLE

A Doctor's Suspicions

Dr. Peter Klementowicz once welcomed pharmaceutical representatives into his New Hampshire cardiology practice. He knew that the detail people push their company's latest drugs, but he rationalized that seeing reps got him free drug samples he could give to his poorest patients. Over time, however, the visits made him uneasy. Once, a detailer told him, "You are my target." Her comment struck the doctor as curious. "You've got to be kidding me," he thought.

What really set him off was a visit in the early 2000s by two reps who had brought free lunch for his staff. They showed him a dot-matrix printout several inches thick listing the prescribing habits of doctors in his region. Other doctors had gotten with the program; why hadn't he? "We want you to change your practice and what you are prescribing," one said.

"Just get out," the doctor responded.

The pharma reps had far greater insights into his and other doctors' prescribing habits than Klementowicz had ever imagined. Incensed, he tossed out the promotional materials and pondered his next move. They knew everything about every drug that he had prescribed for everybody, he realized.

The drugs he prescribed made up his professional signature. "I really thought if they knew my aggregate data of how I work, that that was really stealing intellectual property," he recalled years later. "There was a moment in time I thought, 'Is there a way I can copyright what I do in terms of my therapy?' But it didn't go anywhere."

Klementowicz's anger was especially pronounced, but for many years, few doctors realized that sales reps had access to exact details on their prescribing patterns.[1] Although pharmaceutical reps were sternly instructed never to give any clues about what they knew, some could not resist the temptation to blurt it out. The secret did not hold forever, and when doctors caught on, many fought back.

New Hampshire Takes a Stance

As Klementowicz discovered that pharmaceutical salespeople had meticulous records of his prescribing habits, his wife, Cindy Rosenwald, a freshman Democratic representative in the New Hampshire House of Representatives, also learned about the practice. One day in 2005, an American Association of Retired Persons (AARP) lobbyist named Bill Hamilton handed Rosenwald a few related articles. Knowing she was busy, he hoped that just planting the articles without saying anything might stir her into action. "It is kind of like dropping the hook in the water," he said later. "Someone either bites on it, or you move to something else."

One article was a 2003 front-page *Boston Globe* exposé titled "Drug Companies' Secret Reports Outrage Doctors."[2] The piece revealed the hidden trade in physician-identified data. "Most physicians know drug companies collect some information about which medications they prescribe. But they are often surprised by the depth of detail pharmaceutical makers now are buying about almost every US physician, mostly from large pharmacy chains." The article noted that several drugmakers, including Eli Lilly and Wyeth, and the industry's leading lobby organization, the Pharmaceutical Research and Manufacturers of America (PhRMA), had declined to comment.

"It just amazed me," Rosenwald said, "but it irritated me as well, because not only did I think it was an invasion of physicians' privacy, I thought it was probably an invasion of an individual's privacy. I also thought it clearly was going to lead to higher prescription drug expenses."

When she showed the article to her husband, he told her, "Drug reps do this to me all the time."

The lobbyist's strategy succeeded: Rosenwald was intrigued. Paid just a hundred dollars a year as a legislator and allocated no staff, Rosenwald also worked as an adjunct faculty member at the University of Massachusetts, Lowell, thirty minutes south of Nashua, New Hampshire. The university gave her a little, windowless office off the library stacks. Although she held regular hours, few students came, so in the fall of 2005, she used this time to research physician profiling. Finding very little material, she decided to propose a bill to ban the commercial use of prescription data.

As hearings on the draft legislation started, in January 2006, Rosenwald gave her colleagues a rudimentary chart to show how data flowed from pharmacy to middlemen to data miner to pharmaceutical company. She also handed out an unusually self-revealing article written by two IMS officials and titled "Data Mining at IMS HEALTH: How We Turned a Mountain of Data into a Few Information-Rich Molehills."[3]

She feared looking like a fool if industry experts revealed that doctor profiling had once occurred but had since ended. She need not have worried. The freshman legislator realized she had hit a nerve when several well-dressed IMS officials showed up at the hearing. "They almost exuded a confidence that seemed like, 'We are from a big company, they are a little state, there is not even a nice restaurant in your town,'" she recalled. "You could get the feeling they felt we were a bunch of hicks who didn't know anything."

In a one-page background memo handed out to legislators, IMS warned that the bill would have unintended consequences by impeding the flow of information "used in not only pharmaceutical marketing—but also in public health monitoring, outcomes research studies, pharmacoeconomic analysis, bioterrorism surveillance, Medicare Part D uptake studies and physician feedback reporting."[4]

IMS and the PhRMA lobby argued that they provided a public good by aggregating patient data in important ways the government and public institutions did not. Some who follow the industry found these talking points a diversion from the real focus on sales and marketing. John Mack, the publisher and executive editor of the newsletter *Pharma Marketing News*, considered the arguments about all the public good ostensibly generated by data miners, and he concluded: "If this were true, one would think that the pharma industry would be more proactive in taking credit for this largesse and its positive impact on the well-being of US citizens."

New Hampshire legislators decided to hedge their bets in crafting the Prescription Information Confidentiality Act. The bill, the nation's first of its kind, barred the use of prescription records for "advertising, marketing, promotion, or any activity that could be used to influence sales or market share of a pharmaceutical product." Passed in June 2006, the law did not, however, ban the use of information for public health monitoring and other areas that could clearly benefit society.

As one of the smallest US states by population and size, New Hampshire seemed unlikely to threaten the multibillion-dollar pharmaceutical industry or data miners. Yet the new law in the plucky little state with the motto Live Free or Die attracted nationwide attention, and similar bills followed in neighboring Vermont and Maine in June 2007. "When we found out that IMS was collecting this data without anybody's approval and that they were very self-righteous about it . . . that really sort of galvanized everybody," said David Johnson, who served as the Vermont Medical Society president from 2006 to 2007. "One of the things that caught everybody's attention was how much money was spent on promotion and advertising relative to R&D. . . . It really kind of made everybody angry."

IMS tried to put the best public face on developments, as exemplified in its 2008 annual report: "These three states collectively represent approximately one percent of prescription activity in the United States, so the potential financial impact of these laws on our business, financial condition and results of operations is not expected to be material."

Privately, IMS officials were concerned. "The challenge was: Was this going to be something that really caught fire across the country?" said David Thomas, the IMS chairman and CEO from 2000 to 2005.

The legislative ban on key aspects of their business also hurt IMS employee morale. "Inside the company, there is a bit of shock," said Randy Frankel, IMS Health vice president for external affairs. He was testifying before the Vermont's House Committee on Health Care. "We are entangled in it as though we're doing something wrong."[5]

With a lot of money at stake, the medical and pharmaceutical industry mobilized. The American Medical Association, the largest US physician group, somewhat surprisingly, at least on the surface, sided with the data miners, not with doctors who objected to commercial companies targeting them. One reason is that, as mentioned in the previous chapter, the AMA makes many millions of dollars a year selling its Physician Masterfile of the names, addresses, and educational history on 1.4 million doctors and medical students in the United States.[6] This list, whose history dates back to 1906 and which was initially used for basic membership support and mailings, helps data miners supplement prescription information to create fuller doctor profiles. As the issue heated up, the AMA decided to continue selling access to its

Physician Masterfile database but allowed individual doctors to opt out of salespeople using their information.

The Court Fight

Data miners fought against these new laws and sued in federal court. In April 2007, the US District Court for New Hampshire gave IMS and rivals Verispan and Source International an initial victory, finding that Rosenwald's legislation restricted constitutionally protected speech. In November, an appeals court overturned the decision, bringing the law back into force. Parallel legal fights unfolded in Vermont and Maine. Maine mirrored New Hampshire's rulings at the district and then appeals court level. In Vermont, the opposite sequence occurred: the lower court ruled against the data miners, and the appeal overturned the decision in November 2010.

Throughout, data miners argued that they had a free-speech right guaranteed under the First Amendment to gather prescribing information. "The companies that we represent are publishing companies," argued Tom Julin, one of their lawyers. "They are similar to newspapers in that they focus on gathering and disseminating information." The companies do not report on crimes or on new companies, he said. "Instead, they report about the decisions of doctors such as Tom Wharton of Exeter, New Hampshire, or Dr. Andy Cole of Massachusetts and Dr. Ken Ciongoli of Burlington, Vermont, and other doctors across the land about the drugs that they prescribe for their patients."[7]

Data miners also said that barring doctor-identified data would drive up health-care costs, as drug companies would have to spend more on promoting because detailing would become less successful. IMS official Hossam Sadek gave the example of a company introducing a new Alzheimer's or diabetes medication that might interest fifty thousand out of more than a million doctors nationwide: "Rather than hiring tens of thousands of sales representatives and building or manufacturing a lot of samples, they can basically tailor the resources that they are planning to effectively bring that product to market to the specific target audience that that product is targeted for."[8]

Opponents of doctor-identified data argued that the practice violated physician privacy and led to higher costs by convincing physicians to prescribe newer medications rather than cheaper generics. Jerry Avorn, chief of pharmacoepidemiology and pharmacoeconomics at Harvard Medical School's Department of Medicine at Brigham and Women's

Hospital, mocked the legal objections by IMS and the other data miners: "They obviously, are not going to come in with a statement saying, 'We are making a ton of money selling this data, so we, therefore, want to keep doing it.' They are going to come with objections that are more socially acceptable like 'This is going to hurt patients. Doctors are not going to be able to learn anything about drugs.'"[9]

Avorn also ridiculed the industry arguments that detailers served an important role by informing physicians about the latest drugs: "Most of them don't come in and say: 'Hello, I was an art history major in college, and I never took any training except for the four or five weeks the company gave me and now, I'm going to tell you how to treat you patients.' I'm afraid that doctors don't quite pick up on the fact that this person is not an expert in the field."[10]

Supreme Court Decision

After the appeals court rulings in the three states conflicted, the Vermont case that became known as *IMS Health v. Sorrell* headed to the US Supreme Court in April 2011.[11] Representing Vermont attorney general William Sorrell, Bridget Asay was excited to argue before the nation's highest judicial body for the first time. In the days before the oral arguments, she had had a recurring nightmare in which she had forgotten to wear her shoes to the high court.

When the big day arrived, Asay was fully attired as she stepped in front of the nine justices seated behind a curved mahogany podium under a forty-four-foot ceiling. Standing at the central lectern, she had not spoken even a minute before Chief Justice John Roberts, seated directly before her in the middle of nine tall chairs, cut her off. His question, followed by a rapid-fire series of interruptions from other justices, suggested they were not buying her argument about Vermont's law.

"The purpose is to prevent sales representatives from contacting particular physicians, right?" Roberts asked.

"I disagree, Your Honor," Asay answered. "The purpose of the statute is to let doctors decide whether sales representatives will have access to this inside information about what they have been prescribing to their patients."

Soon Justice Antonin Scalia joined in: "That's the purpose of it, to prevent them from using this information to market their drugs." Then Scalia noted that because Vermont law still allowed doctor-identified data to be shared for academic and scientific research, the law did not afford full privacy anyway.

"How does it increase the prescribing physician's right of privacy that the data about his prescribing can only be given away but can't be sold?" Scalia asked. "Does that make him feel happier about his privacy?"

"What it allows the doctor to do is to avoid an intrusive and invasive marketing practice," Asay responded.

"He can do that by saying: I don't want to talk to you," Scalia retorted.

The tough questioning was not restricted to the more conservative justices nominated by Republican presidents. Justice Sonia Sotomayor, elevated to the bench by President Barack Obama, asked why an opt-out, akin to the Do Not Call Registry for telemarketers, would not suffice to avoid the marketing.

Thomas Goldstein, the lawyer for the data miners, later emphasized that doctors have a choice in deciding whether to meet pharmaceutical representatives: "The doctors do get to say: I don't want you to come visit me. They do that all the time. My dad's a doctor; he doesn't visit with detailers."

Whether patients might object to the sale of their anonymized data was not an important focus of the arguments. "Remember, the patients have nothing to do with this," Goldstein said at one point. "The State doesn't give any control to the patient. That would be true before or after."

Later, Justice Anthony Kennedy asked, "Suppose you had a statute in which the pharmacy cannot give the information or sell the information to anybody; it must remain with the pharmacy."

"That would be a real privacy statute," Goldstein replied. "I think that it would still be unconstitutional, but it would be much closer."

The day had not gone well for the State of Vermont and those seeking to limit data miners, and Asay knew it as she left the courtroom. Less than two months later, Kennedy wrote the 6–3 decision in favor of IMS and other data miners, embracing their argument that gathering information on doctor prescriptions was constitutionally protected. "Speech in aid of pharmaceutical marketing . . . is a form of expression protected by the Free Speech Clause of the First Amendment," Kennedy wrote. "Many are those who must endure speech they do not like, but that is a necessary cost of freedom."

As the oral arguments foreshadowed, the justices were concerned that the law selectively barred pharmaceutical reps, but not researchers, from accessing doctor-identified data. "If Vermont's statute provided that prescriber-identifying information could not be sold or disclosed except in narrow circumstances then the State might have a stronger position," Kennedy wrote.[12]

Data miners continue today to sell doctor-identified data in the United States. Experts have long advocated alternative methods of informing doctors about the latest drugs, but with limited success. Larry Weed, one of the founders of electronic medical records, considers it silly that individual doctors should decide which drugs best treat various ailments. Rather, he advocates a national repository of standard recommendations. "The doctor shouldn't be making a judgment of anything," he said.

Such an idea is not new. In 1905, the AMA set up a Council on Pharmacy and Chemistry to evaluate health claims of drugs and to set standards. From 1930 to 1955, it also issued a Seal of Acceptance for medications it tested in its labs.[13] But as pharmaceutical companies prospered in the postwar wonder-drug boom, they gained significant advertising sway. With the AMA deriving about half of its revenue from advertising in its journals, it eventually backed off from its watchdog role (it was also concerned about liability lawsuits).[14]

"In a perfect world, there would be no need for drug reps," former Pfizer detail man James Reidy wrote in a 2005 memoir. "Physicians would receive sufficient pharmaceutical training in medical school and residency, and this training would last them indefinitely. Doctors would have sufficient time to update this training, if necessary, by reading the latest medical journals throughout their forty-year careers. Finally, pharmaceutical companies would bring to market only those drugs that provide marked benefits over products already in use."[15]

Of course, such a world does not exist. Drug reps can help inform doctors, but these salespeople focus on newer, more expensive medications, ignoring cost-efficient generics. There is a better way, Jerry Avorn said. Through *academic detailing*, a program he devised, neutral experts inform doctors about the latest trends in medicine. "We undo some of the damage that has been created by an IMS-guided world in which we doctors are marketed within an inch of our lives in a very terrifyingly precise manner," he said. However, paying academic detailers to visit physicians requires funding from state governments or outside institutions, so such efforts have been limited to date.

In any case, physicians are increasingly unwilling to see pharmaceutical salespeople. One study found that 49 percent of doctors placed moderate to severe restrictions on reps in 2014, up more than double from 23 percent in 2008.[16] Insurance companies are seeking higher copays for branded drugs than for generics, and the US Food and Drug Administration appears less willing to approve new drugs that are minor variations of an existing medication. All these developments are lessening the effectiveness of detailers.

The gathering of doctor-identified data continues to be debated, but IMS and its rivals have increasingly focused on a new frontier of much more intimate data: dossiers on a patient's medical history, assembled from doctor, hospital, pharmacy, insurer, lab, and other information. As with doctor dossiers two decades before, data miners work behind the scenes without telling patients that their anonymized information is a commercial product. Never before had companies assembled such an intimate portrait of patients, and the march of technology made it easy.

CHAPTER 7

STUDYING PATIENTS OVER TIME

The Infected Water Pump

People were dying fast, and the British medical establishment had no clue how to save them. It was far from the first time a devastating cholera epidemic had swept across England. In 1831–1832, the potentially fatal disease causing severe diarrhea and stomach pains had killed fifty thousand. Another devastating outbreak hit London in 1848. Now, in 1854, the disease was spreading misery and death again.

As a young medical apprentice, John Snow had witnessed the devastation of 1831–1832. He began to suspect that the conventional wisdom about the disease was wrong. Miasmas—gases rising from sewers, swamps, garbage, and other sources—did not cause cholera, he reasoned. After the 1848 outbreak, he suggested that water or food might actually spread cholera. The experts remained skeptical, countering that he had no proof.

When a new wave of cholera hit in 1854, Snow decided to study a large sample of Londoners to look for patterns that might pinpoint the cause of the disease. Two years later, he published his findings in a book, in which he described his sample population: "No fewer than three hundred thousand people of both sexes, of every age and occupation, and of every rank and station, from gentle folks down to the very poor, were divided into two groups without their choice, and, in most cases, without their knowledge."

One group drank water provided by a private company from a section of the Thames River that contained sewage; the second group relied on a different firm, which drew water from a nonpolluted location upriver. Snow found that the sewage-containing water led to far more cholera deaths than did the nonpolluted source of water. Still, medical experts remained skeptical of his findings.

Later that summer, deaths from cholera soared in London's SoHo district. Snow mapped out where eighty-three victims had lived and the nearest public water pumps to their homes. One pump on Broad Street drew his attention. "On proceeding to the spot," he wrote, "I found that nearly all the deaths had taken place within a short distance of the pump. There were only ten deaths in houses situated decidedly nearer to another street pump."[1]

Snow interviewed family members of the deceased and learned that most of the ten who lived closer to another pump still drew their water from Broad Street. Snow convinced local officials to remove the pump to prevent residents from drawing any more water there, and the outbreak subsided. Further study showed that a nearby cesspool was infecting the Broad Street pump.[2] Snow showed that the study of groups of patients over time could reveal new insights. Today, he is regarded as a pioneer of modern epidemiology, which uses statistics and data for insights into how disease spreads.

Survivor

Other modern medical advances have come from gathering *longitudinal data*, or information about patients gathered over time. Toyoyasu Kobatake became a member of one of the world's longest-studied groups of patients just by setting off for high school one August morning.

The sixteen-year-old put on his school uniform and boarded a tram for his new school in the town center. During the ride from his uncle's house, where he stayed because his family lived a few hours away, a siren sounded. It was shortly before 8 AM. The streetcar came to a halt. It was several years into the war, so Kobatake knew the drill. He took cover nearby, waited for the all-clear signal, and then hopped back on the tram.

As the tram trudged along, a second alarm sounded. He took cover again and then attempted to get back on board. After these delays, enough passengers had squeezed in that Kobatake could only hang from the outside. He decided to walk the rest of the way. Along the way, a woman came out of her house and pointed to the sky: "Look up there, a B-29."

Kobatake looked up and wondered about the strange shape of the plane: the rectangular wingspan seemed to be longer than the length of the plane. Then a bright flash filled the sky. The teen felt as though someone had sharply slapped his entire being. Roaring wind pinned him to a traditional Japanese home, and furniture, clothes, and rubble covered him. He had no idea what had happened, but so much debris had enveloped him that he became convinced he could not escape. "I can't survive," he thought before passing out. "I will die."

When he regained consciousness, his will to live motivated his weakened body to shove away the charred wood, tiles, and household debris that had rained down on him. For the first time, he could see himself. The blast had burned away his pants, leaving only skimpy Japanese-style underpants and a white shirt. Whatever he had just endured had burned away much of his skin; the surface of his arms and legs seemed to be writhing and peeling.

He stumbled forward to the river that wound through town. He stepped into the river to cool off his tender skin and then continued toward his school. Dust clouded the view, and the air smelled of sulfuric acid. Many houses had been completely destroyed, yet a few wooden electric poles remained, oddly burned only on one side. Shouts came from inside and outside the rubble. "My kids are still in the house. Please help," one person cried.

As he neared his school, his skin continued to peel and the pain intensified. Someone pointed toward a clinic, yet hundreds were already lined up. He made his way to another emergency center, but the doctors themselves were lacerated with cuts and other injuries. He stopped seeking medical care but a stranger gave him some rapeseed oil to soothe his burned flesh. Bubbles rose underneath the back of his legs, making it hard to walk; he popped them open, releasing a watery puss.

Kobatake knew that something very unusual had occurred, but what exactly had unleashed all this destruction remained a mystery. After finding some school friends, he climbed a hill overlooking the town and saw that everything was on fire.

"Maybe a torpedo hit the city," one friend said.

"The storage house for gun powder—maybe that exploded," another suggested.

Even with all his pain, Kobatake was relatively well off, for he could still get around. Not really knowing where to go, the boy continued to wander and then returned to the spot where he had watched the sky as the blast hit. Scattered on the ground were a few pages from one of his textbooks. As he wandered, he saw people immobilized by broken legs, their skin slashed by glass, some alive, others motionless. Charred horses lay silently on the pavement.

Everywhere he walked, he found only bleakness and despair. Kobatake decided to try to return home, where his parents and six siblings lived. It was normally a three-hour train ride away. He headed toward the train tracks and walked toward Fukuyama. Eventually, at around six in the evening, he heard the train coming along the route. Mustering enough energy, he ran and climbed aboard. Kobatake had not eaten all day; he was exhausted with pain stinging everywhere. As he fell asleep on the train, his burned legs stuck to his seat.

Around midnight, the train arrived and he made his way home. Neither his father nor mother recognized the youth under the charred skin and badly disheveled appearance. Finally, one of his brothers blurted out, "Look, it's Toyoyasu."

The next morning, Toyoyasu Kobatake's father took him to a doctor. Locals could not fathom what had happened the prior day in Hiroshima, and the physician admitted that he did not know how to treat such a badly burned body. In the following days, painful scabs formed across the boy's body as a high fever raged. His father bought a large block of ice to soothe the wounds; relatives brought peaches for Toyoyasu to eat.

With Japan badly hobbled just days before its surrender ending World War II, information and medical supplies remained scarce. A neighbor suggested a home-made cucumber balm. Day after day, Toyoyasu Kobatake's mother dabbed the concoction across his body twice every hour. Another doctor prescribed Chinese garlic chives, so his grandmother served them for breakfast, lunch, and dinner, often with eggs. After about a month, his fever subsided, and by October, he could walk again. In November, he returned to school. Only then did his family stop hiding the mirrors. Later they told him that his face had looked like a monkey's rear end.

Kobatake had been about a mile away from the center of the atomic bomb blast in Hiroshima on August 6, 1945. When I visited him in the Japanese port city of Yokohama in 2015, the eighty-six-year-old appeared remarkably energetic for any man his age, let alone an A-bomb survivor. He drove his car to pick me up at the train station, welcomed me into his home, where he lives alone, and never showed any sign of fatigue over several hours as he recounted his incredible story of survival.

In 1946, Harry Truman, the US president who ordered the atomic attacks on Hiroshima and Nagasaki, approved a plan "to undertake a long range, continuing study of the biological effects and medical effects of the atomic bomb on man." This longitudinal study of atomic bomb survivors continues to this day, and survivors continue to receive free medical treatment following a Japanese law passed in 1957.

STUDYING PATIENTS OVER TIME   65

Studying a select group of patients over time has tremendous advantages because one can compare them with other groups with different experiences or circumstances. When I visited Hiroshima a few months before the seventieth anniversary of the bombing, I was surprised to learn that about two hundred thousand people who had survived the two atomic blasts were still alive. Roy Shore, vice chairman and chief of research of the Radiation Effects Research Foundation, said that of ninety-three thousand people studied who had been within ten kilometers of the blast, between 30 and 33 percent were still alive in 2009, the time of the latest survey. Overall, research has shown that survivors exposed to radiation ended up dying about two years earlier on average than others in their age group, he said. "It is pretty amazing that so many are still coming," Shore said about survivors who still show up for their extensive annual checkups. "It was thought it would shorten life quite a bit, but it hasn't."[3]

Over the decades, researchers have mapped out the exact location of the survivors when the blast hit. Almost anyone within a kilometer died instantly or soon afterward from radiation, unless the person had substantial shielding from the blast. Survival within two kilometers—as in Kobatake's case—depended largely on at least some shielding from radiation. Injury from the blast effects and complications from burns were also significant causes of the early deaths, so, for example, the home-remedy cucumber treatment might have saved Kobatake. Perhaps the small fish he often ate as a boy—and which he considers key to his longevity—had an impact. Maybe he was just lucky to have been shielded by a building or another object at the moment of blast.

Longitudinal Studies

In the first few decades after the blast, researchers did not ask atomic bomb survivors for their consent to use their data in longitudinal studies. Times have changed, and survivors have had a say in recent years. Like most people participating in longitudinal medical studies today, the participants give their *informed consent*, which means that they understand the project and can choose whether to participate.

Another famous longitudinal study started in 1948 in Framingham, Massachusetts, where medical researchers recruited 5,209 men and women for a long-term examination of factors contributing to cardiovascular disease. Every two years, the volunteers return for extensive testing, and the results are shared with researchers. Some from the original group—eighty-six people in total at the end of 2014, all at least ninety-five years old—still participate. The administration of the Framingham Heart Study has cost many millions of dollars over the years but has also led to volumes of groundbreaking medical insights. The research on thousands of patients, augmented by later generations of participants, including children and grandchildren of the original cohort, has helped identify smoking, obesity, diabetes, lack of exercise, high blood pressure, high cholesterol, and other risk factors for heart disease.

The island city of Abu Dhabi has built on the Framingham study by creating the Weqaya ("prevention") program that provides heart disease screening to all citizens every three years. Since 2008, more than 95 percent of citizens—two hundred thousand people—have participated, giving researchers insights on the overall population and individual patients.[4] Other medical longitudinal studies have analyzed the genetic roots of genius, Alzheimer's disease, child development, twins, women's health, and many other topics. There is even a longitudinal study on the impact of pharmaceutical reps on doctors' prescribing.[5]

Whether you live in the United States, England, Australia, or another developed country, your data also end up in longitudinal files. Unlike the Framingham and other studies, not only do you *not* give informed consent for the subsequent use of this information, but rarely do you even know about it. Be that as it may, you are an integral part of the big health-data bazaar.

Data miners such as IMS Health and its competitor Symphony Health compile anonymized dossiers on hundreds of millions of people from various sources, including insurance claims data, which record diagnosis, procedures performed, and medications; pharmacy prescriptions; electronic health records from doctors and hospitals; and blood and urine tests from participating labs. It might seem redundant for a data miner to buy information about the same patient from multiple sources related to the same treatment, but each transaction may contain additional insights. The doctor, pharmacy, insurer, and lab—and various middlemen that process information between all these entities— give data miners different perspectives on medical issues and treatment, much as cameras placed in center field, behind home plate, or aboard an overhead blimp all offer different angles into the same baseball game. The anonymized data from all these sources is linked to the same individual patient (how exactly this happens is discussed in chapter 9). Such multifaceted data may help medical researchers develop new insights and treatments and understand the long-term outcomes of different treatments. The information can also help pharmaceutical marketers discern important patterns such as the tendency of certain patients to switch from one drug to another after some months.

At the same time, linking an ever-growing number of an individual's anonymized files creates privacy risks, especially as computing power grows, said Dennis Turner, a former IMS America president and later a partner with Handel Evans at Source International. "Clearly, you get into a new realm of information because of the ability to link so many different elements of data together in ways that would be highly undesirable for many patients," he said. "The confidentiality issue, in a sense, was always there, but the focus changed as the granularity of the data changed."

Studying Claims Data

Commercial analysis of longitudinal patient files really took off in the 1970s, when large American companies began to look for ways to lower their bills as health-care costs soared. Many employers had expanded their benefits to include doctor's office visits and prescription drugs some years before—for example, the United Auto Workers union negotiated pharmacy benefits for its members in 1967—yet they were vexed because costs rose even faster than the era's high inflation. Several companies, including General Motors, started sending insurance claims data to a pilot project at Boston University for analysis. There, a professor of surgery and vice chancellor, Richard Egdahl, had set up a program to study the quality of health care. He recruited another doctor, Paul Gertman, who had worked in the early 1970s in the Office of Management and Budget and the White House studying Medicare and other health-care issues.

The US government's 1965 creation of Medicare and Medicaid under President Lyndon Johnson's Great Society programs helped spur the computerization of claims data, creating huge quantities of information to study, as well as money-making opportunities for outside firms to handle these claims. One Texas firm, Electronic Data Systems (EDS), founded in 1962 by a former IBM salesman, jumped at this opportunity. It won contracts to process insurance claims for Texas's Medicare and Medicaid programs in 1966 and then for California's programs in 1969. Amid continued expansion and successes, General Motors bought EDS in 1984 for $2.5 billion, making company founder Ross Perot a rich man who later twice ran for president.

While in government, Paul Gertman had wanted to study computerized insurance claims but was told such an effort would not be useful. In

1973, two years after he arrived at Boston University, he got his chance. Medicare gave his team a grant to develop techniques to mine claims to improve insurance options; it sent the team several years of de-identified claims records on hundreds of thousands of Medicare patients. Gertman and his colleagues made considerable strides in learning how to analyze many claims files from companies but faced challenges such as mis-coded data, including claims for pregnant sixty-four-year-old women or odd surges of paperwork for people of the same age or diagnosis filed on Friday afternoons when staff wanted to leave for the weekend. After Gertman's team developed techniques to detect and scrub the bad data, the results showed patterns that gave GM and others useful insights, such as which regions of the country experienced the worst patterns of sicknesses or problems like alcoholism.

Although insurance claims data contain fewer details than doctors' records or lab reports, claims have the advantage of uniformity. Because they capture services wherever patients receive care, the data can be easily compared. By contrast, physicians' notes vary dramatically, as do reports from labs that do not use the same format to record test results.

So many companies appreciated the data-driven insights to reduce expenses and improve quality that in 1981, Gertman formed his own for-profit company, the Health Data Institute.[6] Within a few years, it was analyzing claims from about a third of America's *Fortune* 100 companies, with occasionally unexpected insights. At one large computer company, the data showed that pregnancies and deliveries spiked from nine months to a year after very strong earnings announcements. In another case, Gertman says he and his team uncovered a pattern of fraud among a group of doctors who were funneling money to a suspected Palestinian terrorist organization.

With millions of computer files on reel-to-reel tapes arriving at the company, Gertman's company could have sold information to data miners or pharmaceutical companies, as other middlemen and pharmacies were beginning to do with anonymized prescription information. However, he decided against it, partly because he feared that outsiders could re-identify patients. "We had enough information to show that you could break most of the standard coding," he said, "particularly if you had access to any other kind of corporate personnel files. We got scrambled identifiers, but we also saw the potential that if you had access to other information that was not completely scrambled, you could match up dates and appointments, disability, and identify."

He also expressed a sentiment uncommon among those who could make extra cash by selling medical data: "I don't believe in exploiting people's personal information, for other than their benefit."

Selling Claims Data

Other entrepreneurs also saw value in analyzing insurance claims for companies with an eye to reducing insurance company costs—but decided to go a step further and sell the resulting data. Ernie Ludy, who worked at Blue Cross Blue Shield in Western Pennsylvania in the 1970s, started MedStat Systems in Michigan in 1981, the same year Gertman formed his company. Ludy aggregated details from the claims he collected from Ford, Federal Express, General Electric, Chevron, and other companies, providing them free analysis and benchmark information in exchange for the right to sell their anonymized data to drugmakers, researchers, and data miners. Companies that did not want their data sold had to pay for MedStat's insights. The business grew rapidly, and in 1994, Ludy sold it to Canadian publisher Thomson Corporation for $339 million.

In 2007, the Reuters news agency, where I worked, merged with Thomson. We journalists felt complete surprise when we learned that our new combined company now had an insurance claims database with tens of millions of patient histories. Because reporters love to search through sensitive documents, we could not believe that something as intimate as medical records, even if anonymized, would be in circulation. As attractive as the data were for reporters, the information was worth far more as a commercial asset. In 2012, Thomson Reuters sold its medical businesses for $1.25 billion in a deal that resulted in a new company, Truven Health Analytics. IBM's Watson Health division, in turn, bought the company in 2016 for more than double that price—$2.6 billion—showing the huge value and projected profits that the medical-data business represents.[7]

Insurance claims data also gave rise to a commercial business in Canada, via the unlikely source of the government bureaucracy. In the 1980s, Tom Brogan studied long-term drug costs at Canada's Department of Consumer and Corporate Affairs. He then became director of an agency that monitors drug costs and he worked with provincial governments that control Canada's health-care data. Seeing commercial opportunity, he opened a consulting company in 1989.

In 1992, ahead of SmithKline Beecham's introduction of the antidepressant Paxil, the drugmaker asked Brogan to study how long patients stayed on similar medications and how often they switched to a different drug, something not recorded by traditional data. Brogan made a deal to get patient-level insurance claims data on several hundred thousand patients from a private Canadian insurer. He was convinced not only that he had developed a good business plan, but also that he was acting for the greater good.

Reflecting on cancer, a disease that had struck several relatives, Brogan thought that clues to curing cancer might be hidden in the data, if only the data were made accessible to the right researchers. Eventually, he bought or bartered patient information from about forty private and public Canadian drug plans, paying them a share of revenue and, often, services such as data analysis and trend reports. IMS found the business so attractive that it acquired Brogan's company in 2010.

Dossiers on Individuals

In 1997, years after Ernie Ludy and Tom Brogan started collecting longitudinal patient data, IMS expanded into the area as well. It initially assembled nearly one million anonymized patient electronic medical records from two health-care providers, and insurance claims data from more than 1.5 million US patients, according to Ana-Maria Zaugg, who served as vice president of marketing. It also offered a product called HIV Insight, which gathered medical details from a panel of AIDS patients who agreed to share their information.

Such offerings represented a dramatic evolution into a more personal realm than what IMS had dealt with in its past. In the early days of medical data mining, IMS gathered sales data from a sample of wholesalers and retail stores to calculate the size of the overall market for particular drugs. Over time, it collected prescriptions that were without patient names and that were not linked to other records, and then it started producing profiles on what the individual doctors prescribed. But now, data miners could follow the same individual patient over time.

Even if a new era in medical data mining was dawning, the real action still remained elsewhere for IMS in the 1990s. The company was focusing on products such as Xponent, which profiles what individual doctors prescribe, and its estimates for the market size of various drugs. "When it came down to patient-level data," said Tommy Boman, the IMS North America president until 1998, "the problem was that it was very expensive for us to collect the information, and the pharma companies were not prepared to pay the money we needed to make reasonable profits. We could not, at that time, produce a patient-level database that was commercially possible."

Data mining upstart ArcLight, created out of partnership between wholesale distributor Cardinal Health and large US pharmacy chains, saw longitudinal patient data as another opportunity to challenge the dominance of IMS. It started linking its prescription data into dossiers on millions of patients, telling potential clients that until then, drug companies could see only a shadow of reality. For the first time, pharmas could learn what was actually happening and gain insights on many features of a drug:

Persistency: How long a patient stays on a particular drug.

Compliance: How well a patient follows the prescription.

Switching behavior: Whether patients switch to rival medications.

Concomitance: Which other drugs a patient takes while on the drug in question.

All this percolation in the big health-data bazaar inspired Cardinal rival McKesson and clinical research company Quintiles to create another data mining company, Verispan, in 2002.[8] By the following year, Verispan had gathered de-identified patient data from about a third of all US pharmacies, with more than two billion patient records added every year.[9] It ultimately generated annual revenue of about $100 million, with its biggest customer paying $6 million or $7 million annually for longitudinal data and services, said Peter Castagna, who served as Verispan's chief operating officer.

McKesson was no newcomer to the medical data business but had sold its earlier entity, Pharmaceutical Data Services, in 1988 to investors led by Handel Evans and Dennis Turner. One reason for McKesson to get back in the game was concern that Cardinal spinoff ArcLight would steal customers by giving CVS, Walmart, Kmart, Albertsons, and other retailers a share of profits, a great way for Cardinal to deepen its relationship with the big pharmacy chains. "Walmart was McKesson's largest customer at the time," Castagna said, "and there were some concerns that Cardinal could use ArcLight to potentially target the mass-merchandiser. It gave Cardinal another way into the relationship, to pay for and access data and then potentially turn that data back into information for Walmart to provide more value to them as a future customer."

A New Pathway to Patient Data

As competition in longitudinal data intensified, IMS lined up even more sources for insights on patients. Roger Korman, former president of IMS Canada and IMS Latin America, who was with the company from 1979 to 2004, explained how IMS procured its sources: "When we were buying data, we used to say, 'Look, you are creating data as a by-product. It's an exhaust from your system. What don't you take that thing and turn it into an asset and sell it?' That is the way we would get people to think about data as an asset—with full confidence that we were not violating anyone's privacy or the law."

One important new source of data came from a middleman company called Allscripts, in which IMS invested $10 million in 2000.[10] Originally a service to repackage medications for doctors' offices, Allscripts refocused its services in the late 1990s to enable doctors to prescribe medications electronically to pharmacies. "We knew that if we were to automate this process, take these three billion pieces of paper, and convert them to electronics, we could not only save lives and improve health care, but along the way, we would have valuable data," said Glen Tullman, CEO of Allscripts from 1997 to 2012.

Allscripts later expanded into electronic medical records, a move that gave it access to patient data, which has become a vital component of third-party data mining dossiers. "Most of where IMS is getting their clinical data from is Allscripts," said Bob Merold, a former IMS executive who played an important role in developing the company's databases in the 1990s. "They were one of the first to get the rights to the data from the physicians."[11]

As Allscripts has grown—the company says that one in three US doctors, and half of all hospitals, use its system—data sales have soared to around $30 million annually, up from just $3 or $4 million a few years ago.[12] "Today," Tullman said, "if you look at Allscripts, the data business is the only thing that is driving the growth of bottom-line earnings there. That's a key jewel in the world today, and that's data coming from electronic health records."

Current Allscripts CEO Paul Black emphasized that sharing such information creates a social benefit and that careful anonymization protects patients. "I think that data, used properly, has a lot of value to society, and I think when pharma folks use it, they are extraordinarily judicious with it," he said. "The protections that are in place are extraordinarily broad to insure that there is not a misuse of this information that comes from these kinds of activities," he added, referring to the secondary market for patient data.

I sensed that my questions about such sales—called *licensing* in industry parlance—made Black uneasy. Jacob Reider, a former chief medical informatics officer at Allscripts, later confirmed my suspicions: "They are not comfortable talking about this. If the company's image is, 'We help patients and providers,' then selling data being five percent of your revenue is not something that you want to get out there on the front lines. You don't want that to be part of the image of your company.

"Sometimes the work that involves analytics and insights derived from large data sets is very important to the advancement of science, and sometimes that work is very important to the sales of a given product. It is hard to know for a specific set of questions which and how to differentiate between the two. Many things are in a gray area in between, and that is the hardest part of looking at these activities."

Insurers Selling Data

Over the past two decades, many large insurers have established data analysis companies that harvest details from their claims. UnitedHealth set up Optum, and Anthem has HealthCore; Blue Cross Blue Shield's data analysis company, Blue Health Intelligence, keeps data on 125 million people dating back to 2005, said CEO Swati Abbott. Blue Health Intelligence clients include IMS Health, which incorporates the information into its LifeLink longitudinal patient database.[13]

Some integrated health systems, which act as both the insurer and the health-care provider, have also gotten in the trade. These systems enjoy an unusually rich array of longitudinal data from all the aspects of care, because the care occurs under their own roofs. Kaiser Permanente, which operates in eight states, including California and Washington, DC, has information on more than 10 million members and shares these data with researchers.[14] The Mayo Clinic pools clinical data with Optum's claims data in Optum Labs. Geisinger Health System has set up its own data mining service, MedMining, which offers information—for example, on psychiatry visits, data linking a mother and child, tobacco use, and menstrual-period data—on 467,000 patients.[15] Its clients include leading drug manufacturers, analytical firms and consultants such as Booz Allen Hamilton.

Many big companies you might not immediately associate with health care also participate in the big health-data bazaar. For example, in 2015, IBM bought Explorys, a company with clinical data sets on 50 million people, and Phytel, which had details on 45 million patients, and then IBM obtained insights on another 215 million patients by acquiring Truven in 2016.[16]

GE Healthcare, a subsidiary of General Electric, shares anonymized patient data from its Centricity electronic medical record system (and would rather not talk about it; its CEO, chief spokesperson, and others declined my requests for details). LexisNexis, a data broker best known for its legal and media services, advertises that it has built the largest medical claims warehouse in the industry, with 1.2 billion claims from "almost every payer in the US." The payers include Blue Cross Blue Shield, UnitedHealth, Aetna, Cigna, Humana, Tricare, Amerigroup, Kaiser, and Medicare and cover 250 million patients.[17]

All of these companies highlight the medical and scientific breakthroughs that their data may facilitate. In a recent white paper, two Optum officials summarized the advantages of big medical data: "This information helps health administrators, researchers, and policy makers to understand the cost and quality of health care and identify patients at risk of developing chronic conditions, pinpoint billing fraud, and improve patient care."[18]

The upbeat language used by some of these companies so breathlessly describes the incredibly bright future from health-data sharing that it is often hard to tell what exactly they do or to understand that they are describing commercial transactions in which money is involved. "Smarter Choices. Stronger Businesses. Happier People. Healthier World," the Vitality Group proclaims on its website. I couldn't really tell from the site, but an executive there explained that the company designs insurance programs that offer discounts to those who commit to healthier lifestyles and who agree to be monitored to prove their adherence to the program.

IMS, well aware of the complications of setting up new services, kept longitudinal patient data on the back burner for years, relaunching what it calls anonymous patient-level data with a big push only in 2006.[19] "There was a realization that there was not a lot of commercialization value until we could get a broader sample size and a broader set of distribution outlets," said David Carlucci, the IMS CEO from 2006 and 2010. Carlucci had previously worked at IBM for twenty-six years. "Any major data-set build in our business is about a ten-year-plus run to accumulate enough assets to be able to add value to our clients."

IMS today gathers longitudinal patient information in sixteen countries, including the United States, Canada, Germany, the United Kingdom, China, Japan, Australia, and South Korea.[20] In 2015, Carlucci's successor, Ari Bousbib, illustrated the utility of longitudinal data by saying it helped justify Gilead's charging $84,000 for its standard hepatitis C course of treatment: "Obviously, they needed to demonstrate the drug is effective in a real-world setting and show that the total cost of treatment not the price of the drug itself compared to competing drugs was the relevant measure here."[21]

IMS publishes a bibliography of US-based research that has used its data to better understand medical issues. The publication praises the research: "Collectively, this research represents a substantial advancement in understanding the real-world operation of our health system, and is invaluable to multiple stakeholders."[22] Among many issues for which researchers have used IMS data are the following:

- The use of prescription antiobesity drugs
- The link between unemployment rates and prescription drug use
- Health-care costs for those with excessive sleepiness
- The decline in drug overdose deaths in Florida after a change in state policy
- Geographic differences in antibiotic prescribing
- Heroin abuse
- Changes in how doctors prescribed antipsychotic drugs over a five-year period
- The increased risk of certain other diseases for those with inflammatory bowel disease

In broad terms, IMS and its rivals hail the increasingly comprehensive aggregation of longitudinal data as a game changer that will advance patient as well as business outcomes. "As demand grows for advanced analytics and sophisticated tools to demonstrate the value of medicines, our Real-World Evidence solutions are helping more clients better understand patient journeys and prove performance in real-world settings," Bousbib said in the IMS 2014 annual report. "Drawing on our 500+ million anonymous patient data records, we are enabling a consistent understanding of treatment outcomes, costs and safety over time across every major country."

CHAPTER 8

FIGHTING FOR PATIENTS

Debating Medical Privacy

Psychiatrist Deborah Peel climbs a podium in front of several hundred health-care experts in a Washington, DC, hotel ballroom. The Texas psychiatrist is ready to make her case that the United States does not sufficiently protect patient data, leaving all Americans at risk of privacy invasion and potential discrimination.

For weeks, Peel has been apprehensive about the debate titled "Protecting Patient Privacy vs. Advancing Clinical Research." She is facing off against Daniel Barth-Jones, a Columbia University epidemiologist who believes Peel's cautions would limit scientific progress by curtailing access to medical data. Peel has the advantage of speaking first, but almost immediately, the projector thwarts her. Her PowerPoint images won't advance.

"Technology, right, it's always infallible," she quips. Some in the crowd chuckle at a comment that foreshadows her warning that the wired world endangers our most intimate information.

Peel, who is in in her early sixties, waits for a moment as a technician sorts out the problem. The clicker revives, and Peel describes the hidden trade in medical data. She warns that as these details eventually become public knowledge, the freewheeling trade will undermine patient trust in their health providers. She also fears that advances in computing will make re-identification of sensitive medical information increasingly likely.

Barth-Jones, an assistant professor at Columbia University's Mailman School of Public Health, responds that allowing patients to block the sharing of their data would harm public health research. "People who agree to have their data shared and people who don't agree have been shown to be very different in epidemiological studies," he says. "I think there are a lot of situations where we need to get good counters regardless of consent or not, for public health reasons."

Peel taps her foot impatiently and generally avoids glancing at Barth-Jones. Many people will agree to share their data, she responds, if asked, and if they believe it will help science. They would be less likely to share their data for commercial purposes, which is actually the engine behind most of the huge market in such information.

The Making of an Activist

Peel evolved into a privacy activist as an outgrowth of her psychiatry work. She became chief of psychiatry at Austin's Brackenridge Hospital in 1979 and eventually began speaking out on mental health issues. From the 1990s, she briefed legislators on issues of interest to psychiatrists, first in Texas and then in Washington, DC. She testified before a federal panel for the first time in 1999, discussing the role of middlemen that handle pharmacy data. Her message has not changed much since then. "The breaches of privacy that are so damaging and that affect every citizen in this country are not due to disgruntled employees or hackers; they are due to the systemic corporate practices of these entities," she told a Department of Health and Human Services committee.

In 2004, Peel decided that if no one else would step up to the plate, she would form her own advocacy group that she called Patient Privacy Rights. She sees her work as akin to a warning about the potential impact of a massive hurricane in New Orleans before 2005. Until Hurricane Katrina hit, no one knew exactly what might happen in a disaster. But the danger was always there.

For example, Peel warns that employers use medical data to discriminate, even though the practice is illegal. A boss can always claim that a heathier person had better qualifications to get hired or promoted. For this reason, some patients will avoid treatment to protect their privacy if not given a choice, she said. "Because there is no 'chain of custody' for our health data, it's impossible for us to know who bought, sold, traded, or used sensitive information about our minds and bodies," Peel said. "So if we are offered a higher rate of interest for a loan or credit card, if we don't get a job interview, it's impossible to know if personal health information was used to make those discriminatory decisions and limit our opportunities."

Peel runs the operation on a shoestring budget, funded largely by family and friends, including office space donated by her husband, a real estate developer. Since 2011, Patient Privacy Rights has organized an annual summit on health privacy. Scraping together enough money to put on the show is always difficult. One morning in 2014, two IMS officials agreed to donate $5,000 to sponsor a conference breakfast. Because she is often critical of IMS—she has called the firm "health-data thieves"—she was ambivalent about the gift, saying, "I believe IMS really owes the US public an explanation about exactly what it does with the nation's health data and how they justify using and selling it." The two officials that extended the support, chief privacy officer Kimberly Gray and director of professional relations Robert Hunkler, believe that the good IMS does far outweighs potential harms that concern Peel, but both declined my requests to explain why IMS had supported Peel.

Peel invited Gray to debate privacy advocate Michelle De Mooy at the 2014 conference. A lawyer by training, Gray tried to take a moderate tone and highlight how anonymized patient data help medical research. "I feel that I work for an ethical company," she said. "I've been there five years now, and trust me, I would not stay at a company for five years that I did not believe to be an ethical company."

Things got a little heated when Gray suggested that the public should not be concerned about the IMS' trade in anonymized patient data. "As long as the organization is transparent and accountable, we give the trust," she said. "And that's what we propose."

"Okay, but IMS Health is neither of those," De Mooy said.

"That's not true!"

Gray eventually conceded that anonymized medical data are not impossible to re-identify, but said that doing so is a lot more difficult than Peel and others have suggested.

Victims' Stories

Peel is always seeking out patients to tell their stories of privacy violations. I remember her outrage in 2014, when AOL CEO Tim Armstrong told his staff that he would trim benefits because two employees had cost the Internet firm more than $1 million each by having premature babies. Armstrong's callous remarks generated national headlines and criticism, and he quickly backed down and restored the benefits.

One of the two women involved in the AOL incident spoke at the Patients Privacy Rights annual summit the following year, and was invited back again in 2016. "The damage of health privacy violations might seem abstract—until it happens to you," Deanna Fei told the audience in Washington, DC, in 2015. "Those privacy notices provide nothing more than an illusion. . . . Names don't have to be named for highly sensitive data to be easily traced."

At the annual Patients Privacy Rights conference a few years before that, Peel introduced another woman with a dramatic personal story. Alina is a middle-aged lawyer who was born in Europe and moved to the United States as a girl.[1] She speaks English without an accent, so many people do not know that she came from somewhere else. And because she takes hundreds of dollars of medications every month, even fewer know she has bipolar disorder, an illness that can cause dramatic shifts in mood, energy, or the ability to function normally.

She has experienced three major episodes during which she lost control of herself and needed to be hospitalized. "I was not of this world," she said. "I could have walked onto the highway or something." The first time, the hospital wanted to give her electroshock therapy; her parents refused and took her out of the hospital. In the second instance, she ripped up her passport while in the country where she was born. After the third episode in 2000, she started to see a psychiatrist weekly and take medication.

In therapy, she began to open up to her doctor about her most intimate problems. She had difficult relations with her parents and for a time had not talked to her mother. Alina sometimes struggled to make ends meet, and she had defaulted on her student loans. A friend of her father's had sexually abused her when she was a child. She felt such shame about these issues that she had never told even her closest friends. Confident such details would stay secret, she had disclosed these episodes to her psychiatrist.

One day, Alina felt acute stomach pain and thought it might have been appendicitis. Her regular doctor was on maternity leave, so she saw a new physician. The new doctor looked at her medical records. Instead of conducting a full stomach examination, he asked a direct question.

"Are you seeing a psychiatrist?"

He said he had read her medical records and was not comfortable prescribing any new medication and then launched into a monologue on why she needed psychiatric care. She felt a jolt of indignation. She later learned that any doctor in her health system could read more than two hundred pages of intimate notes on her deepest feelings and secrets shared with her Freudian psychiatrist. She felt violated and traumatized. Sometime later, she obtained a copy of the detailed notes, which included comments such as "Therapy consisted of discussing past relationships, family problems, and job issues. Previous sexual abuse by father's friend discussed in detail."[2]

After she realized that any doctor treating her for any medical issue whatsoever could see all of her mental health records, Alina complained to her medical group. The institution's privacy officer wrote that the group's "handling of mental health records is in full compliance with the law and balances the need for privacy and confidentiality with the need for [our] physicians' access to information on their patients. We feel that if we were to restrict all mental health information, we would be doing a disservice to our patients in that their physicians would be working with an incomplete set of data."

Angered, Alina sent a copy of the letter to an official overseeing the US HIPAA rules on health data. "I am distraught to learn that the . . . privacy policy is so inflexible and indiscriminant as to compromise my human dignity, my autonomy and well-being," she wrote. "[When I go in] with a broken finger, all the people treating me have the 'right' to review my psychiatric records including specific details of my life that have nothing to do with illness or medical issues whatsoever despite my express objection."

She received a bureaucratic response rejecting her request for an investigation: "Your allegation, that psychotherapy notes and other unnecessary information is included in the electronic medical record system and accessible to unauthorized parties, even if fully substantiated, would not violate the Privacy Rule."

Her doctor also wrote her, saying that he had consulted officials in their health plan and those who oversee compliance with US HIPAA privacy regulations: "I was informed that we cannot restrict anyone from your record, and we need to continue to record your information in the Electronic Medical Record. Electronic medical records are now mandated by federal regulations. If you continue to receive care within [our] system, we would need to continue to use the electronic medical record and would not be able to restrict other providers from having access to it if needed to provide care for you."

Alina's efforts to shield her most sensitive records had failed. She remains frustrated and angry and has become keenly aware of her privacy:

"Every time I go to the doctor, it's privacy versus the best quality of care. Several years ago, I couldn't even imagine lying to my doctors. Now it is a constant mental process where I weigh the constant costs— if I don't tell them what is going to happen. I know people who lie about their medical records—medicine they are on. They do not disclose it to doctors.

"You shouldn't have to choose between privacy and the best possible care. It's this huge dilemma—why should I have to make a choice between having a stigma for the rest of my life, including my employer knowing, or people looking at me differently because they know something about you, rather than being safe?"

HIPAA does not address Alina's concerns that too many of her doctors can access all of her records, whether or not the information is related to the problem they are treating. That means a foot doctor can see records related to mental or sexual health, even though such access may cause embarrassment or discomfort. Experts such as Deborah Peel say patients should be able to limit access of particular records to certain physicians, segmentation that is still not commonplace.

Supporters and Detractors

Peel stopped taking new psychiatry referrals years ago, but still sees two long-standing patients. Her office is on the second floor of a two-story business building next to a small strip mall in Austin. Her name is absent from the lobby directory and her door. When I visited, I asked two people down the hall for directions. Neither had heard of Dr. Peel. And that's the way she prefers it, as she does not want others to judge her patients.

Everything about the two-room office is designed to create an environment where the patient trusts that nothing he or she says will go beyond her walls. Visitors enter a waiting room, although Peel has not employed a receptionist since 1980, so no one sees who comes and goes; she writes out the $175-an-hour bills herself.

I first met Peel in 2012 and was struck by her passion, vitality, and lack of pretense. While many advocates carefully package their messages, Peel invariably speaks her mind using language that, when she is speaking privately, might include a string of expletives about privacy injustices (she refrains from cursing in public). When she wants to make an important point, she sometimes grabs her listener's hand or arm until she has finished. In e-mails, she makes liberal use of multiple exclamation points and question marks. She once sent me a short e-mail of just a hundred words that contained eight exclamation points, ten question marks, and ten of the words in ALL CAPS!!!! She signed it, as she often does, "xoxoxo."

One executive at a supermarket chain that sells prescription information about its customers—a practice Peel criticizes—said he personally agrees with many of her positions. "She is a great advocate for privacy, and we need great advocacy for privacy," said the executive, who does not want to be named.

Peel's work has also attracted attention abroad. "Deb's not just a US leader but an international star," said Ross Anderson, a University of Cambridge professor of computer security engineering.

Enthusiasm for Peel and her work is far from universal, however. Detractors, many of whom work at companies linked to the trade in medical data, view her as some sort of crazy person warning that the world is coming to an end when, in fact, the sun keeps rising day after day. They say she exaggerates privacy risks, garbles facts, and makes allegations that are hard to prove. "The Deborah Peels of the world who go out on the warpath terrifying people about the data, that just gives heartburns to these companies," said David McCallie Jr., senior vice president of medical informatics at Cerner, a leading health record company. "She has crossed over into being sort of unreliable and maybe irrational at times."

Jacob Reider, who served as chief medical officer for the Office of the National Coordinator for Health Information Technology at the US Department of Health and Human Services, added, "Deb is very passionate, and sometimes her passion causes the conversation to become less focused on the facts and more focused on the fears that she and others may have on what has happened or what may happen with personally identifiable data."

At the same time, McCallie said he likes Peel and thinks she provokes an important discussion: "It is not bad to have somebody out there holding down that corner of space, so you can sort of triangulate where you are, so you can say, 'I am not quite as crazy about it as she is,' but she has raised some interesting points, particularly about the ability to keep certain mental health issues private and keep them off the grid, even if they could help your care in other places."

Peel responded that any advocate will get criticized, but she does not ramp down her outspoken approach. "My passion scares certain people," she said. "But I'm too old to learn new tricks."

"They think I am a raving lunatic from Texas," she added. "None of these people understand that health care is the big kahuna. . . . If we don't hold to this critical right we have had forever to control the use of our health information, how will we ever build our way out of the total surveillance of everything online?" As far as criticism that she sometimes exaggerates, Peel said she is doing the best she can, given the lack of transparency among companies trading personal health data: "I'm hungry for facts. I'm not in this to make this up. Show me where I am wrong, and I'll correct it."

Experts such as Jerry Avorn, a Harvard Medical School professor who started studying Medicaid claims data in the early 1980s for insights on drug utilization, would like to have access to as much information as possible. But he worries that privacy advocates will tar all anonymized medical data and make it hard to conduct effective research. "Those people are well intentioned and doing good work as it applies to what some companies are doing with data," he said. "But the side effect of that emphasis is that some people look at medical researchers like me and my group, who strip out all identifiers and who only want to learn about the next Vioxx before the drug's been on the market for five years giving people heart attacks and strokes, and they think that work is somehow part of the same invasion-of-privacy problem."

He referred to his team's efforts in 2003–2004, when they analyzed data on more than fifty-four thousand Medicare patients and found that those taking Vioxx had a higher risk of heart attacks within the first ninety days of taking the pain killer.[3] They obtained the data not from commercial sources such as IMS Health, but from state programs in New Jersey and Pennsylvania aimed at helping low-income seniors. Later in 2004, the manufacturer, Merck, withdrew the drug. Avorn said it is important to assess the different motivations behind groups that want aggregated patient data: "Some people don't seem to be able to distinguish between conscientious, responsible researchers who only want to learn about a medication's good and bad effects in a university medical school setting versus somebody sitting in the backroom at Target trying to figure out how can they sell more of product X by invading someone's privacy."

Drawing the line as to which patient data can freely be used and which should be restricted remains complicated. "In a very different political climate than we have," Avorn said, "one could consider that there could be legislation that says that aggregation of personal data only for purposes of marketing would be prohibited, but at the same time allow for that kind of use of anonymized data . . . for medical research."

Ask Us

After many hours talking to Peel, visits to her home in Austin, and seeing her speak at a number of conferences, I asked what she really wants. Simple, she said. Pharmacies, doctors, hospitals, and the long chain of middlemen should all have to obtain permission before sharing our medical data, even on an anonymized basis. Actually, she didn't say "simple." Her actual answer encapsulated her passion, style, and bottom line: "The point is just ask us," she said, adding an expletive in the middle for additional emphasis. "They don't want to ask, because they want to steal it!"

Those opposed to allowing patients to opt out of the sale or distribution of their anonymized data say that science benefits from as complete a data set as possible. Tom Brogan, the aforementioned Canadian pioneer in commercial longitudinal databases, explained: "You get some people who have serious medical conditions that you really need in the database, and if they started saying no, they don't want their data in the database, well, then you have got this massive hole."

A second objection involves the complication of administering a patient choice system. "I don't think people really understand or would understand or could understand, even if they were smart and well trained," said Jonathan Wald, a Harvard Medical School instructor and the director of patient-centered technologies at the Center for the Advancement of Health IT, part of the nonprofit research institute RTI International in North Carolina. "If I say no to distribution by the pharmacy, by this particular company, in this particular way, in this particular organization, that doesn't stop thirty other pathways from existing that have nothing to do with that particular consent that I gave."

Clearly, consumers would need some sort of system to indicate their preference for anonymized medical data in general, rather than ask a myriad of providers and middlemen to abide by their wishes. The US Do Not Call Registry offers one opt-out model that puts the burden on companies to check before calling. As of late 2015, the registry held 222 million numbers that preferred not to receive telephone solicitations.[4]

A similar approach might work for medical data. However, opponents say it would be impossible to attach a patient's consent to the hundreds of millions of existing anonymized patient files. "That would require re-identification, which we can't do," IMS chief privacy officer Kimberly Gray said at the Patient Privacy Rights debate.

I wondered if she might be mistaken. Data miners add new anonymized patient information from multiple sources to their dossiers all the time. Could the same techniques accommodate opt-out requests? For an answer, I set out to understand the behind-the-scenes details of how data miners take anonymized files for the same patient from different pharmacies, doctors, and labs and group them into the same person's longitudinal file. The techniques are remarkably sophisticated, so much so that some, even a few outspoken data miners, find them increasingly invasive and potentially troubling.

CHAPTER 9

□ □ □ □ □

HOW SAFE IS "ANONYMIZED"?

Data Pioneer

In the 1950s, Alfred Kuehn, a chemical engineer by training, started teaching marketing at Carnegie Institute of Technology's business school (part of today's Carnegie Mellon University). He focused on consumer buying behavior, trying to understand how people decide what to buy. He examined large amounts of company sales information, lots of numbers in the era before big data. His 1958 PhD dissertation analyzed thousands of purchases of frozen orange juice concentrate in Chicago to understand how pricing and advertising influence what brand people buy.[1]

To crunch the numbers, Kuehn rented access to an exotic machine, one so rare at the time that it cost millions of dollars—a computer. Starting in 1956, he used one at a large accounting firm. Later he rented time on the computer used by Bettis Atomic Power Laboratory in Pittsburgh, where engineers had developed the first nuclear-powered submarines as well as the first nuclear-power cruiser and aircraft carriers. He grabbed whatever free hours they had available, often at odd hours such as during the wee hours of 2 AM to 3 AM on weekends. Even at off-peak hours, the cost was so high that a suspicious Internal Revenue Service audited his taxes for all the deductions he declared.

In 1963, while he was still teaching, Kuehn formed Management Science Associates (MSA), which advised consumer product companies such as General Mills, the maker of Cheerios and Wheaties, and Lever Brothers (part of Unilever), known for margarine, Pepsodent toothpaste, soaps, and detergents. MSA specialized in analyzing data for new-product launches such as Cool Whip dessert topping (1966), Clairol

Herbal Essences (1971), breakfast cereals, and other goods. Eventually, managing advertising placements for TV stations became a big part of his business.

From its earliest days, companies entrusted MSA with confidential data about their sales and products. Even if the information only concerned a dessert topping, millions of dollars were at stake. In the 1950s, he was already working on medical data, and that field became a growing focus from the 1980s. In 1992, for example, MSA studied longitudinal patient data from clinical trials counting breast tumor cells. All of this history made the company a good candidate to help study anonymized patient data for commercial use in the 2000s.

The Secrets of De-identification

Health-care entities covered by US HIPAA laws must de-identify medical information before selling it to data miners. That means removing eighteen fields of information, including birth date, name, and Social Security number, or having an expert determine that the risk of re-identification is "very small."

De-identifying a single patient record under these rules is straightforward. The challenge for data miners comes in assembling dossiers that draw from multiple anonymized data sources, and continually updating such records for hundreds of millions of patients. A patient may get a prescription from Walgreens one day and CVS the next, then switch jobs and generate claims from a new insurer.

The solution to this problem is a software program known as a de-identification engine (or de-ID engine), which allows data miners to link anonymized records from multiple sources. Such engines work by converting identifiers such as the name, birth date, and city of Janet Williams, thirty-seven, from Reno, Nevada, into a longer version of a code such as "x5f7jj46sh8." Whether a new prescription comes from CVS or a rival pharmacy using the same de-ID engine, the software deletes Janet's personal identifiers and replaces them with "x5f7jj46sh8," allowing the prescription to link to other files about her with the same code.

Before HIPAA came into force in the early 2000s and tightened the rules, data miner ArcLight could test whether its encryption keys would repeatedly generate the same unique identifier for a person. It took the code and went back to check the results against the named patient files. They were correct 99 percent of the time, said Fritz Krieger, ArcLight's chief operating officer (complications included identical twins and those who paid cash for their health-care services).

The company knew full well that it could trigger a public backlash if it was not especially diligent in how it handled the data. "We were concerned," Krieger said, "not because we were going to freak out the public, but we were more concerned what [effect] a public freak-out would have on our data vendors. We wanted to get in front of that to really, really, really well establish that our stuff was a hundred percent blinded, that there was no way we are going to be able to find out that Suzie Q on Main Street had herpes."

ArcLight's ambition to create anonymized patient dossiers was perhaps a little ahead of the technology at the time, and the company went out of business after a few years. "Frankly we weren't getting the job done," Tom Ludlam, ArcLight's CEO, reflected years later. Consistently matching anonymized data to the same person proved more difficult in reality than in initial tests. "We couldn't get the encrypted data to link up one to the other with a high level of confidence or repeatability such that we could make a commercial product out of it."

Only toward the end of the 2000s—after ArcLight's demise—could computers more easily handle huge amounts of de-identified data. "More research came into play, more tools came into play," said Jani Syed, an MSA technical group director who works on its de-ID system. "Before that, it was impossible to do, due to the processing power of the servers."

Nowadays a large pharmacy chain typically sends transactions to MSA's computers in Pittsburgh regularly, perhaps weekly or monthly. MSA takes a few hours to sort through the millions of new files to match them with preexisting patients. In an ideal situation, each prescription file contains multiple confirmations of a person's identity such as a Social Security number, name, address, phone number, and e-mail. Often, a file lacks details such as Social Security number, so Syed said that MSA scores the likelihood that the file is for the same person. In other cases, MSA must sort through errors. It may be that "Janet Qilliams," thirty-seven, from Reno is indeed the same "x5f7jj46sh8" but has a typo in her surname. When the process is complete, MSA de-IDs the files and uploads the anonymized files to the data miner. "Some people," Kuehn said, "whenever they hear what we do, initially think, 'But that isn't legal, is it?' But in many cases, I can tell them, 'For you it would not be legal. For us it is legal.'"

Convincing pharmacies and other suppliers to install de-ID software took some effort, said former IMS America president Bill Nelligan, who announced a new IMS push into longitudinal data in 2006. "In partnering with the pharmacies, we would demonstrate our capabilities because they . . . obviously were extremely sensitive to the risks associated with breaches," he said.[2]

More recently, IMS and other companies have moved to bypass de-ID companies such as MSA, according to Mark Degatano, a consultant who was at Merck for twenty-four years and has advised IMS and worked at Symphony Health. They can do this by installing their own de-ID engines at the data sources with their permission, a move aimed at aggregating longitudinal patient data faster and more cheaply in the long term.

"I know from my work at IMS that IMS has a de-identification engine which is basically taking PHI [personal health information] at a source and converting it to an IMS patient key that can't be reengineered," Degatano said. "If they install that de-ID engine at every source and it has the same algorithm, that means everyone with the same PHI will get the same IMS patient key."

Anonymization ensures that IMS and its rivals such as Symphony Health never see identified data. "We focused strongly on making sure we never got it," explained David Thomas, the IMS CEO from 2000 to 2006. "We never had it in house, so we could never let it get out of our house. You create a reputation in the company for not having patient-identifiable data, and I think that you live by that, you operate by that, and if you ever violate that, your business would be in deep jeopardy. So I don't think you would ever violate it."

Other former top IMS officials have echoed similar themes, as does rival Symphony Health. Don Otterbein, Symphony Health's senior vice president for marketing and product development and a former IMS official, agreed with the focus on anonymized data: "We have a dedicated team that reviews every project, every data set, every engagement, so that there is no chance of re-identification. So I would say no, I don't think it is something that you should worry about. Even if somebody hacked it, there wouldn't be information there that could be linked back to an individual. . . . I think there is very little risk."

Re-identification

Despite such assurances, a growing number of data scientists and health-care experts say that the same computing advances that allow the aggregation of many anonymized patient files into a longitudinal dossier also make it increasingly possible to re-identify those files. "It's very difficult to protect data from re-identification through most processes that are used to anonymize it," said Jonathan Wald, the Harvard Medical School instructor and RTI International expert mentioned earlier.

He said that re-identification is easy when a patient has a rare condition and when there are a few other pieces of information on the patient. "It is getting easier and easier because of the amount of electronic publicly available data and the amount of analytic engines to turn through it. So it seems like a determined individual or organization that is willing to throw resources at the problem is probably going to be successful in many cases."

Since MSA's Syed is at the center of the technology that de-identifies patients, I asked him about this risk. He surprised me with his candor. "In the area of big data, there are always problems with the privacy," he said. "No matter what you do, no matter how much data obfuscation you are going to do, if you have enough data, it is always possible to identify a particular person. It's not that hard to do."

I asked if he personally worries that someone could cause trouble for him or his family through such techniques. "Definitely, I would be worried," he said. "If I have traces of all the electronic data myself, my health records, there is always a way to find out if I go to many places, if I am suffering from something. . . . There is always a way to find out who I am."

This risk is not only theoretical. One scholar has built her career on showing that many de-identification techniques are indeed breakable. As the Supreme Court reviewed the *IMS Health v. Sorrell* case over doctor-identified data in 2011, Latanya Sweeney filed a brief for what is really a future battle over how companies anonymize patient data with little outside oversight. The computer scientist argued that widespread aggregation of medical information threatens individual patient privacy. Her arguments made little impact on the Supreme Court's ruling, which upheld the right of data miners to assemble dossiers on what individual doctors prescribe. Her work may, however, have a more lasting impact on future debates.

In two court filings, Sweeney, the founder of Harvard's Data Privacy Lab, argued that the privacy protections devised in the 1990s are inadequate, given present-day computing power: "There is no external review of IMS' de-identification process, no public detailed statement describing it, and what is reported about it, exposes known vulnerabilities for re-identifying patients. . . . Society has experienced an explosion in the amount of data collected on individuals, challenging HIPAA's 1990s-styled protection. Yet, IMS has expressed no desire to adapt or seek less privacy-invasive approaches."[3]

Sweeney has long been a thorn in the side of data miners. Not only has she become one of the nation's leading experts on re-identification, but she is also a compelling public speaker with an upbeat personality that disarms critics. The first black woman to receive a PhD in computer science from MIT, she served as the chief technology officer at the US Federal Trade Commission in 2014. She has also influenced this and my previous book by sponsoring me as a fellow at Harvard, where she is a professor, and by sharing her insights.

She first came to public attention in 1997 as an MIT graduate student when she analyzed the medical insurance records of state employees and their families—information that the Massachusetts Group Insurance Commission intended to share widely. The commission, which provides insurance benefits to state employees, had removed all names but had left in birth dates, home ZIP codes, and gender. Cross-referencing the records with public voter registration rolls in Cambridge, where Governor William Weld lived, Sweeney identified the governor, to his apparent displeasure. She calculated that with just the birth date, ZIP code, and gender, an analyst could identify as many as 87.1 percent of all Americans.[4]

In 1998, after a local newspaper received documents on Illinois cases of neuroblastoma (a cancer that typically affects children five years old or younger), Sweeney re-identified twenty of twenty-two children on an anonymized state registry. She looked at diagnostics and medical procedures performed and matched them with hospital exit data and public records. Illinois courts ruled that only a top computer scientist like Sweeney could achieve such re-identification, so they barred her from sharing the technique with others.[5] Instead of embracing the cloak of genius, Sweeney said that what she had done was simple: "Given today's data rich networked society, a high school student could, in less than an hour, easily re-identify the data using information readily available on the Web."[6]

In 2011, she analyzed data made public in the Personal Genome Project. In this research effort, which is aimed at helping researchers advance science, volunteers share intimate details, including a sample of their genome, medical history, and basic demographic information, and all this information is made public. Some participants list past drug use, child abuse, abortions, alcoholism, and mental health issues. Cross-referencing the birth date, ZIP code, and gender of 579 people with information from data brokers, she identified 84 to 97 percent of the profiles.[7] To illustrate how powerful just these three pieces of information can be, Sweeney set up a website, aboutmyinfo.org, that allows anyone to enter a date of birth, gender, and ZIP code to find out how many others match that profile.

Critics of Sweeney's experiments often respond much as the Illinois courts did: Yes, perhaps a few exceptional experts can re-identify patients from anonymized records, but an ordinary person would not be able to replicate her techniques. Wondering if someone without an extensive background in computer science, cryptography, or mathematics might succeed, I picked out three Personal Genome Project subjects with especially long histories, and I cross-referenced their details with a publicly available database. With just these steps, I found the identities of the two women and one man I was seeking to re-identify. When I telephoned the surprised volunteers, they confirmed their participation in the Personal Genome Project.[8] Since then, others have also shown vulnerabilities in other forms of publicly posted genomic data.[9]

Like the great magician Houdini, who demonstrated the weaknesses of locks by devising increasingly difficult escapes, Sweeney, in her next experiment, analyzed medical data released by Washington State, one of a number of US states that make such information public. The twist this time was that the files did not contain exact birthdays but gave the patient's age in months and years, so she had less precise information than in the William Weld re-identification.[10] She took eighty-one medical records released by Washington and attempted to match them against media articles that contained the word "hospitalized." Many of these articles mentioned vehicle accidents, assaults, or hospitalizations of well-known people. She succeeded in thirty-five instances, for a match rate of 43 percent.

I witnessed firsthand the unhappiness of one official when Sweeney explained that she had re-identified anonymized users of Boston's Hubway bicycle sharing program. In a contest aimed at producing interesting data visualization, Hubway posted data on half a million rides in 2012. Sweeney entered the contest by conducting a re-identification experiment in which she searched tweets and social media to identify people with their anonymous rides.[11] Holly St. Clair, director of data services at the Boston region Metropolitan Area Planning Council, had no idea that the data were vulnerable to re-identification. She had hoped the contest would build enthusiasm for the bike sharing program. "When we got the submission, we all freaked out," she told Sweeney. "They nearly pulled the whole contest."

The response was fairly typical. Inside health care, many regard Sweeney warily, saying she seems intent on throwing rocks at their industry. "Re-identification is very disruptive," Sweeney told me, "but every effort I made to soft-shoe it and work with them on their timetable failed miserably. They never had time. Many in health care seem intent on ignoring possible remedies that I and others have provided, electing instead to force an all-or-nothing choice. It does not have to be that way."[12]

Re-identifying Without Demographic Information

Data mining companies emphasize that they anonymize medical information according to HIPAA standards, which offer more privacy protection do than many of the anonymized files Sweeney has cracked. For example, US rules allow the sharing of just three digits of a ZIP code and just the year of birth rather than the exact date of birth. This point is accurate but ignores the vulnerability of anonymized longitudinal dossiers to be matched against other kinds of data.

Several recent successful re-identifications highlight this weakness. In one case, two *New York Times* reporters re-identified a woman among 657,000 anonymized Internet users by analyzing twenty million searches released by AOL.[13] What the woman searched for on the Internet gave enough clues to determine her identity. In another, graduate student Arvind Narayanan and one of his professors showed that they could identify people from among half a million anonymous users by studying the users' publicly released Netflix video rental histories and comparing them with reviews on the movie website IMDB.[14]

"A lot of traditional thinking about anonymous data relied on the fact that you can hide in a crowd that's too big to search through," wrote Narayanan, who today is an assistant professor of computer science at Princeton. "That notion completely breaks down given today's computing power: as long as the bad guy has enough information about his target, he can simply examine every possible entry in the database and select the best match."[15]

Even anonymous taxi data contain potentially sensitive information that can be re-identified. In 2013, the New York City Taxi and Limousine Commission, responding to a Freedom of Information request, released a year of GPS trip data for the city's taxis. Anthony Tockar, an Australian data scientist, showed that it was not hard to pinpoint specific individuals within this anonymized data set. He searched the Internet for "celebrities in taxis in Manhattan in 2013" and found images of actors Bradley Cooper and Jessica Alba (who played a pharma sales rep in the movie *Little Fockers*). From that, he was able to identify their exact taxi routes and fares. He wrote that Alba, whose wealth *Forbes* estimated in 2015 at $200 million, did not leave a tip. He also tracked taxi journeys that originated outside a sex club between midnight and 6 AM that year, to their exact destination, often to specific addresses in places such as Long Island or New Jersey.

GPS data can also link someone to sensitive medical location such as an abortion or a cancer clinic. If patients drive themselves somewhere, data brokers may photograph the license plate and sell the car's locational data. A few years ago, when I looked up the license plate number of a relative (with her permission) recorded by one data broker, I learned the day and time the car was in a doctor's parking lot.[16] Likewise, a Twitter posting can indicate someone's location on a certain day and thus give clues to re-identify.

"Clearly, common practices need to change when it comes to protecting the individual," Tockar concluded. "Put another way, is it fair to citizens and consumers to use their data without even being able to guarantee their privacy?"[17]

Combining different data sources may unlock medical data that was de-identified to HIPAA standards. For instance, longitudinal data could show that a forty-six-year-old patient sees two doctors, one where the patient has a primary home and the second doctor across the country, near a vacation home. These data include height, weight, and allergies, which further narrows down the field of possible candidates for re-identification. With a specific ailment or series of problems, that person may suddenly become the only one who could fit the description and thus become identifiable. With people giving off more and more information, including location from cell phones, car devices, health apps and devices, Internet searches, store purchases, and lots more, it is increasingly possible to re-identify people's anonymized data.

Max Petzold, director of the Swedish National Data Service Institute, said it would be easy to identify patients with HIV or other ailments in Sweden's medical data that is made available to researchers. "It is just a matter of time until something happens, because as a researcher, you can get really sensitive data," he said.

"I am positively surprised that there has been no known misuse of data," he continued. "Just as an example, just myself, I am working with the complete HIV registry for Sweden. I have never done it, of course, but . . . potentially I could identify individuals within that one, especially if I combine it with other data."

Researchers have also shown that it is possible to identify a man by his DNA using a few additional clues such as age, and state of residence posted on other sites with DNA information.[18] Yaniv Erlich, one of the authors of a 2013 study that showed this connection, suggested that researchers explicitly tell potential subjects in scientific experiments about such possibilities. "The emerging consensus is that consent forms should include re-identification as a potential risk for the participants," he told me.

He cited the stark warning given to potential participants in the Personal Genome Project. George Church, the Harvard geneticist who heads the project, says it cannot promise anonymity even though the data do not include names or other easy identifiers. When Church receives an annual anonymous survey from his department, he writes his name on the top of the form, saying anyone could have figured it out anyway. "The same thing goes for medical studies, especially as we go forward with more and more in-depth information about your genes, your environment, and your traits," he said. "Any small subsets of any of those classes of data are identifying. Any promises of keeping data secure are also false, if the intention is to share it, which it almost always is."

The US Genetic Information Nondiscrimination Act of 2008 bars discrimination based on DNA differences, but sensitivities around the issue remain high. Genetic data are basic personal identifiers akin to a person's face and, at the same time, may lead to dramatic new medical insights. A 2014 White House report outlines these issues: "The information that stands to be discovered by predictive medicine extends beyond a single individual's risks to include others with similar genes, potentially including the children and future descendants of those whose information is originally collected. Bio-repositories that link genomic data to health care data are on the leading edge of confronting important questions about personal privacy in the context of health research and treatment."[19]

In broad terms, people could be harmed just by knowing their intimate data are in circulation. "Imagine if nude pictures of a woman, uploaded to the Internet without her consent though without identifying her by name, were downloaded in a foreign country by people who will never meet her," Richard Posner, a US Court of Appeals judge for the Seventh Circuit in Chicago, wrote in a 2004 decision related to abortion. "She would still feel that her privacy had been invaded. The revelation of the intimate details contained in the record of a late-term abortion may inflict a similar wound. Even if there were no possibility that a patient's identity might be learned from a redacted medical record, there would be an invasion of privacy."[20]

Security Breaches

Another way outsiders may be able to identify anonymized files is by cross-referencing them with other sensitive files that hackers and thieves have obtained in recent years. Unfortunately, details about you from medical files may already be in circulation on the Internet or in hacker circles. I know about this possibility from personal experience, as I am one of many millions whom medical insurers and providers have notified as victims of such attacks. Between 2009 and early 2016, the US Department of Health and Human Services recorded more than 1,300 data breaches involving at least 500 people. All told, breaches have exposed more than 170 million patient files, and barely a week goes by without new breaches occurring.[21]

Some of these breaches are startling in their scope. In January 2015, Premera Blue Cross revealed that attackers had obtained records on about 11 million users. The stolen records included "name, date of birth, e-mail address, address, telephone number, Social Security number, member identification numbers, bank account information, and claims information, including clinical information."

Weeks later, Anthem announced the theft of personal data on 78.8 million people in its Blue Cross Blue Shield plans. The hackers obtained personal information, employment data, and Social Security numbers, but not medical information (among the many affected by the breach were employees of IMS Health). Even if only part of someone's personal information is obtained, the stolen information provides additional clues that bad actors can use for mischief or crime, such as re-identifying other medical records. A lawsuit filed after the Anthem breach alleges that criminals filed tax returns in victims' names to obtain refunds, stole money from bank accounts, and took out credit cards and loans.[22]

Massachusetts doctor Gary Lasneski was among the many victims. Not long after he learned of the breach, the Internal Revenue Service wrote him saying they suspected a fraudster had filed a tax return in his name. Initially, he shrugged off the news. "Because I pay every year, I thought, 'Good, let them file and pay for me,'" he said. It is no joking matter however, because criminals file returns hoping to receive tax refunds. Soon, someone tried to set up fraudulent accounts at Best Buy, Office Depot, and Capitol One using his information. He later joined the class action lawsuit against Anthem.

From inside, the picture is even more worrisome than the public realizes. For example, hackers continuously try to get into Microsoft

HealthVault, a site storing patient-controlled medical records, said Sean Nolan, the former general manager of the service. "It tended to be kind of your very classic, mostly overseas, very low sophisticated attacks," he said. "People trying from zombie machines, using well-known penetration attacks to try to capture this data."

With enough details about someone's health records, people who are uninsured, criminals on the run, or undocumented immigrants may succeed in receiving free medical care or prescription drugs.[23] One report estimated that 2.3 million people were victims of medical identity theft in the United States in 2014, an increase of 22 percent over the prior year.[24] One reason for the increase comes from the forces of supply and demand on the shadowy "dark web," where criminals sell hacked data. There, a glut of stolen credit cards has made medical data relatively more lucrative for thieves. "You can use these profiles for Normal Fraud stuff and/or get a brand new healthcare plan for yourself and with all the advantages that comes with," said one posting shared by the security company RSA to illustrate the underground market.

Hackers have also demanded—and received—payments by taking control of medical records and holding them hostage until they receive a ransom. For example, in 2016, Hollywood Presbyterian Medical Center in Los Angeles paid $17,000 for an encryption key after malware locked the hospital out of its own files. "The quickest and most efficient way to restore our systems and administrative functions was to pay the ransom and obtain the decryption key," said Allen Stefanek, the hospital's president and CEO. "In the best interest of restoring normal operations, we did this."[25]

Certainly, all signs suggest that the number of medical breaches of personal health information will to continue grow. "Many doctors' offices, clinics and hospitals may not have enough resources to safeguard their patients' PHI," a report by data broker Experian concluded.[26] It is not hard to imagine criminals also threatening to unmask stolen, de-identified patient dossiers in future ransomware attacks.

Sometimes, hacking will hit even those without a direct connection to the company whose records are penetrated. I received a letter from Anthem in 2015, telling me my data had been stolen. Since Anthem has never provided me insurance, I called to ask how it had any information about me in the first place. After a few weeks of investigation and a fair amount of prodding, Anthem replied that it had gotten my data from the pharmacy benefit manager CVS Caremark, which had handled my previous employer's drug plans. Caremark, in turn, outsourced the administration of one of its plans to Anthem. Multiple layers of outside entities I was unaware of possessed my medical information, and one of these entities, unfortunately, was unable to protect it against penetration.

Data Miner's Reaction

Companies that buy and sell medical data discuss potential flaws in security and anonymization with as much enthusiasm as a typical patient undergoes a colonoscopy. Current IMS officials, including the chief privacy officer, declined to discuss this and other issues in detail, although IMS spokesman Tor Constantino issued a written statement: "Protecting patient privacy through the collection and use of anonymous health information is a cornerstone of IMS Health's business. IMS Health treats its privacy and security obligations very seriously, striving not only to comply with the laws and regulations where it operates, but to adhere to the highest standards of business practices."[27]

But in a 2002 filing to the European Commission probing allegations that the company had abused its dominant position in five European Union countries, IMS argued against what it sees as excessive requirements for anonymization:

> It should not be the case that to anonymise personal information . . . an organisation has to destroy the identifiers and be sure that there is no conceivable method, however unlikely in reality, by which the identity of individuals can be re-established. This is a highly impractical approach and extremely difficult to achieve in reality. It may for example require the destruction of valuable identifiable data sets residing outside the control of the anonymising organisation. The rights, freedoms, and legitimate interests of individuals can more than adequately be protected if data is anonymised in such a way that all means *likely reasonably* to be used to identify the said person will fail. The value that can be gained in protecting individual privacy through de-identifying personal data is lost if the law makes it prohibitively difficult to anonymise the information.[28]

Former IMS officials also stressed to me that the company is truly interested in ensuring that patients are not re-identified. "If we screw up our privacy—the people we are getting data from are very, very cautious—we'd be out of business that day," Tom Brogan said. "So guess what: We are pretty damn careful."

Despite this caution, data scientists say companies could employ more secure, cutting-edge anonymization techniques that still preserve the utility of the data. One promising method, *differential privacy*, introduces a tiny bit of noise or fuzziness into a data set to block the possibility of an outsider's identifying any particular individual. Under this method, if researchers are studying how many people are HIV positive among an anonymized group of people, the addition or subtraction of one person would not give any clues to that individual's identity—even if the researchers have additional outside information about some of the people in the data set. The math and logic behind differential privacy is rather complicated, and those who work on it use pages of equations to explain its logic. The bottom line is that differential privacy works best for larger rather than smaller data sets, and many consider it a more promising approach than current anonymization techniques.

Why Re-identify?

It is worth asking why anybody would try to re-identify medical data. "My argument to the privacy guys is, it's much easier to steal the real stuff than identify the anonymized stuff," said Bob Merold, a former IMS senior vice president who in 2016 was working as head of strategic initiatives for the CancerLinQ platform at the ASCO Institute for Quality. "If I'm hacking, why am I going to hack the de-identified people?"

To date, there is no publicly recorded incident of hackers getting into the individual patient dossiers held by firms such as IMS Health and its rivals. Nor are there reported instances of re-identification of anonymized medical records in the United States other than academic experiments. Even if thieves did hack such records, they would face the additional complication of re-identifying anonymized records. The reward for all that effort would be a potentially richer array of insights into a patient than from single-source files, as anonymized patient data may contain pharmacy, claims, doctor, and even lab information.

Experts identify a variety of possible re-identification scenarios, including a nosy neighbor, a business competitor, a journalist, an intrusive employer, extortion, or medical identity theft.[29] The dramatic increase in online data theft in recent years shows that shadowy hackers routinely steal and release personal data, even though such activity is illegal. In any case, it is not illegal to re-identify anonymized data, although such action might constitute a breach of contract, depending on the conditions set by the source of the information.

Michelle De Mooy, a privacy expert at the Center for Democracy and Technology, spoke about the challenges of anonymizing large amounts of personal data: "Health information, in particular, which can encompass a variety of things, from sleep patterns to diagnoses to genetic markers—the data gathered about us can paint a very detailed and personal picture that is essentially impossible to de-identify, making it valuable for a variety of entities such as data brokers, marketers, law enforcement agencies, and criminals. Traditional methods of anonymization from commercial entities, such as the use of patient identifiers, have also become more of a problem with the amount of data available about individuals—there is, of course, an entire industry in vendors matching records retroactively."

It is not hard to imagine a US senator condemning a foreign country, only to find his or her intimate medical data plastered on the Internet, or an unscrupulous political operative leaking information about a rival candidate (the bitterness of the 2016 US campaign makes such sleazy tactics easy to picture). Rogue investors might be keen to learn inside details about the health of key corporate leaders before stock prices react to future revelations. A fanatical sports fan may want to humiliate a rival team's star player.

"That's the key challenge," said Sean Nolan, the former Microsoft HealthVault official. "Unlike financial fraud, it's not that broad-scale sort of identification that matters. It's the VIP identification that matters. Because that's where you actually have actionable, real data that you can use."

He added, "The dirty not-so-secret is that data HIPAA considers anonymized isn't."

You don't need to be famous or prominent to face such a threat. A rival at work who wants your job or simply does not like you may know when you took medical leave and other clues that could help identify you in a batch of anonymous patient files. Suddenly, your re-identified files might appear in circulation. In a crime of passion, a romantic rival—or an angry former lover—might want to spread such information on the Internet, a variant of revenge porn, in which former partners post intimate photos online.

Medical data, both de-identified and re-identified, could also become national security weapons against high-ranking officers or other members of the armed forces and their families. "It is not just that the information might embarrass a general or embarrass a senator," said one military official who did not want to be named, "because we also see VIPs and so forth in our system. It is that the aggregation of certain health data in our context is potentially classified information. If I were to aggregate immunization data for a particular region of our country, like, say, Fort Bragg, I might be able to learn where special operators are ready to deploy in the world, given the timeline."

Outside commercial companies have access to sensitive medical information on members of the military, but are subject to stricter restrictions than those applied to the civilian world. For example, RelayHealth, a subsidiary of McKesson, has provided secure messaging services between members of the US Army, Navy, and Air Force and their doctors.[30] Its privacy policy typically allows the outside sharing of aggregated patient information, but US military rules expressly forbid the secondary use of such information.[31] According to the military official who asked to remain anonymous, RelayHealth accepted these terms only reluctantly. RelayHealth officials declined repeated requests for comment on the record, but one who asked not to be identified said the company has accepted the Department of Defense terms without fuss since first doing business with it in 2009.

IMS also analyzes the health records of the US military and their families for the federal government and confirmed that "the government precludes any subsequent use of anonymized data specifically from the military," according to Wes Watkins, an IMS director of strategic health insights and an expert on US military health data.[32]

The agreement by companies such as RelayHealth and IMS to forgo any secondary sale of anonymized patient data in dealing with the US Department of Defense carries a certain irony: apparently nothing short of the world's most powerful military can slow the momentum of the data mining industry's quest for ever more details on patients. The military's caution illustrates that aggregated information about groups of certain types of people can also be very sensitive, even if no one re-identifies the information of any single person in the data set.

The vulnerability of anonymized medical data came into focus when two whistle-blowers in South Korea shared with a local journalist and prosecutors large anonymized data sets that their companies had been selling to IMS. Very quickly, South Korea, one of the world's most technologically advanced countries, emerged as a front line in the fight over the commercial use of patient medical data. It turned out that re-identifying the patients there was far easier than anyone had imagined.

CHAPTER 10

□ □ □ □ □

KOREAN WAR OVER PATIENT DATA

Guilty Conscience

One evening, Korean businessman Minjae Baek (a pseudonym) was so upset by an evening television news report that he began questioning whether he had acted unethically and maybe even illegally at work. South Korean prosecutors had launched an investigation into whether firms had illegally sold patient data to IMS Health Korea. About half of the country's pharmacies shared these data using software that did a poor job of masking patient identities, the TV report said. So poor, in fact, that it was almost child's play to re-identify the resident registration numbers, South Korea's social security numbers, contained in the data.

Until recently, Baek had worked at one of South Korea's middlemen companies, handling the flow of data between doctors, pharmacies, insurers, and other health-care providers. Selling anonymized patient data to IMS accounted for about a third of the profit for the company where Baek worked. "Did I also commit a crime?" he wondered. "Am I also part of this criminal act?"

The December 2013 television report triggered a serious self-examination of his role in facilitating the trade in sensitive patient data. "I started to question whether I was a bad man," he remembered later. "Although I wasn't directly in the process, because I wasn't the CEO, being part of something coming out in the news makes you feel bad."

In the global picture, South Korea represents an increasingly import-ant pharmaceutical market, with growing opportunities to profit from data mining. Once mired in poverty akin to Africa and Asia's least devel-oped countries, the country has grown dramatically since the 1960s and is now the world's thirteenth- or fourteenth-largest economy.

Despite his nagging conscience, Baek did nothing for several months. From time to time, he wondered if he should speak out and share his knowledge about Korea's trade in patient data. He weighed the pros and cons. On one hand, stepping forward could create complications. Why get involved, he wondered, when so many others could speak out? Also, South Korea does not have protections, like those in the United States, to protect whistle-blowers from retaliation.

Still, the issue gnawed at him. Baek had always thought of himself as a good person leading an exemplary life, so he was troubled by what he had learned from the television report. He really wished the whole moral dilemma would disappear, as easily as if he would awake from a bad dream. He consequently came up with a compromise so that he could live with himself. He would e-mail the reporter who had aired the original report as well as a second television correspondent at a twenty-four-hour Korean news channel. If they replied, he would tell them what he knew. Yet he really hoped that they would not write back, so that he could drop the whole matter and at least say he tried.

He sent the e-mails, and a day passed without any response. Baek felt both relief and some disappointment that the television reporters did not want to hear his story. He left on a trip and did not bother to check that e-mail account for several days. When he returned, he found several messages from the reporter who had aired the TV piece that had stirred Baek's pangs of conscious. He would get involved after all.

The Brain Surgeon

By any standard, Dongcharn Cho possesses exceptional qualifications for a journalist. Not only did he work as a medical doctor, but he is also a brain surgeon who has participated in twenty-six hundred brain and spine operations. To master one of medicine's most demanding specialties, he spent six years in medical school, one year as a hospital intern, four years in a neurosurgery department, three years in a military hospital, and six months in fellowship training at a university hospital. His specialist knowledge and gentle bedside manner put patients at ease.

Yet after all this training, Cho decided to make his mark by translating the complex world of medicine into the images and scripts of television news. An unlikely event triggered his decision to switch careers. As he toured the Uffizi Gallery in Florence, Italy, he became enchanted by a painting of early Renaissance master Sandro Botticelli. Mesmerized by the image, he felt his heart beat faster, a response no art had ever before triggered. He started to think about what he was doing with his life. He had gone to medical school because society values doctors as a profession. But he realized he might be happier doing something else.

In 2008, he heard about a medical journalist position at the private television station SBS, Seoul Broadcasting System. He applied and got the job. It took a while to get the swing of things, even if journalist work is not brain surgery. "To be honest, I assumed being a journalist would be easier, but it was not that way. The first three to four years were as intense as working as a neurosurgeon. Now I think it is more difficult!" he said, citing the complexity of penetrating the reserve of government and corporate officials to uncover what is really happening in health care.

One day in 2013, Cho received an intriguing tip from an official at the Korean Medical Association, where Cho is one of the group's hundred thousand members. The source said an official troubled by the secretive trade in Korean patient data had come forward. The whistle-blower worked at the Korea Pharmaceutical Information Center (KPIC), an offshoot of South Korea's pharmacy lobby. KPIC had developed the PM2000 software used in about half of the country's pharmacies. Provided free of charge, the program helps pharmacies manage their prescriptions and insurance claims and links them to doctors and hospitals.

Afraid of being unmasked, the source did not meet Cho personally. But he told the Korean Medical Association official how data middlemen sell patient information to IMS. Cho learned that to process prescriptions, PM2000 uploads patient data, including name, gender, doctor, medication, and illness code (such as G404 for epilepsy, B200 for AIDS, or K520 for gastritis) to a central server. The records include the national ID numbers, thirteen digits that are especially revealing. The first six numbers give a person's year, month, and day of birth; followed by a digit indicating gender; then four digits pinpointing the birthplace city and district; then a digit sorting out those born on the same day; and a final digit calculated from the other numbers.

The whistle-blower said the KPIC funded the free PM2000 software program by selling data to IMS Health for $300,000 a year, with the name removed and the national ID number thinly disguised. Cho listened with amazement as he learned about the secretive trade in medical data. "What game are KPIC and IMS playing?" he wondered.

Cho had a stake in the data sale not only as a reporter and a citizen, but also as a doctor, since the files included information about which medications doctors prescribe. "Why is my information as a doctor being sold without my consent to IMS?" he wondered.

He recalled that when doctors remove organs, such as those extracted because of cancer, Korean patients must consent before anyone can do research on the samples, even if the study benefits science. "In this case, the patient personal data was not subject to consent, and I found that problematic," Cho said. "It is still a problem even if it is anonymized. First, even if it is anonymized, the consent of the patient is essential, and second, they did anonymize it and it was so easy to figure out the codes."

Despite being upset and intrigued by the allegations, Cho remained cautious about airing the story. The source declined to meet with him, so the journalist doctor wanted an additional confirmation before going forward. He contacted criminal prosecutors and briefed them on what he had learned. That intervention prompted action, and in December 2013, criminal investigators raided the offices of the Korean Medical Association and KPIC. Only then did Cho air his story.

Within ten days, the South Korean government issued new regulations regarding the protection of personal data. In February 2014, the Korean Medical Association teamed up with twelve hundred physicians and nine hundred patients who felt aggrieved by the data sales. The group filed a lawsuit against the Korean pharmacy lobby, its KPIC offshoot, and IMS Health Korea. In July 2014, prosecutors pressed criminal charges against the Korean Medical Association and KPIC—but not against IMS, as they lacked concrete evidence linking IMS to the data purchases.

Cho hoped that someone else might come forward with more details. That's when former middleman executive Baek sent his e-mail. Initially, Cho did not see the message buried among the hundred or more he receives daily. When the reporter did finally read it, he immediately put aside a planned report on breast cancer and frantically tried to get in touch with the author of the message.

A Criminal Investigation and Lawsuit

Baek finally agreed to meet with Cho, even though the businessman remained wary about serving as a whistle-blower. "I'm not Dirty Harry," he said later. "I'm not Superman or Batman. I'm just a civilian, and I knew it was a hassle to be involved. So I was not so happy about Dr. Cho's enthusiasm."

Baek knew nothing about the reporter's background as a brain surgeon or Cho's integrity. He had never met a reporter and did not know if he could trust him. He had heard that unscrupulous Korean journalists sometimes went to a company after gathering information against it to demand money to withdraw the story. If that happened, Baek might be vulnerable and exposed to his former employer without bringing what he knew to public attention. In short, he was scared.

With his gentle manner, Cho put Baek at ease and convinced him to record an anonymous interview. Although Baek had feared that nothing would come of his involvement in the case, Cho's reporting not only garnered attention, but also put South Korea on the front line of the international battle over the trade in personal medical data. The reporter again waited for prosecutors to act before airing the segment with Baek. So many months had passed, in fact, that Baek was shown wearing a short-sleeved shirt even though winter had arrived by the time the segment aired. In any case, Cho blurred the whistle-blower's face and altered his voice so that Baek would remain unrecognized.

In early 2015, a prosecutor invited Baek to his office and, at a meeting attended by several others, highlighted the sensitivity of medical data. "Imagine that I can't get an erection on my own, so I need Viagra to get it up," the prosecutor said. "Then I arrange for a blind date through a matchmaker. She checks me out and finds that I come from a very good family, but also learns that I need Viagra. Imagine the position I would be put in if she knew in advance that I take that medication."

Baek completely understood the sentiment—that's why he had come forward. "Personal medical data is very high-quality data because there are no tricks involved," he said. "How could someone sell these personal high-quality data? For example, if I have a problem with the stomach and that is exposed to the insurance company, the insurance company may not accept me as a member. One could not continue to live as a normal person in Korea if this data was exposed."

Visit to Korea

I learned about South Korea's fight over patient data through a brief mention in the 2014 IMS annual report, which referred to the Korean Pharmaceutical Association and Korea Pharmaceutical Information Center affiliate that distributed the PM2000 software: "The civil lawsuit alleges KPA and KPIC collected their personal information in violation of applicable privacy laws without the necessary consent through a software system installed on pharmacy computer systems in Korea, and that personal information was transferred to IMS Korea and sold to pharmaceutical companies. The plaintiffs are claiming damages in the aggregate amount of approximately US $6 million plus interest. We believe the lawsuit is without merit, reject plaintiffs' claims and intend to vigorously defend IMS Health's position."[1]

The money at stake was relatively small for a multibillion-dollar company, but the case could set an important precedent. Since I could find little published information about the lawsuit, I visited South Korea's capital, Seoul, in 2015. Early in my stay, I went to see Sung Bae Kim, a general family doctor and one of the twelve hundred physicians suing over the data sharing.

"When I first found this case, I was shocked by it," he told me in fluent English. "If it's syphilis or hypertension or diabetes, if you have information about me without my understanding, it is very shocking. I want justice on this. Nobody has any right for this information."

"If IMS and KPIC want my health data, they should get consent," he continued. "If they do not get consent, they have no right. It is very unethical."

As we talked more, I understood that Korea's turbulent history has contributed to sensitivity about personal data. Divided after World War II from the ruins of the Japanese imperial empire, South Korea was nearly vanquished by the Communist North in 1950 before a three-year war restored the previous division. The continued threat from the North, just thirty-five miles from Seoul, helped justify decades of authoritarian rule, including the introduction of especially revealing national ID numbers after a 1968 attack in which North Korean agents penetrated the South Korean president's residence.

While a typical American might use a Social Security number only occasionally, such as to open a bank account, obtain a credit card, or file taxes, South Koreans routinely give their numbers to join social media, get cell phones, join loyalty programs, or conduct other commerce. As in many countries, South Korean companies have suffered from hacking in recent years, often with personal ID numbers stolen because of their widespread distribution. Eventually, the government realized that too many organizations were using these revealing numbers, so they created an optional second ID number for everyday transactions. Yet the national ID number remains the same, whether or not criminals have hacked them in the past.

Worrying About the Future

Kim arranged for me to see his cousin, Minso Kim, one of the nine hundred patients suing over the sharing of medical data. We met at one of Seoul's myriad Western-style coffee shops near Ewha Womans University where Minso Kim studies Chinese literature and business. Kim and the other patients only stand to gain about $2,000 each for mental anguish; doctors are seeking $3,000 for exposing their license numbers and prescription histories. With the amounts relatively small, I wondered why she had joined the lawsuit. "Even though I am young—I have lived about twenty years—there will be an amount of information in the database about me," she said. "People can predict from it my future, so I think it is really dangerous that people can sell the data."

She said she has had occasional periods of enteritis, an inflammation of the stomach that she says worsens when she feels stress. Even though she is young, she—like other South Koreans—works relentlessly, an attribute that, en masse, has fueled the country's rapid economic growth. She also fears that her medical files will reflect genetic conditions that could cloud her future health. Two grandparents have had strokes, as have other relatives. "Getting my family history and my data, they can predict my illnesses, and for me that is scary," she said.

Even though South Korea offers all its citizens national health insurance, she is concerned that her health history could affect future employment or insurance if she lives abroad. She hopes to spend time in both China—whose literature she studies and whose language she speaks—and New Zealand, where she spent a year and a half as a girl.

Doctors Fighting Pharmacists

What makes the South Korean fight so interesting is that patients and doctors, two key sources of medical data, are fighting against the unauthorized distribution of *anonymized* as well as identified files. They are arguing that medical data are private even if the information is stripped of name, national ID number, and other direct identifiers.

Another layer of complexity complicates the picture. Until the year 2000, South Korean doctors supplemented their income by selling the drugs they prescribed.[2] That year, the government barred physicians from selling medication and required prescriptions for a wider range of drugs sold at pharmacies. South Korean doctors responded angrily, even going on strike at one point. They are still lobbying the government to overturn the restriction.

"There has been a conflict for fifteen years between the Korean Medical Association and the Korean Pharmacists Association," said Lee Yong Jin, the vice president of planning at the Korean Medical Association. A neurosurgeon by day, he heads a "special committee for the protection of medical information" behind the lawsuit at his organization.

"For five thousand years, Korea doctors have examined patients and dispensed medication," he continued. "The doctor's prescription is their technique, their authority, and should be something exclusive to the relationship of a doctor and patient." But then Jin told me something that surprised me in the context of the big dustup over Korean data mining. He said that his and other doctors' clinics had themselves sold data directly to IMS Health Korea. Quickly, he suggested I not include that information in this book. That hardly seemed fair, I countered, so he explained why such sales differed from the current controversy. First, he said, doctors obtained the explicit consent of patients, who sign a waiver (only about 30 percent gave their approval, he said). Also, he explained that such information was used only for broad statistical data such as how many patients use a certain drug.

"Because of the lawsuit, a lot of companies and people know about the sale of data, so it will not be easy for IMS to collect this information in Korea," Jin continued. "To justify the practice, IMS Korea needs to take an initiative to explain how the data is going to be used for positive purposes and how the data is very safe and protected."

I had hoped to learn more from the Korea Pharmaceutical Association, KPIC, and IMS Korea. All declined to talk. IMS Health's US-based spokesman did respond to written questions—a rare exception to the company's policy of noncooperation with me, because at the time, I was also researching a magazine article—but he provided few details about the situation in Korea.

"IMS Health only receives anonymous healthcare information. IMS Health then takes further steps to ensure the information remains anonymous, such as additional cryptographic coding," Tor Constantino said. "Furthermore, IMS Health provides its clients with syndicated market research based on aggregated healthcare information, further generalizing the healthcare data it receives from its suppliers. Information within IMS syndicated market research only reports aggregate, anonymous information and reveals nothing about identified patients."[3]

Despite these precautions, the anonymized patient information that was leaked by whistle-blower Baek was easily re-identified. Harvard data sleuth Latanya Sweeney and a young researcher studied more than twenty-three thousand of South Korea's national identification numbers included in the data that IMS had received in anonymized format. They published a paper explaining that encryption was a surprisingly simple substitution, with a letter representing each digit, depending on whether it came in an odd or even numbered position.[4] With this simple code, an outsider could take an anonymized South Korean medical record and cross-reference it with consumer profiles containing national ID numbers that had been hacked from other businesses. With re-identification so straightforward, it's no wonder that people who know about the sharing of their data, even people who benefit from the big health-data bazaar, are often uncomfortable about it. "I don't want to share my data," said Ji-Hyung Lee, who uses IMS data as Korea director of business development and licensing at Takeda, the largest Japanese pharmaceutical company, which expanded into South Korea a few years ago.

Outside companies should seek Lee's permission and pay her for such data, she said. "Without it, I don't think I want to do it. I think they should ask. If I know my data is used without my consent, I will be a little upset. Or they should give money—they should pay."

Lee is one of many marketers who appreciate insights from personal data while feeling personally concerned about an outsider's assembling of dossiers about themselves.

Caution in Japan

In neighboring Japan, the world's second-largest pharmaceutical market, I found many current and former medical officials uneasy about the more freewheeling patient data collection practices of South Korea and the United States. The commercial collection of patient information in Japan is especially opaque, operating in what many call a gray zone, but the data collection has grown rapidly into a market whose scope few fully understand. For example, IMS Health advertises the sale of Japanese longitudinal data, including "actual prescription data from pharmacy records for individual patients."

In the United States, many health-care insiders accept the trade in patient data to third parties as a current reality. Among their counterparts in Japan, however, many find such practices distasteful. "The difference between IMS in Japan and in the United States: In Japan, they treat data and privacy in a more sensitive way," Yoshitake Yokokura, president of the influential Japan Medical Association, told me. "Medicine should be for the public benefit, not for business. If someone acquires any profit, the fundamental thing is to get the consent of the patient."

Osamu Nagayama, the chairman and CEO of Chugai, a subsidiary of Roche, said that firms obtaining data should explain to patients the scientific benefits of sharing this information and obtain their consent. "I would not be surprised that if the people were asked, they would be very cooperative—if they understood the significance of the contribution," he said.

I heard a similar sentiment from Emi Kuramae, a marketing manager at drug company Otsuka. "I think in the future we need informed consent for anonymous data. We don't like to be like Korea," she said. "If there is a person who cares about their information—maybe we can just have a system of opt-out."

Chugai, which makes many oncology drugs, buys commercial data from local Japanese data miners and IMS. The leader of its customer relations e-promotion group surprised me by saying he did not want outside firms to sell his family's data for any purpose. "For my daughters, this data is going to somewhere else. I am really scared of that," said Katsuya Yano, whose daughters were aged four and thirteen when we met. "I object personally."

Henry Marini, a retired pharmaceutical company official living in Japan, also objected to the sale of anonymized longitudinal data. "I would draw that line at the individual doctor level," he said. "I, as an individual, I consider it an invasion of privacy. What the doctor prescribes is between him and me. I'm along in years. I guess it doesn't really make a difference. I talk freely about my physical problems. If I was my son's age, I would appreciate the fact that someone could learn what diseases I am afflicted with. If I am going seeking a job, if I have a cancer, I am not sure I would want my employer to know that."

Even former IMS officials in Japan agreed with this sentiment. "During my time, the IMS principle was always that data they provide were only on a consolidated basis and no individual data were disclosed even anonymously," Shunsuke Keimatsu, who served for many years as the IMS Japan CEO, told me. "I have a simple question of what value such anonymized individual data has to IMS clients and how clients can use the data. Secondly, wouldn't it break the privacy law even if it is anonymous data? To be blunt, I feel that they went too far unless there are legitimate answers to the above two questions."

Current IMS Japan officials declined repeated requests for interviews.

For Tohru Omoi, who headed up the IMS Japan production in the early years, the issue is especially personal, because he recently recovered from cancer of the esophagus. "If my data is sold on that level, I would be very uncomfortable," he told me. "I don't like that. Too much personal data should not be kept and used for business purposes. There is always a risk of the data leaking, no matter how severely how they try to protect the privacy of the data."

It took a while for me to understand the extent of Japan's trade in patient data (I spent five weeks researching the issue there in 2015), but the business was certainly growing, even if firms were far more cautious than in the United States. Overall, the examples of Japan and South Korea show that in the absence of guidance or government restriction, market forces will continue to expand personal data collection quietly, even in a traditionally conservative business climate. During interviews with dozens of Japanese health-care and business officials, I found that few had a clear sense of this growing business of data gathering. In that regard, Japan shares the same fundamental problem afflicting the United States and other countries: Until the public has a better understanding of the opportunities and risks from the big health-data bazaar, informed debate to shape future rules is impossible.

Yet even when everybody knows what is wanted in health care, the goal can remain frustratingly elusive. That has certainly proven true in the United States when it comes to the half-century-old vision of creating easily available and comprehensive electronic medical records to improve patient care.

CHAPTER 11

□ □ □ □ □

THE PATIENT'S DATA TOWER OF BABEL

Epic Challenges

As a presidential candidate in 2008, Barack Obama promised to usher in a new era of electronic health records. Within weeks of taking office the following year, he signed the Health Information Technology for Economic and Clinical Health (HITECH) Act, which offered billions of dollars in grants to doctors and hospitals to make "meaningful use" of digitized records. He spoke of computerizing America's health information within five years.

Since then, computers have indeed become commonplace in doctor's offices and hospitals, fueled by more than $31 billion in subsidies paid out through the end of 2015. Yet hundreds of different electronic medical systems still communicate in a babble of different languages, a problem health-care officials call *interoperability*, crippling patients' ability to access their lifetime records.

Craig Barrett, the former CEO of computer chip maker Intel, has experienced the problem firsthand. Not long ago, he had a heart attack while visiting his ranch in Montana. To get the records of his emergency treatment to his regular doctor at the Mayo Clinic, he had to send an old-fashioned paper request. When I asked Barrett if he had since gotten access to a complete set of his own medical records, he answered succinctly: "Be serious, no."

Denny Briley, who helped computerize pharmacy records in the 1970s, is another person who you might expect would have access to his own medical files. Not long ago, he transferred his own records by hand when moving from Chicago to Kansas. "The only way to get that historical data from there to Olathe, Kansas, was to carry it," he said. "Ridiculous."

The inability to access records from different providers has flummoxed even Neal Patterson, the cofounder and CEO of Cerner, which calls itself the "world's largest independent health information technology company" and which operates a major electronic health record system. His wife has had breast cancer since 2007 and visited thirty-five providers across the country for treatment, yet she has to carry around her records by hand, he told a Senate committee in 2015. Patterson may have to do the same himself: He announced in 2016 that he was diagnosed with soft-tissue cancer.

"My wife is stage-four cancer, since 2007," he told senators. "I think it is a failure of all of us to have in 2015 the fact that Jeanne carries shopping bags to all of her appointments where she is going to see a new doctor or specialist.

"It's of course not just cancer patients who live this reality. It's almost all people with chronic conditions who have to see specialists, and people who move, and people who rely on emergency rooms for their care. If it is you or your loved one and that information is vital, I consider it immoral for people to block that data and force us to carry it in bags."[1]

In the worst-case scenario, a patient could take a turn for the worse or even die if health-care providers do not have easy access to comprehensive records. Indeed, in 2016, I was working as a lecturer on a cruise abroad when a seventy-nine-year-old man with diabetes suddenly collapsed while seated on a bench during a tour. A nurse and doctor who happened to be nearby struggled to learn his previous conditions from his wife, a Chinese-born New Zealander with limited English. The man died within minutes. It's entirely possible that no intervention could have saved him, but more information could only have helped. In an emergency, physicians might treat a patient in a way that clashes with preexisting conditions or medications they do not know about. So the question is obvious: After billions in spending, why does this straightforward goal remain elusive?

Some experts say certain electronic records system providers, hospitals, labs, and others are more interested in wedding their customers—and their health-care dollars—to their own particular systems rather than addressing the puzzle of interoperability. "Some health care providers and health IT developers are knowingly interfering with the exchange or use of electronic health information in ways that limit its availability and use to improve health and health care," the Obama administration's Office of the National Coordinator for Health Information Technology wrote in a 2015 report to Congress. "This conduct may be economically rational for some actors in light of current market realities, but it presents a serious obstacle to achieving the goals of the HITECH Act and of health care reform."[2]

The report cited no firms by name, but detailed "information blocking" techniques such as restrictive contracts, prohibitive fees, systems that make it hard to share data, and technology that locks in users: "The persistent lack of transparency and access to reliable information about health IT products and services, including for electronic health information exchange, is a significant problem that not only causes and exacerbates information blocking but substantially impairs the efficient functioning of health IT markets. The precise nature and extent of information blocking remain obscured in large part by contractual restrictions that prevent the disclosure of relevant evidence."

This last point repeats a theme that runs throughout this book. Companies that handle our medical information often obfuscate what is going on behind the scenes, complicating a level-headed discussion of key issues in health care. The reason is that big firms have business reasons to keep their information segregated and isolated, said David Brailer, who served as national coordinator for health information technology under President George W. Bush. "Health systems compete to retain patients within their delivery system so they don't want to cooperate with competitors," he told me. "Also, vendors want to create switching barriers to make customers stickier."

Some experts, including in a recent RAND report, have singled out electronic health records company Epic in particular for a lack of interoperability.[3] "I feel that Epic is the elephant in the room," Senator Bill Cassidy, a Republican from Louisiana, said at a 2015 Senate hearing. Elephant or not, the company has won over many clients within medicine, including the Cleveland Clinic, Kaiser Permanente, Massachusetts General Hospital, and Johns Hopkins Medicine.

A computer programmer named Judy Faulkner founded Epic in 1979. As a graduate student at the University of Wisconsin, she had taken a Computers in Medicine class that patient-power advocate Warner Slack cotaught. Around 1972, while still in graduate school, Faulkner began working on a system to keep track of patients. Today, her company remains privately held, and she is personally worth $2.5 billion, according to a 2015 estimate by *Forbes*.

Faulkner rarely speaks to journalists, so I was pleasantly surprised when she telephoned me one Friday evening and also responded to several e-mails. She said Epic started addressing interoperability in 2005, before other electronic records companies did so, after one of her pediatrician husband's patients died when the girl went to the wrong emergency room and the attending doctors did not have the medical records that might have saved her.

Systems operated by different companies struggle to communicate because each uses its own codes to describe procedures and information, Faulkner said. "Most of the data elements we had to define ourselves because there were no definitions," she said. "That's across all the vendors. It doesn't matter if we are talking about Cerner, Meditech, Allscripts, Athena, Epic. And it would be highly unusual if we all defined them alike. Someone says 'throwing up,' someone says 'vomit,' someone says 'code thirty-seven,' someone makes a code number three."

Epic breaks down the world of health into 150,000 data codes. Industry standards exist in some areas such as medications, but not in others such as allergies. "Is it a rash, is it fever, is it throwing up, is it you practically die? One group may have eighty-seven different ways of putting down reactions to allergies. Someone else may have twelve. How do they map into each other?" Faulkner said.

The Epic founder says the government and various committees need to organize electronic health system vendors to agree to common standards. When I ask how long it might take until all these different systems speak a common language, she said there was a possibility that it would never happen. Despite these obstacles, she said Epic exchanges twenty-one million records a month as of 2016, putting it far ahead of the competition. "When stories emerged about Epic not being open or interoperable, we didn't take them as seriously as we should have," she said. "By the time we started to address the misinformation, the amount of confusion around interoperability had mushroomed."

Critics note that Epic is the only major electronic record vendor that has not joined CommonWell Health Alliance, a health-care exchange network that is seeking to ease interoperability. Faulkner explained Epic's reluctance to join: "Requiring everyone to use one technology would be like requiring iPhone developers to use BlackBerry technology because you mistakenly think that's the only way people on iPhones and BlackBerries can talk with each other. One platform is not necessary and would stifle innovation."

Ultimately, the paradox that patients cannot access their own lifetime medical dossiers while a for-profit data miner can compile its own anonymized versions is also a failure of government policy and regulation, which failed to foresee how industry would behave. In short, US officials blundered by failing to demand that systems be compatible before it handed out billions in HITECH subsidies, said Julia Adler-Milstein, a University of Michigan expert on health-care IT. "I do not believe that [electronic health record] vendors are the bad guys here, that they set out to fragment health information and sort of make money hoarding data," she said. "But I do think we set up a set of incentives for them where it is not obvious that it is really in their best interest to make it easy to share information, either.

"We did not set up a business model where it made sense for Epic to invest their own money figuring out how to talk to and connect to the hundreds of other vendors that are out there. That would have been very expensive, and it is not clear that it would have really benefitted their bottom line."

David Blumenthal, the federal government's health information czar under President Obama, ushered in HITECH. He said the primarily goal at the time was to encourage medical providers to digitize their records, with the hope that the different providers later on would adopt their systems to share records. "I wish we could have done interoperability early on, but I don't think it was practical," he told me.

Over time, it became clear that getting different providers to share information was going to be more difficult than officials had hoped. "One of the things I didn't anticipate—didn't understand at the time but came to understand—was that there was no business case for interoperability," Blumenthal said. Getting electronic health record vendors to cooperate is akin to getting Target and Walmart to share information about their customer bases, their customers' buying patterns, and the prices the retailers charge, he said.

Exactly because electronic health record companies do not have a business interest in embracing interoperability, it is up to the government to mandate standards. "The vendors cannot be expected to solve this problem on their own," said William Yasnoff, the CEO of the nonprofit Health Record Banking Alliance. "By analogy, it is not really reasonable to blame manufacturers of telephones if their customers cannot make calls to phones from other vendors if there are no standards for telephone communication."

He advocates a system akin to banking, which puts the individual in control of his or her own money. Once upon a time, you had to go to a branch of your own bank to make a withdrawal. Now you can get cash from ATMs all over the world. "In my vision, patients engage a third party to receive and manage that data with their consent," Yasnoff said. "The bankers don't decide where your money goes. You do. And presumably if they do send your money somewhere without your consent, they go to jail."

Google Gives It a Try

The vision of an easily available, patient-controlled medical dossier remains stubbornly elusive, even for the world's most successful tech companies. The ambitious goals that pioneers Larry Weed, Warner Slack, and others had begun decades before continues to elude all those who pick up the torch. With all of its brains and money, Google thought it could present patients with easy access their medical records from multiple providers in one central location. Google's CEO Eric Schmidt described a scenario when he announced a medical record bank called Google Health in 2008: "If, God forbid, I were in the emergency room here in Florida, I'd want whoever is sitting there trying to keep me going to have access to the last N years of my radiological experiences, and I'd like them to have it instantaneously. And we can do that now."[4]

Schmidt explained that Google Health would store data for patients, who could use it for everything from checking up on their vaccinations to providing access to doctors in an emergency. To help patients import data, Google signed up pharmacies (Walgreens, Duane Reade, Longs Drugs), test labs (Quest Diagnostics), middlemen (Allscripts), insurers (Aetna), and health-care providers (Cleveland Clinic, Beth Israel Deaconess Medical Center). It promised never to share data without the user's permission, saying that profit could come from generating more business for other Google services. Schmidt noted that in 2008, there were two hundred US personal record systems, most linked to a specific company or health system. "Any scenario where information is sort of isolated is a scenario where health is not well delivered," he said.

With past success in search, browsers, maps, and many other areas, it seemed that if anyone could succeed in attracting users, especially for a free service, it would be Google. "You sit there and say, 'Well, this will never happen . . . five percent of people will adopt this stuff,'" he said. "That's always true in year one. But in year ten, it is usually 70, 80 percent that have adopted it."

Such bold pronouncements from Silicon Valley have often come true. But not so for medical dossiers. In 2011, Google gave up and closed the service. "Google Health is not having the broad impact that we hoped it would," the company wrote in announcing its demise. "There has been adoption among certain groups of users like tech-savvy patients and their caregivers, and more recently fitness and wellness enthusiasts. But we haven't found a way to translate that limited usage into widespread adoption in the daily health routines of millions of people."[5]

Microsoft Health Vault

When Google announced that it was suspending the service, Microsoft quickly put out statements reminding the public that its HealthVault was still operating and ready to convert Google data into its system. Not only did Microsoft's free service outlive Google's, but HealthVault also started a year earlier.

Despite HealthVault's relative longevity, Sean Nolan, HealthVault's general manager, said by the time he left Microsoft in 2014, only some two million people had signed up for the service, far below Microsoft's goal of ten million. "Anybody with any sense of logic can come in and look at this industry and say this is effed up, this is ridiculous. I could fix this overnight," he told me. "Getting people healthy doesn't pay, and so nobody invests and nobody changes."

Just transferring information into the user's vault from different doctors, hospitals, and providers has proven intractable. "How many times we had to fight with health systems to make the data available—how many conferences we had to go to and how many lawyers I had to talk to," lamented Peter Neupert, the vice president who oversaw Microsoft's health division. Among the electronic health record companies that did not smooth the flow of data into HealthVault are Epic and Cerner, Neupert said.[6] Microsoft HealthVault lost something shy of $100 million from its concept stage through 2015. "It's still real money, but we launched it in 2008, so over nine years, that's not a lot of money," Neupert said. I wondered if Microsoft had considered following Google's footsteps in shuttering the service. "Every day," Nolan said.

Like many others who have dabbled in the field, Neupert is convinced that one day, health record banks will catch on. "It is going to happen," he said. "There will be a need for consumers to take charge of their health data. The device where people may enter and engage with it and how they do it may be the phone, which we weren't anticipating as much then as the Internet itself."

Health care is just far slower than other sectors in embracing these logical changes. "You used to deal with the bank on their terms. Now the bank deals with you on your terms," Neupert said. "Health and education are the last two industries to do that."

Another Silicon Valley Try

Other important players in Silicon Valley have also thought they had the solution to empowering patients with their records. For Craig Barrett, the former Intel executive, his inspiration came when he was feeling pain in his mouth and went to see his dentist, who took a full set of X-rays and concluded he needed root canal treatment with another specialist. The specialist took another set of X-rays and advised that Barrett visit a third practitioner, who—you guessed it—took another full set of X-rays. After a successful career of over thirty-five years at Intel, Barrett could easily afford the cost of additional tests, but he thought the repetition was wasteful and inefficient amid rising health-care costs. So in 2006, ahead of Microsoft and Google, he formed Dossia, which allows patients to access their own records.

Barrett convinced Applied Materials, BP America, Intel, Pitney Bowes, and Walmart to advance $1.5 million each to become the first customers, giving the start-up potential access to 2.5 million patient records. "We thought one of the ways to arrest the ever-inflating medical costs was to empower employees with an electronic medical record," he said. "We concluded that the US government was not going to do anything about health records, because of its complexity and bureaucracy, and thought the private sector might be able to get together much faster."

Early media accounts expressed enthusiasm. But privacy advocate Deborah Peel said individuals should entrust their health records to a neutral third party, not an effort backed by employers, which could discriminate because of such information.

Dossia had hoped to get off the ground by mid-2007, but it had a disagreement with the company contracted to provide the underlying technology. By the time the suit was settled in 2008, Dossia had spent $12 million and was quickly running out of cash, according to Steve Munini, the chief operating officer, who joined at that time. It restructured and pressed on.

To date, no company using Dossia has paid to make medical records available to its entire workforce. Instead, firms pony up about $2 per month per employee who signs up (a large firm such as Walmart gets a big bulk discount). At the end of 2014, Dossia had 140,000 registered users, less than 3 percent of the 5 million employees offered the service. Did Dossia end up saving companies money, as originally intended, by motivating workers to get more tests such as cholesterol screenings or colonoscopies? "If it worked wonderfully, Dossia would not be struggling today," Barrett said.

Vermont Pioneers

Google, Microsoft, and Dossia are all relative newcomers in the quest for electronic health records. For the ultimate perspective on the problem, I drive up to Underhill, a rural area of northern Vermont near the Canadian border, a week before Christmas. The temperature hovers at a few degrees above freezing, but snow has already blanketed the region. I turn off a country road and make my way up a long, sloping driveway lined by tall trees. At the end, I find a remote T-shaped house on fourteen acres, much of it forested.

A mile and a half away lives Underhill's most famous resident, merchant marine Captain Richard Phillips, whose harrowing survival of a Somali pirate takeover of his ship was made into the movie *Captain Phillips*, starring Tom Hanks. I am visiting another determined survivor, Larry Weed, a doctor in his nineties who lives alone in the woods. I want to hear his reflections on why America failed to embrace his half-century-old vision of easily computerized medical records.

Lured by the offer of a professorship, Weed moved to Vermont with his team of medical data pioneers in 1969 to usher in a revolution they called PROMIS (Problem-Oriented Medical Information System). Programmer Jan Schultz led the team in writing hundreds of thousands of lines of computer code so that doctors could record patient histories in a consistent manner, an approach Weed called the problem-oriented medical record.[7] The PROMIS system also allowed doctors and nurses to look up information on hundreds of medical problems decades before the Internet, an effort aimed at lessening the importance of any one physician's insights. "We were doing real patient care with these systems, many, many years earlier than anybody else, probably in the world, really," said Schultz.

At the time, some outsiders waxed poetic about the system. "Recently I spent eight hours, spellbound before the PROMIS monitor screens, watching the green glow cast by the pages of medical logic and personal history that marched in precision on and off the screen," one researcher wrote in 1978. "There is no other word to describe it but awe inspiring."[8]

For all the tech wizardry, Weed's personal approach was old school. Dressed in a white lab coat, shirt, tie, and brown trousers, he would walk briskly through the hospital ward and check up on his students. He was a man in a hurry, and others had to trot alongside to keep up. Sometimes he would read a record out loud in front of a patient to review how accurately the student had recorded the problem-oriented medical record. He displayed an extraordinary intellect and conviction that his ideas would win the day. "He was very sure of himself. He has a gigantic ego. He had all the answers, basically," Schultz said.

Weed's cocksure preaching on what medicine needed alienated many in the hospital. He was disrupting health care—which was exactly what he intended. Other doctors resisted a system that allowed others to see their notes. He thought they arrogantly presented themselves as all-knowing when in reality one person could possess only a fraction of total human knowledge about medicine. "If you are telling somebody their 'MDeity' doesn't mean what the public thinks it means and they are making a living doing it, do you expect them to kiss you, throw their arms around you? Of course, it's threatening!" Weed said.

The hospital's business side thought billing deserved priority, as billing made rather than lost money. "It became quite apparent," Weed said, "that there was a real conflict between the computers in the business part of the hospital and academic people like myself who wanted to have everything start with the patient." The tensions between the PROMIS innovators and traditionalists became so great that a group of University of Kansas anthropologists studied the dynamics from 1976 to 1977 and wrote a book about it.[9]

Funding for PROMIS eventually dwindled, and Weed left the university. In 1982, he started the PKC Corporation, which aimed at promoting *knowledge coupling*, his system that allows doctors to enter a patient's symptoms into a computer and receive likely causes of the problem. Yet he chafed at the business world's emphasis on the bottom line, expressing indifference to cashing in when computers and the Internet offered the potential of big returns.

This tension between science and commerce came to the fore in 2005, when Steve Case, the cofounder of America Online, came calling. Case, who created Revolution Health with the goal of doing for medicine what AOL did for e-mail, met PKC officials, including Weed, who displayed his usual brilliance and intensity. Case offered $40 million to buy PKC, and a deal was struck. Weed owned a third of the company and stood to do very well financially. But two days before everything was to be finalized, he got cold feet and e-mailed the board expressing his concerns. Executives at Revolution Health heard about Weed's reservations and called him; he happily shared the e-mail with them as well. "He sent an e-mail to all of the key players that was sufficient to kill the deal," said Howard Pierce, the CEO of PKC. "It looked like a crazy person with founder's remorse." (Weed counters: "It was a very rational note.")

Weed's action on the potential Revolution Health deal dismayed the PKC team, and he retired soon after. In 2012, Sharecare, a social network set up by the founder of WebMD and television host Mehmet Oz, bought the company. Today Weed's knowledge couplers, the descendant of PROMIS, are the engine behind the site's AskMD service, which may invite users to sign in, and thus be in the company's database, to get answers. Like Facebook and Google, Sharecare does not sell personal data, but makes money by targeting sponsored content and advertising according to what it knows about users.

Weed Looks Back

As I step out of my car and approach Larry Weed's house, he appears rapidly at his door, remarkably fit and lively for a man in his nineties. He immediately sits me in front of a computer on his dining room table and launches into a rapid-fire explanation of knowledge couplers. There is no time for pleasantries, no questions about the drive up from Boston. He has lots to explain—so much, in fact, that he has suggested, very persistently, that I read several books before arriving, including his 2011 *Medicine in Denial*.[10]

Knowledge couplers were at the heart of his company PKC, where he had hoped to create the pinnacle of human knowledge related to medicine. I ask what he thinks about the fate of the company, which relies on web advertising and sponsored content to present medical content to consumers, today. Not surprisingly, Weed finds the mix of health care and commerce distasteful. "I really got disgusted with the business world," he says. "I don't want to say anything negative, because I don't want to get into trouble, but the business world is something else. You have to come from the Harvard Business School and just see dollar signs in your sleep in the business world."

He fires out nonstop facts for more than three hours, until the late autumn afternoon light starts to fade in his living room. My relative youth is no advantage; his energy level seems indefatigable. Seeking a pause in the action, I ask if he still plays the Steinway grand piano in his living room. He leaps up and races to the piano bench. The living room window overlooks a field and woods beyond, the perfect setting for a contemplative song. But he plays presto, tackling challenging compositions by Sibelius, Bach, and others quite well for a person of any age.

Before leaving, I ask not about science, but about his feelings. Is he surprised that society has not yet embraced his proposed innovations in medicine? "I've been depressed. It's horrifying," he says. "The disaster in medicine is far bigger than most people realize.

"Am I frustrated that fifty or sixty years have gone by and nothing has changed? If I was a suicidal type, I would have committed suicide long ago. Am I frustrated? Well, yeah, but I'll drop dead one of these days."

Before leaving the neighboring town of Burlington, I go to say good-bye to his former programmer Jan Schultz. "A lot of people said the reason it didn't succeed was because of Larry, and that is bullshit," Schultz says. "The reason it didn't succeed was it was way too early, and it was threatening to doctors. If you look at what has happened, it's all these little [data] silos. It's pathetic. It's horrible."

Nothing sums up the continued shortcomings of today's electronic medical records better than my earlier visit to David Miller, the director of Cleveland Metropolitan General Hospital when Weed began some of his pioneering work there in the mid-1960s. Miller also moved to Vermont in 1969 and worked with Weed again in the 1970s. Born in 1930, Miller had had a number of health problems, including surgery for bowel obstruction and a bladder cancer correction. Yet even he does not possess his own complete medical dossier. "I don't think even Larry Weed has one," Miller said.

Weed does not and adds frankly, "I'm in my nineties. I'm at the point where I say to the kids, 'I don't want to wake up in an intensive care unit. Don't worry about me surviving. I couldn't care less.'"

Miller instead relies on a rudimentary solution. He keeps two pieces of paper bearing the letters EMT on the entrance stairs of his home. When he and his wife leave the house, whether for a quick outing to the store or on holiday, they bring the two sheets of paper with them, so that if something happens, emergency medical technicians can get quick access to their vital information the old-fashioned way.

By contrast, recent years have brought significant advances for data miners, giving them ever greater capabilities to gather anonymized patient information from a surprisingly wide spectrum of sources.

CHAPTER 12

□ □ □ □ □

TWENTY-FIRST-CENTURY ADVANCES

IMS Today

When IMS Health celebrated its fiftieth birthday in 2004, its CEO compared its success with companies that dominated business when Ludwig Frohlich and Arthur Sackler formed their secret alliance behind IMS (a partnership the CEO did not mention). David Thomas looked up the *Fortune* 100 list from half a century before, only to learn that these lists only began in 1955, a year after IMS's official formation, so he compared the company to that year's list. "Only about 10 percent of the companies still exist," he told an annual IMS investor meeting. "There's something unique about a company and a brand that can survive fifty years.

"We have a product that doesn't go out of style. It changes with the times. It doesn't get replaced by something else; it just gets enhanced."

The company continues to expand, most recently through a May 2016 merger with Quintiles, which conducts drug clinical trials and provides other services helping pharmaceutical companies bring their products to market.[1] The merger greatly increases the company's access to medical data, an asset that Quintiles and IMS companies highlighted when they first revealed an October 2015 strategic alliance leading up to the merger. "This collaboration greatly enhances access to healthcare data from across the world—providing customers with the critical information and the related services needed to demonstrate the value of their medicines to physicians, payers and patients," Scott Evangelista, the president of integrated health-care services at Quintiles, said in a statement.[2]

The merger marks the latest IMS move in a long history of outmuscling or buying out rivals as it seeks to update its business and dominate the health-data field. "IMS has been a fast follower and an acquirer throughout its history much more than an innovator," said Greg Ellis, a former top executive at rival Symphony Health. "When innovators come along, IMS has often bought those innovators but has not directly spawned a lot of innovation."

Frohlich's advertising agency is long gone, but his side business, IMS, continues to dominate medical data mining and grow in value. Dun & Bradstreet bought IMS in 1988 for a little less than $1.7 billion. IMS became independent again a decade later, and in 2005, Dutch publisher VNU offered to buy it for $6.8 billion. The deal collapsed amid shareholder grumbling over the high price, but in 2010, several investment funds bought IMS for nearly $6 million. When IMS went public again in 2014, the IPO established its value at $6.6 billion, and a rise in the stock price lifted its value to more than $10 billion by the summer of 2015. The May 2016 merger with Quintiles boosted the combined company's value to $17.6 billion.[3] Also adding to the value of IMS Health in recent years has been the growth of its consulting services—which became a half-billion-dollar-a-year business by the 2000s—where the company offers tailored insights to pharmaceutical firms on issues such as how to best introduce a new drug.[4]

IMS CEO Ari Bousbib, a former Otis Elevator Company executive, did very well in the IPO, earning $25.9 million, which included a big stock bonus, in 2014. In researching this book, I contacted his office a number of times over several years; no one ever responded. I finally called him at home one Sunday. "I'm so sorry, this is a bad time," he said in French-Canadian-accented English. There was never a better time, and we never spoke again.

The amount of data IMS collects continues to increase dramatically, boosted both by a long series of acquisitions and mergers as well as by advances in computerization and big data storage. As in its earliest days, IMS gathers invoices from drugmakers and wholesalers, but now from more than fifty countries; panels of doctors record their diagnoses and therapies in more than forty countries. It also obtains prescription information from more than ten countries, as well as insurance claims submitted by doctors' offices, hospital discharge records, and lab tests from a variety of nations, including about two-thirds of all US claims.[5] It is expanding significantly into developing economies, including China, Russia, India, and Brazil. In total, the company gathers information on more than fifty-five billion health-care transactions a year, with anonymized records on more than half a billion people, according to its 2014 annual report.[6] Whenever possible, IMS barters for data, offering IMS reports and analysis instead of cash. "We are moving from fee-based to service-based," said Doug Long, the IMS vice president of industry relations. Such an arrangement works well because "there is interdependency."

Data Mining Competitors

IMS continues to face competition in the ever-growing market for patient information. One long-standing rival has been Source, which Indian-born Silicon Valley billionaire Romesh Wadhwani bought for his private-equity firm Symphony Technology Group in 2012. Although a number of its executives have come from IMS, Symphony sued IMS in 2013, alleging monopoly behavior. The suit said IMS had a 90 percent overall global market share and 86 percent market share of the half-a-billion-dollar US targeting and compensation data market, which allows pharmaceutical companies to target individual doctors according to dossiers gathered about them and to base pharma reps' pay on their effectiveness in boosting sales.

"After swallowing every other major U.S. competitor by acquisition," the complaint stated, "IMS has engaged in an unlawful scheme to protect its monopoly and to eliminate from these markets the only formidable competitor left standing: Symphony, a company that provides often better products than IMS but which is dwarfed by IMS in size and market power."[7] IMS said the lawsuit is without merit, as "customers have a broad range of choices in this highly competitive marketplace." It countersued Symphony, alleging patent infringement related to the de-identification of longitudinal patient records.[8] The suits were dropped in 2016 as part of a deal in which IMS bought a company owned by Symphony Technology Group.

The demise of ArcLight and other rivals over the years illustrates the difficulty in challenging the leading medical data miner. It is very costly to buy enough data to offer robust competition, noted Robert Weissman, the former chairman of Dun & Bradstreet when IMS was part of the company. "Anybody who thought about the potential of competing broadly with IMS would recognize that, generally speaking, collecting 10 percent of the information which IMS was collecting would not translate into 10 percent market share," he said. "To be competitive, someone would have to build a database which, generally speaking, duplicated the IMS database. That was a very expensive proposition."

Don Otterbein, Symphony Health's senior vice president for marketing and product development, concurred with Weissman's analysis: "It is very expensive data, so therefore the idea that you could have a small piece of it and it was sufficient to compete doesn't make sense to compete with IMS."

Medical Direct Marketing

In the days of Frohlich and Sackler, drug companies advertised only to physicians. By the 1980s, US authorities allowed direct-to-consumer messaging, and by 1998, the practice had become common enough that former US senator and Republican presidential candidate Bob Dole pitched Viagra in television spots. Since advertisers want to reach an audience most likely to be interested in their products, greater sophistication in targeting medical advertising has become commonplace.

Although health-care *data miners* such as IMS Health and Symphony Health deal only in anonymized patient dossiers, related firms known as *data brokers* sell identified profiles about hundreds of millions of customers. The profiles include names, addresses, phone numbers, e-mail addresses, and medical conditions. Name a condition—Alzheimer's disease, a weak heart, obesity, poor bladder control, clinical depression, irritable bowel syndrome, erectile dysfunction, even HIV—and some data brokers will compile a list of people who have the condition, and will sell the list to companies for direct marketing.[9]

Such patient-identified trade is allowed because HIPAA applies only to health-care providers such as doctors, labs, health plans, insurers, and middlemen. Everyone else can freely trade medical data by tracking patients' various activities: online purchases, surveys, sweepstakes, coupons, magazine subscriber lists, health-related purchases, fitness apps, health websites, and other sources, even DNA information. "Genetic data outside of HIPAA-covered entities isn't protected generally, just like all other health data," says Washington, DC, privacy consultant Bob Gellman. There is a "big gap in protections here, and as genetic data comes into broader availability and use, it may pass into data broker, profiling, and marketing files—just like other health data. Except that genetic data may be about your kids too."

In recent years, millions of people have tested their DNA, seeking insights into their future health, longevity, paternity, ancestry, and more. Few realize, however, that some commercial firms offering DNA tests share by default. For example, Veritas Genetics, a Personal Genome Project spinoff that in 2016 generated headlines by announcing full gene sequencing and interpretation for $999, shares "de-identified" data with public databases aimed at helping science. The sharing is detailed only in item number 19 of its "informed consent for genetic testing" section, one of eight privacy documents posted on the website.[10]

Some companies do take a different approach and say customers should be able to decide for themselves what happens with their DNA information. "It's our industry's ethical responsibility to drive towards standardized language so when an individual shares their data they know exactly who has it and for what purpose—and feels confident their data is contractually protected," said Warren Little, the CEO and founder of Sure Genomics, a Carlsbad, California, company that offers full DNA sequencing. "If personal privacy is not protected, then data monetization without informed consent potentially becomes a reality. It's a slippery slope."

Even the rare few who carefully read the fine print of privacy policies are often left confused about what actually happens with patient data. "If you look at enough terms of service and privacy policies, you will see the word 'may' or 'might' being used a lot—as in we 'may share,' which leaves the door open," said Jan Charbonneau, a PhD candidate at the Centre for Law and Genetics, Faculty of Law, University of Tasmania, Australia.

When the fine print admits to selling data, rarely do companies reveal what exactly they put on the market. For example, the dating website EliteMate writes: "The information we collect is also sold, licensed, transferred, rebranded, updated, appended and/or shared with individuals and companies engaged in the sales, marketing, advertising, and publishing industries for various products and services in which you may be interested." Yet a search among commercially available data broker sites reveals that among EliteMate's named mailing lists for sale are those with AIDS/HIV.[11]

"A lot of people don't connect what they are doing with future marketing," said Tim Burnell, principal owner of data broker Complete Medical Lists. Even though he has worked more than two decades in direct marketing, he has no illusions of what most people think about his trade: "The majority of people would say they hate it."

DataMasters, a broker that sells medical information and postal addresses on 92 million Americans, sees the following groups as potential clients:

- Pharmaceutical companies offering a new or a competing medication
- Market research companies doing studies for pharmaceutical marketing organizations or other medical research related organizations

- New physicians needing to build a medical practice
- Physicians that limit their practice to a certain type of ailment or patient group
- Companies offering medical devices or medical services intended for specific ailment sufferer groups
- Attorneys needing to contact prospective clients for class action lawsuit participation.[12]

Many companies offering free services vacuum up your personal data to target advertising. Your information is the price for their service. RealAge, which estimates the apparent age of your body, asks for name, e-mail, date of birth, and gender.[13] Consumer health site WebMD targets ads according to online searches at the site (although not for certain sensitive conditions such as AIDS) and asks users for personal information in surveys.[14] A WebMD site called eMedicineHealth.com has a straightforward piece of advice: "If you do not want your Personal Information used by WebMD as provided in this Privacy Policy, you should not register as a member or for any specific tool or application that collects Personal Information."[15]

Even visiting a website anonymously can sometimes provide enough details for a company to guess who you are, an observation highlighted by birth-control website your-life.com, which is supported by drugmaker Bayer. The site gathers the name of your Internet service provider, your computer's IP address (a unique code assigned to your computer), and the websites you came from and are going to. "This data could possibly lead to your identification, but we do not use it to do so," the site's privacy policy says.[16]

Many insiders worry that the competition will continue to drive some firms to push the boundaries in medical targeting and to tarnish the whole industry. "Has the industry tried to discover who are the patients with diseases? Absolutely. [Have] they had their hands slapped? Repeatedly," said Roger Korman, a former senior vice president at IMS. "The instinct of the industry is to sell more stuff and identify patients."[17]

Stan Crosley, an attorney who previously worked as chief privacy officer for drugmaker Eli Lilly added to the discussion of competition: "What you worry about are the ones who are the one-offs, the fly-by-nights who try to jump into the middle of the mix because they think there is a lot of money to be made, and then you can have some really significant issues."

From a drugmaker's point of view, finding patients who might need its medication makes good business sense. For example, Lexicon

Pharmaceuticals turned to IMS Consulting to calculate the numbers of patients with inadequately controlled carcinoid syndrome, a condition that causes severe diarrhea. IMS data can also help the company target doctors with these patients to prescribe their treatment, said John Northcott, Lexicon's vice president of marketing, commercial strategy, and operations.[18]

Naked on Social Media

Postings on Twitter, Facebook, blogs, patient groups and other Internet sites also give outsiders a new fountainhead of medical insights. In recent years, companies and scientific researchers alike have paid more and more attention. For example, one study tracked more than two hundred thousand Twitter messages referring to Adderall, a prescription stimulant, and found that mentions peaked around university exam periods.[19]

Mark Dredze, a computer scientist at Johns Hopkins University, is one of a growing number of researchers who mines social media for health insights, including data on depression, suicide, schizophrenia, posttraumatic stress disorder, eating disorders, and other issues. Initially, he found it hard to believe that patients would reveal themselves on the Internet.[20] "For the mental health stuff, for example, I was incredibly skeptical that we would find enough data to do anything, because I thought that people would never post such intimate things," he said. "I was completely wrong. There are plenty of people who go online and share in a completely public forum details about what they are doing. Some of them do it anonymously . . . but other people are using accounts where it is not hard to figure out who they are."

For his studies, he searches Twitter for key words such as "diagnosed with," which might lead to a posting such as "today I started therapy, she diagnosed me with anorexia, depression, anxiety disorder, posttraumatic stress disorder." Some experts in his field make conclusions about broad public health trends; others want to help individuals by, for example, identifying potentially suicidal people before it is too late.

As with so much in the world of digitized medical data, the ability of outsiders to discern an individual's health details can add to greater public health insights, but it also has a downside. "If you are a nefarious individual, you can use these things to do evil. . . . That's just the reality of the data world we live in," Dredze said. "But I think overwhelmingly the interest here is using these for good."

Privacy experts worry that outsiders will exploit this information in ways that social media posters may not have considered. You may not realize that data brokers harvest names from patient forums and hospital sites to add to lists of people linked with a particular disease. The largest data brokers assemble elaborate profiles that list wealth, real estate holdings, employment, religion, ethnic background, sexual orientation, hobbies, and many other categories, which may include health. Since some niche brokers focus on producing named lists of individuals according to ailments, social media can enhance the details they can obtain.[21] "If you post anything related to your health condition online anywhere that is outside of HIPAA, it becomes fair game," said Pam Dixon, the founder of the World Privacy Forum and author of several books on privacy.

Dixon recommended caution in places such as online forums where people trade details about specific diseases, or hospital sites that invite patients to leave comments such as compliments to a specific doctor for curing a disease. "People will leave these in a moment of happiness and joy that they have had a good result, and they have no idea that those pages are public and their names are being harvested," she said.

Medical data miners are also paying more attention to social media, with IMS Health buying an analytics company specializing in the area in 2013. Murray Aitken, executive director of the IMS Institute for Healthcare Informatics, spoke about this new trend in a news release: "Increasingly, patients are turning to social media as an essential forum for obtaining and sharing information related to their health. This trend only heightens the need for relevant, accurate content that can be accessed and used throughout the patient journey."[22]

Start-ups such as Treato—which invites clients to "see what millions of patients are saying"—monitor what patients say about drugs and treatments. With offices in the United States and Israel, Treato uses computers that crawl the Internet seeking to discern new trends and insights. "We get to discover things that people did not know what to ask," CEO Gideon Mantel said. "This is, in my view, the ultimate wisdom of the crowd. . . . If I see many of those [comments about a drug or a treatment], there is something here."

Sometimes, the findings are rather unexpected, such as several hundred postings that suggest Robitussin can help women get pregnant, Mantel said.[23] Overall, Treato focuses on the wisdom (or, sometimes, nonsense) of the crowd, but does not profile individual patients. "We are not going to say, 'Adam had switched from drug A to drug B, and here is a lead for a sales guy,' and say, 'Hey, Adam, here is a coupon for the drug,'" Mantel said.

Fitness and mobile health apps and devices, to say nothing of implanted medical devices and biosensors transmitting data wirelessly, also create vast amounts of additional data unregulated by HIPAA. These data could allow outsiders to detect conditions such as depression, alcoholism, posttraumatic stress disorder, or cancer. Sensors in our cars and homes will grow dramatically in the years to come, with many gathering health-related information. That could put companies such as Google, Apple, or even Samsung in the position of becoming major health-data gatherers whose insights could dwarf what is now in circulation. "The amount of health data that is going to be collected in cars and the home is going to increase dramatically in ways I think will boggle people's minds," Dixon said.

The availability of such health data raises many ethical issues. "In theory, a health insurance company can look at your online behavior that might be publicly available through a Twitter account," Dredze said. "Can they use that information to somehow affect policy decisions, pricing decisions? Is that fair?"

Using Anonymized Patient Dossiers to Target Ads

As the sophistication of data analytics grows, companies are increasingly able to combine different data sets about individuals to produce powerful insights for medical advertising, even if individuals are not targeted directly by name. In one growing area, medical data miners cross-reference anonymized patient dossiers with named consumer profiles from data brokers, whose leading US companies include Acxiom, Experian, and Epsilon. The merged results give drug companies unprecedented ability to gather a picture of the consumers mostly likely to buy their drugs.

This technique, known as *propensity modeling*, illustrates the power of big data to reveal intimate information even when anonymized. As recounted earlier, data sources such as pharmacies replace a patient's name, address, and other direct identifiers with a unique patient code such as "x5f7jj46sh8." Propensity modeling uses the same technique to match anonymized medical information with the hundreds or even thousands of facts contained in one individual's consumer profile.

Data scientists batch together millions of these fused medical and consumer profiles to target those most likely to have a specific ailment. That means that even if you never filled out an online survey, entered a sweepstakes, ordered a related product, or posted a social comment on

Facebook, companies can target advertising to you by deducing that you may have an affliction.

For example, the data might suggest golfers of a certain economic profile aged fifty-five to sixty-five in specific areas of the country might be the right market for skin cancer treatment ads. "We take anonymized medical records . . . and we correlate the medical information with demographic lifestyle and interest information," said Jennifer Barrett Glasgow, the chief privacy officer at Acxiom. "You end up with a much bigger, if you will, target audience. You have to understand that many people in the audience do not have the condition, but a lot of them, far more than in a normal audience, do have the condition. It does improve the marketing results without getting very, very specific."

Firms at the heart of medical propensity modeling are typically wary about saying too much publicly. On a webpage aimed at potential advertising clients, Crossix, a New York analytics firm that matches consumer profiles with prescription and medical data, explained its work: "Our data network incorporates a national sample of retail and specialty pharmacies, PBMs and switch companies. We partner with Acxiom to collate consumer profile data that informs campaign targeting and optimization."[24]

To go to an Internet site and see an advertisement for a condition you might have can certainly prove jarring. "The sophisticated profiling that they are doing on search now is scary in terms of how much they know about you," said former IMS executive Bob Merold. "Companies like IMS are selling 'Here [are] four million patients with erectile dysfunction and here [are] their profiles,' and then Google puts it into their algorithms so that the Viagra ads show up when you are searching fishing or whatever the heck the things are that correlate."

Ryan Olohan, who oversees Google's efforts to partner with health-care advertisers, told me that Google conducts four to five billion searches a day and that many of the users are logged into their Google accounts linked with other activities such as what videos they watch on YouTube. "We are sitting on a ton of data," he said. This information can track the spread of disease or medical concerns, giving researchers insights to changing health patterns. It can also help pinpoint related advertising on any topic video. "Between IMS, WebMD, Google, there are a million" data points, Olohan said.

Through Internet tracking tools such as cookies, companies gain additional information, and data miners and drug manufacturers augment their consumer insights by sharing cookies, Barrett Glasgow said. That means that if you visit sites such as Viagra.com or Lilly's Cialis.com without sharing your name, your computer still shares its IP address, which gives the drugmakers insights for future ad targeting. And they can learn even more by exchanging data with Acxiom.

Clever or Creepy?

Propensity modeling requires sophisticated data crunching, but Internet advertising often uses far simpler techniques. You've probably noticed that after researching a vacation in Florida, ads may pop up days later on different webpages. The same thing happens when you search for medical terms or visit health-related websites. If you look up birth control, a marketer could follow you to different sites later on to deliver an ad with a dancing condom or some other kind of eye-grabbing graphics—just when you are making a presentation from your computer at work. I recall attending a lecture at Harvard a few years ago in which the speaker shared videos from YouTube. As the clips played, ads offering treatment for depression flashed on the side of the screen. I could not help but recall the scene when I saw the person recently. Live Internet video is increasingly common in public presentations, giving speakers vulnerability they might never have imagined when looking up medical problems online.

However anonymized targeting is delivered, and whether others are watching or not, some people find such targeting downright creepy. "I personally worry a lot about the use of my data or data more generally in a variety of settings being used for nefarious purposes by private interests," said David Newman, executive director of the Health Care Cost Institute, a nonprofit that gathers claims data from leading insurers to make the information available only to academic researchers who have a university e-mail address.

He cited his mother, who lives in South Florida, as an example. "You could go into our data set hypothetically and look that there is not a significant demographic difference between Broward and Dade County in south Florida, and all of a sudden you see in Broward County there are certain prescribing patterns that are advantageous to us, and in Dade County, for some reason, docs are not marketing Cialis or Lipitor or whatever. I don't want my mother being marketed to, even in an indirect fashion, off of aggregated data."

Advertising Age highlighted this concern in an article headlined "Sophisticated Health Data Industry Needs Self-Reflection." The piece, whose subheading read "Pharma Targeting Feels Like a Personal

Violation to Consumers," described the disturbed feeling an editor at the magazine had after receiving a robocall asking if someone in the family suffered from a specific disease.[25]

Clearly, targeted medical ads can touch a sensitive nerve; people may wonder if advertisers know their actual medical condition. If marketers show you ads for $700 high-heel Manolo Blahnik shoes but you can only afford flip-flops, the ads have done no harm. Medical ads are different. If an advertiser believes someone has AIDS and directly targets a message to the person, it can cause great offense and possibly humiliation or other consequences. "Communications can get creepy pretty quickly," admitted Barrett Glasgow.

Companies do get it wrong from time to time and cause offense. Robin Gegauff-Brooks knows how this feels. She started to receive direct solicitations addressed to her husband from Idaho's Saint Alphonsus Health System and other health-care providers. But her husband was in no condition to receive medical care: he had died a few years before. She moved to Idaho from California to make a new start and does not want to be reminded of her personal loss every time the mail arrives. "They have crossed the boundary," she said angrily.[26]

Barrett Glasgow of Acxiom said she sympathizes. "My husband passed away in 1999. I still occasionally get mail addressed to him," she said, adding that there is no master list of deaths from which data brokers can update their files.

Another danger in targeted advertising is redlining, a practice in which certain people receive offers and others do not. Stan Crosley, a lawyer and a former chief privacy officer at Eli Lilly, expressed his concerns: "Is it appropriate to target a subpopulation you know is going to stay on the therapy while not targeting or reaching individuals who could still benefit from the therapy if they had either the finances or the knowledge about it?"

In the consumer and social media world, people concerned about such sharing can try to control what they reveal about themselves to the world. Unfortunately, in health care, you rarely have a choice on how your data will be shared. And nowadays the sharing often begins soon after you enter the doctor's office.

CHAPTER 13

□ □ □ □ □

INTIMATE, ANONYMIZED, AND FOR SALE

Getting Between You and Your Doctor

After I recently changed health insurance plans, my new doctor signed me up for an online health record portal, run by eClinicalWorks, which calls itself the largest cloud electronic health records system in the nation. I looked up the company's privacy policy and found this sentence: "eCW may provide aggregated information related to Your Personal Information to some of our business partners."[1] It used the word "may," but did not describe its actual practices.

I tried to learn more by calling my doctor's office manager. She had no idea that such information could possibly be for sale. Nor did my doctor. When I asked if a patient could opt out of data sharing, the office manager researched the issue and ultimately said no: "This is common practice by EMR [electronic medical records], insurances, and health organizations to share data." After contacting eClinicalWorks by telephone and their website to find out what it actually did with my data, I waited a long time for a clear response.

As doctors and hospitals have embraced electronic health records, many companies operating these systems have stepped up sales of anonymized patient information to data miners. For example, IMS Health advertises the extent of its data gathering: "We capture over 33 million records for unique, de-identified patients."[2] This commercialization of intimate details discussed behind a doctor's closed doors has occurred without public debate, often without even physicians' realizing their work generates a commercial product. The practice does test the modern-day meaning of the Hippocratic oath dating back to antiquity, and could rupture patient trust once the public realizes what is going on.

While most companies make it difficult or nearly impossible to find out what they do with data from their patient record systems, a few are commendably open. One especially interesting start-up in this area is Practice Fusion, which combines the goals of two of the pioneers chronicled in this book, Larry Weed and Ludwig Frohlich, in creating electronic medical records while also delivering advertising and selling data to pharmaceutical companies.

The Lure of Free

When Ryan Howard created a cloud-based electronic records system targeted at smaller medical practices in 2005, he thought he could charge them three hundred dollars a month. After all, Practice Fusion's program not only records patient data electronically but also acts as an intermediary between physicians, patients, and insurance companies. Only one office signed up at that price. Physicians receive a lot of things, such as drug samples, for free and were not interested in paying so much. Howard slashed the price to fifty dollars, but still doctors resisted. One day, a physician telephoned him to bargain over the price.

"I'll give you twenty-five dollars a month," the doctor said.

"You've got to be shitting me!"

"Ryan, I don't really need this. It's nice, but my philosophy is, everyone in the value chain is benefiting more than me, so why should I pay?

A native of New Hampshire, Howard had started his career in supply chain management, making sure large retailers such as Walmart efficiently sourced products. He worked for a San Francisco network of doctors, then a communications company whose founder preached the virtues of cloud computing. This background provided great training to create a medical records start-up. The real breakthrough for Practice Fusion, however, came after it stopped charging doctors altogether and embraced the power of free. Instead, the company makes money by collecting fees from middlemen between doctors, pharmacies, labs, and others; by advertising to physicians using its system; and by selling anonymized patient data from the electronic health records.

Even offering a free service, the company struggled in its early years. Howard used the $2,500 rent he collected from a duplex he owned in New Hampshire to cover Practice Fusion's costs, fell four years behind in his taxes, and let the real estate go into foreclosure rather than cover his loan. He put off two expensive root canal operations. When one software developer held the company's code hostage over some missed paychecks, Howard sold his 1998 BMW M3 and sent over a cashier's check.

He kept his beloved 2001 Ducati 996s Troy Bayliss edition, but one day, a car hit him while he was riding the motorcycle back from the gym. The $13,000 insurance settlement funded payroll rather than a torn rotator cuff repair. The storied bike now sits in the reception area of Practice Fusion, a reminder of the firm's lean early years.

The company aggressively promoted any media coverage it received. "I had a PR technique where I would generate press," Howard told me. "And when I did, I would syndicate that press to any potential investor, like every month. If I bumped into that investor, they would be like, 'Holy shit, I keep hearing about you!' And they had been hearing about me because I had been e-mail-blasting them perpetually for the last year, and that built a lot of momentum."

It took several years before enough doctors signed up for the electronic health records system for advertisers to start paying to reach physicians while they were treating patients. Walmart pharmacy ran its first ads in 2009–2010, and within a year or two, Practice Fusion's advertising business started to thrive.

Today, the company's early hand-to-mouth days have long since passed. Its office, across the street from a division of software maker Adobe, displays all the trappings of San Francisco's start-up culture. Visitors pass video games in the building lobby before arriving at the office, a series of large open spaces where coders, salespeople, and top executives sit side by side. Employees enjoy free gourmet food around the clock, and some bring their dogs to the office.

By 2015, Practice Fusion had signed up 6 percent of US doctors, about 112,000 active users across thirty thousand doctor's offices, connected to seventy thousand pharmacies, and 450 labs. "It is really, really, really hard to get in front of a lot of doctors in one place," Howard said of advertising. "Even with only six percent of the market, six percent of the market is more than any other aggregated group of doctors on one platform."

In 2014, the company started aggressively marketing its anonymized patient profiles, seeking prices of $50,000 to $2 million for longitudinal data sets, depending on how large and how rare they were, Howard said. But selling data is a difficult endeavor, he says: "You are competing against IMS; you are competing against a lot of big contenders. It's a complex, gnarly business. Media [advertising] is a larger business for us right now, and data is smaller. Data has, potentially, dramatically more potential."

I planned a trip to San Francisco and had arranged to meet Howard at Practice Fusion's office; shortly before our scheduled office meeting, he invited me instead to his home overlooking a charming oval park near the city's baseball stadium. When we met, he explained the change of plans. Shortly before I came to town, the board of directors had lost confidence and had abruptly fired Howard. It is a common story in Silicon Valley: the brash visionary who sets up the company may lack the seasoning and insights needed to captain the ship when it matures into a larger entity. The possibility of a lucrative IPO may have contributed to the decision.

If the company continues to grow, investors are likely to give Practice Fusion a warm embrace. But it still faces criticism from those who object to the idea of advertising to doctors as they are treating patients, and to the sale of anonymized data. "Why do you even have our health-care records?" one reader wrote in response to a 2015 article about Practice Fusion in the *Wall Street Journal.* "I never gave you permission to have access to any of it. Who gave you access? How do you have 100 million health records at your company to do, sell, market in any way you choose?" Another reader wrote: "I just love someone making money off my personal data without even notifying me."[3]

As soon as privacy activist Deborah Peel learned about Practice Fusion, she, too, was sounding the alarm. "Doctors get the software free, but patients pay dearly," she said in 2011. "At best, this is a reckless business model, because Americans have very strong rights to health privacy. . . . Practice Fusion is not alone. This widespread, yet under-the-radar practice will destroy trust in doctors and in the healthcare system when the public finds out."[4]

When I asked Matthew Douglass, a cofounder and vice president, about Peel, he became very animated. "She is incredibly bombastic," he said. "I think her ideas that medical information should be severely locked down are dangerous."

For Douglass, who is in his mid-thirties, the issue is especially personal, because he was recently diagnosed with an inflammatory skeletal disorder so rare that his doctors published a paper using him as a case study to describe the condition.[5] He was bedridden for three months and walked with a cane when I visited. He believes that everyone who receives medical care should be obliged to share their data to help others. "It is inhibiting my health by not having someone else opted in to share their medical information," he said. "What's more important: Do you want your life . . . or are you incredibly concerned about protecting every little thing about yourself?"

His comment reminded me of my meeting with Tokyo University law professor Norio Higuchi, one of Japan's top experts on medical privacy, who has successfully undergone dialysis treatment for kidney problems. "My treatment derives from the past information of various past patients," he said. "I want to return my benefits to society. My basic thinking is that health data is not private information but public information. . . . It should be shared for good use."

The Sometimes Elusive Truth

Howard openly discussed his story and his business, but many health-care companies struggle with how much to tell the public about their data sales. For example, Cerner, a major electronic records provider that had a profit of $539 million in 2015, has sold access to its large patient database, said David McCallie Jr., a senior vice president. "They do it carefully. They do it through something called 'data enclaves,' where you don't actually get the data yourself, but you can do analytics against the data," he said. "That prevents you from being able to join the data from an external source of known data."

Others at Cerner did not embrace McCallie's openness. Neither the company's online customer portal nor its spokesperson provided an answer when I asked about the sale of anonymized information. "People are extremely cautious about talking about that," McCallie said.

McCallie understands that sharing anonymized data could make people feel uncomfortable, but he said that transparency is almost always a good thing. How companies explain what they do with medical data will, however, shape how the public responds. "If you ask the question along the lines of, 'Were you aware that your sensitive private health data are sold to the highest bidder, and do you think that is a good idea?' [the public would answer,] 'Oh, my God, no,'" he said. "If you said to them, 'Were you aware that all those discounts that you get at the supermarket depend on their ability to use that data . . . and would you want them to take that card away from you?' And they go, 'Oh no, don't take that card away from me. Use my data.'"

Eventually, I did receive a thoughtful e-mail from Cerner's cofounder and CEO, Neal Patterson. "Research is the basis for advancement in medicine, and that the digitization of medicine is unleashing huge potential for knowledge and discovery," he said. "We support the use of HIPAA-compliant, de-identified data for research, including research by pharmaceutical and biotechnology companies."

By contrast, Judy Faulkner, the founder of Epic, which does not share data, said she was uneasy about the commercial use of her anonymized information: "I would feel fairly uncomfortable about that." Faulkner does believe that scientists should have access to anonymized data to advance medicine without patient consent. But if the data are used for sales and marketing, she thinks patients should be able to call the shots. "Personally, if it is for legitimate research purposes, I would like to see all the data accessible," she said. "Anything other than that I think it is fine if the patient has a say over it."

Cerner's CEO said his company is moving in the direction of giving patients more control. "I fundamentally believe that the person owns their own health data, and that the provider is also a legal steward of their shared portion of that data," Patterson said. "Cerner believes the individual should have to give consent for their identified data to be shared beyond the process of direct care, and we're actively creating this ability through our work on the CommonWell platform for consent-based sharing." He also said if a patient believes he or she is a target for snooping, there is a way for the data to be flagged so they will not be shared.

Oddly, it is sometimes difficult to get a straight answer even out of companies that do not sell patient-derived data. Aetna took two weeks to respond to my question of whether it made money from its claims data as many other insurers do. "Aetna has long had a policy of not selling or monetizing its data," the company finally said in a statement. "This policy decision emanates from a strong belief that our data should only be used to support efforts which advance the health of our members."

When I asked why it was so hard to get this response, especially since a no-sharing policy might give the company a competitive advantage, an Aetna official who did not want to be named said, "This is so sensitive."[6]

I found the same reticence from eClinicalWorks, the electronic health record company used by a doctor I had visited. I had written and phoned customer service but could not get an answer as to whether it sells anonymized patient data. So one Saturday morning, I called the company cofounder and CEO, Girish Navani, on his cell phone to get to the bottom of the matter. He adamantly said the company has never sold or shared anonymized patient data. "It is a bad practice because people don't know it is happening," he said. "Without the knowledge, I believe it is invading their privacy."

"I don't believe in the Cerner/Practice Fusion model unless the patient and doctor agree—the patient has to be in the know," Navani added. At the end of a half-hour conversation, he had one question for me: How I had gotten his cell phone number to reach him on the weekend? I told him that the same aggregation that we had been discussing in health-data mining makes it possible to find such numbers through commercial data brokers.

Blood Tests for Sale

Much as at the doctor's office, patient data mining now takes place in test labs as well. Not long after a nurse jabs a needle into your arm to extract blood or hands you a little plastic cup and sends you off to the bathroom, the results become a commercial product. Few patients know that anonymized data extracted from these intimate samples are for sale, and often the lab's front office team and nurses don't know, either. It took me a while to figure out what was taking place behind the lab's curtain.

In May 2014, I wrote a leading US lab chain, Quest Diagnostics, to ask if it sold anonymized results to data miners. "Quest is committed to protecting the privacy of our patients' health data, and we maintain data in alignment with applicable laws and regulations," customer service supervisor Maria Rumrill wrote. "We do not currently provide data to commercial data aggregators like IMS Health."

I remembered this opaque response when I later learned about New York start-up Medivo, cofounded by Jason Bhan, who started his career as a family physician. Because of his computer savvy, colleagues often asked him to help install electronic health record systems in their offices. Eventually, the entrepreneur got so many requests that he stopped seeing patients and made such assistance his full-time business. Over time, he began to notice that once doctors digitized their records, many wondered what benefit these systems brought to patient care. Bhan became interested in what insights could be garnered from digitized data—lab results in particular.

In 2010, he and two partners formed Medivo, with the goal of buying and bartering anonymized results from US labs to sell to drug companies and others. Data miners such as IMS had long wanted to add test data to their patient dossiers but had trouble convincing the labs. Medivo may have come along at just the right moment, for some key players such as Quest were beginning to reassess their traditional reluctance to sell de-identified patient information.

When Steve Rusckowski became Quest's CEO in 2012, he decided that the company should do more than just administer medical tests. Formerly the CEO of Philips Healthcare, Rusckowski set Quest on course to become an active player in the medical data market, with the stated goal of helping health care in the long term. In the spring of 2014, Quest decided to sell to Medivo rather that IMS because the start-up offered about 20 percent of the resulting revenue, compared with just a few percent from IMS, according to Dermot Shorten, Quest's vice president of strategy and ventures. The sales generated additional annual revenue of a few million dollars, a number expected to grow in the future.

Other labs, once they were convinced that anonymized data sales were legal under HIPAA, signaled that they too would work with Medivo, although many initially wanted unrealistically high prices, Bhan said.[7] In the end, the labs signed up for more modest payments or services such as cleaning up their data and analytical insights. By mid-2015, Medivo had access to more than 10 billion lab test results on 150 million US patients. IMS has also started buying substantial amounts of laboratory data, and as of late 2015, said it collects nearly half of all US tests performed.[8]

Lab data also open up a new realm of opportunity for pharma reps, because they can learn which doctors have patients who have tested positive for a disease—even before the physician next sees the patient. The lead information gives the detailers a chance to pitch the physician on their latest products before the doctor breaks the bad news to the patient. Here's how that process might take place: A lab gives you a blood test and sends out the results simultaneously to the doctor and to the outside commercial data miner. The result tells any drug company buying Medivo's data that Dr. Jefferson in Houston has a patient who has tested positive for a disease (the patient's name is anonymized, but the doctor is identified). Jefferson's office calls the patient to schedule an appointment for next Tuesday to go over the lab results. The drug company rep rushes to visit the doctor on Monday before the next consultation. Perhaps the rep informs the doctor about a new drug that truly is the best treatment for the condition. Or perhaps a generic medication might be just as good, but the detailer does a great job persuading the doctor to prescribe the new, more expensive concoction.

Medivo says selling doctor-identified lab data is justified because the practice funds the collection of scientifically important information. "To make real progress in health care," Bhan said, "we have to be able to look at data, analyze it, and come up with clear insights from it. The advances we will make in the next five years looking at and analyzing data will dwarf the number of medical breakthroughs in the last fifty years. The rules in place protect people's identities and privacy. To require an individual's consent or permission for this type of research would slow us down by years.

"The business of medicine and patient-care aspect of medicine are forever intertwined, and somehow along the line, money has to be generated to do this. If there is something that pharma can contribute their dollars to that, that forwards this sort of research, then I am happy about that."

Quest's Rusckowski outlines a bold vision for his company, which he says collects test results on about half of all Americans over a three-year period. But when we first talked, he was hazy about whether his company gave patients a right to consent in the sharing of their anonymized information. "Yes, we share with patients that—ask their permission, if you will—if data should be used, can be used, and then we de-identify the data if it is used," he said.

When I pushed back and said that I thought it unlikely that a patient actually had that choice, an awkward silence ensued. Then the CEO admitted that he was not sure, but added he thought an opt-out was the best option since few would not want to help science. He promised to find out more, and later that day, he sent me an e-mail: "We comply with all HIPAA requirements, which do not require obtaining patient consent to use de-identified patient data."

When Open Trade in Your Identified Data Is Allowed

Data miners trade anonymized information, but in some instances, drugstore chains and pharmacy benefit managers are allowed to sell named data about you, typically to insurance companies. "As an underwriter, wouldn't it be great if you could gather greater insights into your applicants' prescription history?" ExamOne, a subsidiary of Quest Diagnostics, asks on its website.[9] Naturally, the question provides an opening to describe its ScriptCheck service, which assembles a seven-year history of an individual's prescription information to share with life and health insurance companies.

ExamOne says it has access to 85 percent of US pharmacy benefit managers. "Identify potential diseases based on an individual's prescription history," its website promises. "Recognize specialties of all the doctors prescribing medication to your applicants."[10]

All of this information helps insurers make quick decisions on applicants, as ExamOne's rival Milliman explains: "Milliman IntelliScript delivers complete and current prescription histories that allow insurers to make instant underwriting decisions with confidence."[11]

Under HIPAA, ExamOne and Milliman require consent from insurance applicants, who would have to read the fine print of an application to realize what is going on. After getting the authorization, the insurance company connects with ExamOne or Milliman, which gathers the patient's information from their data suppliers. Within seconds, the insurer has a list of drug names, dosages, when they were filled, inferred diagnosis, doctor names, and sometimes a score set up according to the insurer's preference. One early company in this field, IntelRx (which was bought by Milliman in 2005), used to advertise that in light of these prescription histories, insurers changed 10 to 30 percent of their underwriting decisions, a reference presumably to application rejections.[12]

Both Milliman and Ingenix (a company founded in 1997 and the forerunner to ExamOne's ScriptCheck) received some public attention in 2007–2008, when they ran afoul of the Federal Trade Commission. The FTC charged that the firms failed to provide proper notification about their activities and thus did not comply with the Fair Credit Reporting Act. The two companies agreed to abide by the act in the future but were not assessed fines.[13]

Another company that shares information about insurance applicants is the Medical Information Bureau, often known as MIB. Formed in 1902 by a group of insurance companies, the bureau seeks to reduce risk when companies write health and life insurance policies by allowing members to see what other insurers know about an applicant. Details including "different medical conditions, hazardous avocations or adverse driving records that affect the insurability of the proposed insured" are recorded in confidential codes and shared only with members who receive authorization from an insurance applicant.[14] The association does not share information beyond its 430 member companies.

Pharmacies also sell identified patient information to a competitor when closing a store or going out of business. In such cases, the buyer pays $15 to $20 per prescription filed annually, hoping the store's former patients will transfer their business to it.[15] Only rarely have customers complained. "What gives CVS the right to sell or give my family's medical information to another company without my consent?" Charles Doebler wrote to the *Pittsburgh Post-Gazette* after CVS closed his local branch and sold his files to a rival.[16]

In 1999, one New Yorker went a step further and filed a class-action lawsuit. Diagnosed with HIV in 1986, the man bought his medications from Trio Drugs on Manhattan's West 57th Street. When he learned that CVS had purchased his prescription records under its "independent file buy program" he was horrified, fearing that tens of thousands of CVS workers could access details about his condition. His law firm placed ads to find other such patients. "If you are HIV-positive or have AIDS, and your prescription or medical information has been sold or disclosed by your pharmacy without your knowledge or permission, your privacy rights may have been violated," one notice said.[17]

The case attracted media attention. "Then 9/11 happened, people were not as concerned about individual privacy at that point. They were more concerned about individual security," said Richard Lubarsky, who represented the HIV patient. A 2004 settlement after years of court proceedings provided a very modest amount for only the customers of Trio Drugs. Today, it remains commonplace for pharmacies to sell patient files when the stores cease operations.

All told, the details from electronic health records, prescriptions, tests, and other sources amount to an unprecedented flood of personal information. "We are at the bottom of Niagara, and we can't stop it," said Bill Castagnoli, the former advertising executive and historian of medical advertising.

□ □ □ □ □

CHAPTER 14

AT THE BOTTOM OF NIAGARA

The Paradox of Medical Data

IMS founder Ludwig Frohlich could never have imagined how the world of medical data mining he helped create would evolve. Likewise, the pioneers of electronic health records did not foresee such a tortuous path to creating easily accessible lifetime records to help patients. What we are left with today is the paradox of medical information: the sophisticated, anonymized dossiers that data miners maintain about us help market drugs, yet very few people can access their own complete medical records, which could help provide the best possible care.

IMS emerged during the postwar era of new wonder drugs, fueling demand from pharmaceutical companies for more insights about their markets to boost sales. The genius of Frohlich and his secret partner, Arthur Sackler, was to anticipate this demand and build a service that became indispensable to drugmakers. In the early days, IMS never considered buying prescriptions from pharmacies or claims from insurance companies. Back then, such activities were simply beyond the pale. "We were not allowed to do it in those early years," said Lars Ericson, the former IMS CEO who had worked closely with Frohlich and David Dubow. "You were intruding on somebody's privacy, and we never contemplated doing it."

Such restraint ended when medical records could be digitized, paving the way for doctor-identified files and then anonymized patient dossiers on hundreds of millions of patients. "What was radical a generation ago is commonplace now," said Bob Merold, who helped build the IMS doctor-identified database. "People's attitudes evolve and shift as you get used to the fact that there is doctor-level data and that is old news and the world hasn't fallen apart. And now we want this clinical data, and we just take one step further into the swamp here."

In some parts of the world, the caution Ericson describes remains the accepted standard, even for anonymized patient data. "No matter that it is anonymous, the consent from the data owner is the most important," Sabrina Chan, executive director of the Hong Kong Association of the Pharmaceutical Industry, told me when I visited her. "My principle is, without the patient's consent, actually it is unethical to disclose their data to anyone." Europe is also far more protective of personal data, including health information, than the United States and shuns data miner offerings such as doctor-identified data.

Obscuring the Facts

Companies that declare they are helping save the world while profiting from the trade in patient data are exceedingly reluctant to talk about how the whole process works. As a test of how difficult it is to learn what companies do with patient information, I did an Internet search for the following phrase: "We sell your anonymized medical data. Here's why." I figured since many health-care officials enthusiastically tout the benefits of big data for science, some should be willing to explain the trade. The first ten search items linked to media articles and blogs. The second page included a mention of Betterpath, a free site that helps patients store medical data. Its page explaining the service provided a description remarkable in its clarity and simplicity: "Betterpath is free because we anonymize the data that comes from our health summaries—that means we remove all personal, identifying information from it—and sell it to other healthcare entities, with the goal of reducing cost and improving care." Yet clarity and honesty does not necessarily translate into business success. When I last checked the Betterpath website in mid-2016, it was no longer functioning, although the founder said the company continued to operate.

Several pages deeper into my Internet search, the results mentioned social network Carenity for people with chronic diseases. "We sell our studies to companies that are developing and distributing medical products," it tells users. "Because we believe in transparency, we tell our members what we do and do not do with their data."[1]

Such openness remains rare. As I recounted earlier, many pharmacies decline to say whether they sell anonymized prescription records, or they give wrong or contradictory answers or proclaim self-righteous justifications. Since US law presently does not require patient consent to trade anonymized information, many companies see no reason to add the additional step and complexity of giving customers a choice. "We are not required to offer a means or mechanism for patients to 'opt out' of lawful uses or disclosures of de-identified information," said Lynette Berggren, director of privacy and pharmacy compliance at Albertsons, which also runs Osco pharmacies. IMS echoes a similar approach on its website: "We will be open about our services and products and, *where required*, offer appropriate choices for information collection or use to stakeholders in the healthcare community."[2] I've emphasized "where required" because under current rules, "where required" means patients get virtually no say.

Joel Kallich, the founder of Big Health Data, used to work at Amgen and has consulted for IMS. He described the state of the health-care business in discouraging terms: "The entire US health-care system, as well as the entire political system, has devolved into this shadow game where nobody tells the truth, they lie, they scheme, they manipulate, they steal data from the people it should belong to—i.e., the people—and they hold up the health-care system in the US." He has grown so discontent with the industry's lack of transparency that he has vowed never to work with IMS again.

Ironically, one reason health-related companies get away with obscuring what they do with medical information is that patients are not treated as their customers. Data miners cater to those who buy their services, from drug companies and government agencies to hedge fund managers. Websites such as *WebMD* or data vaults typically rely on advertisers for revenue, often drug companies selling related goods and services. Even though a doctor or pharmacist is providing goods or services to a patient, insurance companies or government programs pay most of the bills.

Why Data Traders Stay Silent

Medical data officials confide a number of reasons for clamming up. Many worry this complicated topic will alarm ordinary folks. They want to avoid government scrutiny that could limit the valuable trade, and they fear lawsuits from speaking openly. "I suspect it is more driven by a desire to just avoid any embarrassing accusations that they can't go public and defend and a desire to avoid any new regulations to complicate their life," Cerner's McCallie said.

One day, I met a division head of a middleman company that serves as an important source of anonymized patient information to data miners, pharmaceutical companies, and others. An intelligent and engaging individual, he answered all of my questions clearly and directly and gave a robust explanation of the benefits of sharing data. Later, he said he was worried about his fate after this book appeared. "To be honest with you, I do not want to lose my job," he said.

Robert Hooper, the former CEO of IMS North America, said such sentiment is, lamentably, commonplace. "It is a shortcoming. If they continued that thought . . . they could educate the people more about the benefits of it," he said. "I volunteer for hospice here, and all of my cancer patients are dying to get into a database. 'Take anything, take anything that you need, just tell me how you can cure me.'"

Added Greg Ellis, a former top executive at Symphony Health: "The fact that we can connect patient claims data with other data and anonymize the appended data sets yields great patient health insights. The resultant data have the potential to spook people, regardless of how careful the health information industry is in ensuring that an individual's personal health data can't be uncovered and re-identified."

Many working for companies that buy and sell patient data strongly feel that they are helping society. "Everybody who works at IMS believes that there is ultimate good that is being produced," said Ana-Maria Zaugg, a former chief marketing officer and vice president for strategic planning who left in 2011. "That's how we recruit people. They come to us not because they want to deal with data, but because they believe health data improves health, and especially via anonymized patient-level data. Ask anybody on the market research side of the business or anyone in consulting in outcomes work. You don't have to dig very deep to find an absolute conviction that good comes of our stuff."

David Carlucci, the former IMS CEO who left in 2010 after outside investors took the company private, remains a true believer in anonymized longitudinal data: "The more information you could get in that format, the more you could do, not only for the business, but for governments and others to be able to track abuses and other forms of illicit activity, and the more insight you have to health economics, outcomes research, things that evolve from anonymized data with huge sample sets."

But Zaugg said IMS has done a poor job of conveying to outsiders the upbeat message of how anonymized data can help patient outcomes: "I absolutely think IMS should communicate more and better with health-care folks (including the government) about what valuable applications can be done with the data and expertise." She nevertheless does not think aiming this message directly at patients is the appropriate course: "I just have the feeling that going straight to consumers has a lot of potential to blow up."

Carlucci adds that as companies such as Google, Facebook, and Apple capture ever more personal data, including information from health-related devices in real time, IMS will pose a relatively minor privacy concern. "Obviously, concerns about privacy and data privacy are going to be exponentially higher in the coming years than they have been in the past, but I would think that IMS is a relatively small part of that in the grand scheme of things," Carlucci said.

We should certainly closely monitor what Google, Apple, and other tech giants do with our data as health devices and the Internet of things expand dramatically in the years to come. Some of these newcomers to health have already seen the wisdom of highlighting protections in the realm of health privacy. Apple HealthKit, which allows health and fitness devices to communicate with Apple's health app, bars outside developers from "disclosing Health data to third parties for advertising or other data mining purposes."[3] The company also says, "Apps can share data for the purpose of improving your health or health research, but only with your permission"—a policy that gives users more control than traditional health-data miners offer.

Giving Patients a Say

"Only with your permission" are still words rarely seen when it comes to our medical data. The reluctance of medical data buyers and sellers to discuss the trade in the United States and elsewhere illustrates a widespread uneasiness, at least as far as public disclosure, leaving our most intimate secrets in a gray zone of digitized zeros and ones.

Right now, an individual can control the privacy of his or her medical data only with difficulty. I decided to test this point when I learned that my new doctor used an electronic health record system whose privacy policy left open the possibility of selling my anonymized data. I felt I might be more comfortable opening up to a doctor who used a system that does not sell patient information. I had to call half a dozen doctors' offices until I found a physician whose record system does not sell patient data, and then I had to have another complete examination just a few weeks after I left the other doctor. It was a big effort just to test how someone might control some of the flow of medical data.

Somewhat surprisingly, quite a number of former IMS executives favor empowering patients in this area. Roger Korman, who served as IMS

Canada and IMS Latin America president, said that as a start, companies should openly tell us that they sell our medical data. "Maybe anyone who traffics—ah, that word, 'traffics,' yes, drug traffickers, dope traffickers, info traffickers—people who sell information commercially, maybe they need to do a disclosure," he said. "It's hospitals, it's insurance companies, claims processors."

Tommy Boman, a former president of IMS America, wavered a bit when I first asked whether medical data mining companies should get patient consent. He changed his mind after we talked about the possibility of future re-identification. "Damn it, I kind of agree on this," he said. "Somebody who knows how to deal with it might have a chance to say, 'Oh, that is actually Adam.'" Former IMS CEO Ericson also agreed that patients should have the right to opt out of anonymized data collection.

I had an especially interesting conversation on the subject with Robert Weissman, the CEO of Dun & Bradstreet when it bought IMS in 1988 and who served as chairman of IMS after it was spun off into an independent company in 1996. "We live in a world today," he said, "where every month, thousands of pieces of data are being collected on each of us, used for a whole variety of purposes, and they form a halo around us that characterizes us. Our habits, our activities, our interests, and, in many cases, our foibles. Those halos are going to become larger and more intense at a rapidly expanding rate over the coming decade. In the broadest sense, it's scary as hell."

Weissman has no regrets about IMS's past practices. But he does wonder what will happen as increasing amounts of anonymized data are collected. "That's the tough, big-picture question. You say, 'Is what we are doing now, is that beneficial to our customers and to society?' And my answer is, as far as I know, what IMS is doing today, I think they are a very positive influence on the human race. And I am very comfortable with that answer—today," he said. "If we extrapolate it out twenty years from today, thirty years from today, will this process that we as a society are going through evolve, and will we regret having gone along the path? Possibly."

"The question is in today's world—and it gets down as basic as opt in or opt out," he said, referring to policies in which a user has to approve (opt in) the sharing of data before it can happen or say no (opt out), blocking sharing that will otherwise take place. "I consider myself to be a relatively sophisticated consumer. If somebody says to me 'Opt in or opt out,' my default answer is 'Opt out.' I don't want my data collected without my permission."

Others said not only should patients determine the fate of their data, but they should also receive financial benefit if they agree to share. "I think the principle is very important," said Michael Pierce, who joined IMS when the company bought rival data miner SDI (Surveillance Data Inc.) and who remained until 2013. "I mean, this is America, man. You've got to give people choices even if they are too dumb to take them."

Warner Slack, the originator of "patient power" in the 1960s, concurred, especially when it comes to using patient specimens. "I certainly think that the patient's privacy should be protected," he said, "and I think the patient should be a participant in the remuneration. No clinical information should be given out from the institution, and that's a radical position. The insurance companies and the federal government do not need to know the specific information about the patients without the consent of the patient."

Jason Bhan, cofounder of Medivo, the data miner that buys and sells lab test information, also sees wisdom in such logic, at least for the long term. "In an ideal setting, probably patients should get paid for having their data used somewhere. I think that would be the ultimate," he said. Since any one patient's data may not be that valuable, compensation might to go to the patient's preferred charity. One researcher, David Kim, a fellow at Texas Medical Center, estimated that if a commercial business empowered patients to sell anonymized medical records, it would likely pay each person between $1 and $15, with $3 to $7 the most likely range.

Bill Marder, a senior vice president at Truven Health Analytics, which has longitudinal files on 215 million people, mostly from large and medium-sized US companies, would like to offer compensation to patients for those willing to share *identifiable* data. Under his idea—which is not a company policy—data miners could supplement information from insurance claims with comments directly from the patient. "I'd love to have information on how people feel," the health economist said. "At the end of the day, do they feel better?"

Some recent initiatives offer possible models of patient choice that could be expanded while still allowing scientific study of anonymized patient data. For example, in 2014, Rhode Island became the first state to allow residents to opt out of its anonymized insurance claims sharing. Out of a population of one million people, 1.5 percent have opted out, or about 15,000 as of mid-2015, according to James Lucht, informatics manager at Rhode Island's Office of the Health Insurance Commissioner. "We hope that you will choose to be a part of Rhode Island's health care reform effort," the Rhode Island Department of Health suggests insurers tell policyholders in explaining this option. "However it is your right to choose to have your information kept out of the database, even though it is anonymous."[4]

Since 2001, the pioneering longitudinal Framingham study has also given its participants an innovative degree of control. In the spirit of advancing science, the study's organizers have long made their patient data available to researchers, and in recent decades, they have also shared their insights with pharmaceutical and other commercial companies. But Framingham also now gives participants a say in whether they want their data shared with such commercial entities. Less than 5 percent of Framingham's participants have opted out of the commercial use of their data, according to Greta Lee Splansky, the director of operations.[5]

With so many entities trading people's anonymized data, the easiest way to allow individuals to express a preference might be a national list that data miners and suppliers must follow in the same way that telemarketers must comply with the Do Not Call Registry, an idea suggested in chapter 8. Thus, you could state your preference once, rather than at every turn in the health-care system.

Who Is the Best Custodian for Data?

Joel Kallich, the founder of Big Health Data, believes that digitized information on millions of patients will prove very valuable to the future of science. But he objects to what he sees as overcharging by firms more interested in the bottom line than in advancing medicine. "This is what grinds me about the whole thing," he said. "It is an example of how capitalism has infected data. People are trying to make as much money as they can off of selling patient data and using it as an exclusivity monopoly, where I don't believe that they have a right, actually, to that monopoly."

In many countries, governments collect and make available patient data to qualified researchers for little or no money. Britain's National Health Service has done so for years, charging only for its administrative costs for UK researchers and an academic price to those abroad.[6] One recent study illustrates different countries' approach to anonymized patient data. Using British, Canadian, and US records, researchers found a greater risk of diabetes from patients using high-potency statins. The authors used government-collected information from Britain and Canadian provinces, but turned to a commercial company, Truven, for US data.[7]

The Nordic countries have also long made health data available to legitimate researchers for a nominal administrative cost. Researchers studying registries of everything from cancer to HIV patients have published more than five hundred papers between 2005 and 2010.[8] Such registry information is available a bit more slowly than data miners might provide it, with a lag of a few months. Because patient identities are less masked, there is greater reliance on the honesty of researchers not to re-identify, said Max Petzold, a statistics professor at the University of Gothenburg and director of the Swedish National Data Service Institute. "That is the drawback to having free data: if it was commercialized, someone would be very eager to get the data in shape very quickly," he said. With anonymous public data, "quite often you can identify the individuals, but it is illegal."

In the United States, some federal and state agencies, including the Centers for Medicare and Medicaid Services (CMS), release anonymized medical data. CMS allows researchers to study a 5 percent sample from these programs for the poor or elderly. In 2015, CMS also started releasing physician-level prescribing information to the public for the first time, with Excel spreadsheets containing millions of records immediately downloadable on the Internet for free.[9] More than a dozen states have made public what they call "all-claim patient databases," and more are thinking about or already assembling such aggregated records for research.[10]

Some experts say the United States should do more to make anonymized hospital, doctor, prescription, patient record, and other data available via a national repository to help advance science and allow oversight to a process already occurring with little public scrutiny.[11] Some kind of public-private entity might be the best repository to advance science, said Chesley Richards, deputy director for public health scientific services at the Centers for Disease Control and Prevention.

One existing effort in this direction is the Health Care Cost Institute, which pools data from Aetna, Humana, and the UnitedHealth Group to share only with legitimate academic researchers.[12] Other possible US repositories are part of the US Department of Health and Human Services: the National Institutes of Health, which calls itself the "nation's medical research agency," or the Centers for Disease Control and Prevention, which includes the National Center for Health Statistics. Patient consent could be a feature of data collection for whichever institution might become this storehouse for researchers, and the institution could set the rules so that researchers only can access the data sets—marketers need not apply.

CONCLUSION

What Needs to Change

Unanticipated shortcomings in US government policy have allowed today's troubling paradox of medical data to evolve. By acquiescing to an unfettered commercial trade in anonymized data, HIPAA has allowed a vast market for intimate information to evolve in ways that may lessen patient trust in the health-care system and may create dangerous privacy vulnerabilities. And because the effort to digitize health-data records—an effort costing US taxpayers billions of dollars—failed to require easy patient access to these data, we still cannot gain access to our own complete records when we need them most.

In the big picture, what we need in the big health-data bazaar is not so complicated: more transparency, more consent, and more control. What you tell your doctor behind closed doors and the lab work on your blood sample contains sensitive information. You should have control over what happens to it. This means that in the United States, HIPAA protections should extend to *an individual's health information*, not just to the category of "individually identifiable health information," which is covered by the regulations today.

Anonymized patient data need protection for two reasons. Most importantly, patients must have full assurance that they can confide in health practitioners without fear that outsiders may learn of their conditions. Such trust is fundamental to a successful health-care system. A second reason is that anonymized data will be increasingly vulnerable to re-identification. "It is getting easier and easier to identify people from anonymized data, so I think having more discussions about how health data are used and who has it is really important," said Chesley Richards of the Centers for Disease Control and Prevention.

Government protections should extend more broadly to whoever gathers health information. HIPAA today only applies to "covered entities" such as doctors, health plans, and middlemen. But a growing amount of our medical data comes from, and goes to, places outside HIPAA—entities such as health device makers, fitness trackers, smartphone apps, and DNA ancestry websites. Overall, patients should decide how and whether to share their information with outside medical researchers; the patients' options should be expressed in clear language that does not require an advanced degree in law or medicine to understand.[1]

Such control will not curtail science, as many patients will gladly share their information to help science, as opposed to helping Viagra gain market share from Cialis or supporting other marketing activities. President Obama outlined these issues while speaking at a 2016 conference on his medical research initiative to gather DNA samples from a million volunteers. "We've got to figure out, how do we make sure that if I donate my data to this big pool that it's not going to be misused, that it's not going to be commercialized in some way that I don't know about," he said. "We've got to set up a series of structures that make me confident that if I'm making that contribution to science that I'm not going to end up getting a bunch of spam targeting people who have a particular disease I may have."[2]

Outside of the government, universities and others are gathering DNA samples for the insights they may reveal about human health. Examples of such research efforts include the BioM Biobank Program at the Institute for Personalized Medicine at the New York City's Icahn School of Medicine at Mount Sinai, where patients give consent to share their de-identified medical records, which include DNA sequencing for research. One recent study using these data from over eleven thousand patients identified three subtypes of type 2 diabetes, a finding that could help improve patient care in the future.[3]

Yet people donating DNA samples to such efforts need to understand that especially when it comes to genes, anonymization is a false promise. "DNA is so unique, and there are so many data sources out there that it is incredibly hard to fully anonymize, and more so to promise and provide any absolute guarantee that the data are anonymized," said Laura Lyman Rodriguez, the director of policy, communications and education at the National Human Genome Research Institute.

Linda Avey, the cofounder of the popular DNA testing site 23andMe, agrees: "It's a fallacy to think that genomic data can be fully anonymized."

Still, many DNA testing companies, including 23andMe, either share genomic data by default or encourage customers to do so, both for science and for commerce.[4] "We encourage data to be shared if anonymized and consented," says Jay Flatley, chief executive of Illumina, which made a splash in 2014 by announcing the first full genome sequencing for one thousand dollars. "This is the only way we are going to ramp the discovery rate in human genomics."

The Gold Standard

Even in the age of big data, the most effective medical research comes from randomized, double-blind, controlled clinical trials, which test the effectiveness of a drug on a limited number of patients. Randomized refers to the random assignment of treatment to the study participants, and double-blind means that neither the participant nor the researcher knows which treatment the participant received. Controlled means that some participants receive no treatment or a placebo, to ensure that the effect of a treatment is real. Clinical trials are expensive and complicated to organize, thus the appeal of using patient data that are already collected to gain new medical insights.

The ever-growing for-profit trade in longitudinal patient data, however, has so far brought neither the wave of revolutionary medical breakthroughs promised by data miners nor the worst-case-scenario patient violations feared by privacy advocates. Both sides struggle to come up with dramatic examples highlighting their arguments. Take Blue Health Intelligence—which advertises itself as having "the largest, most comprehensive database in the industry, by far." It has shared its claims data on 125 million people from the Blue Cross Blue Shield insurance systems with IMS Health since 2012. I asked its CEO, Swati Abbott, for examples of the most compelling insights learned from the data so far. "There are so many of them," she said.

When I pushed further, she replied, "I don't have a specific example per se," before citing greater accuracy in predicting hospitalizations for people with diabetes. Other industry executives, questioned about the great benefits of the big health-data bazaar, cite categories such as a "more holistic view of the patient" and "cost efficiencies" amid a growing trend favoring compensating doctors for value-based health care rather than fees for services.[5] Under such a system, physicians earn more if their patients stay healthy; the topic has generated a lot of attention and study in recent years.[6]

Some critics question whether the commercial sale of anonymized patient dossiers—rather than a public or nonprofit program to share data for science—is the best approach to advance medical research or health-care efficiency. Several researchers grumble that they find it difficult or too expensive to access IMS information for their studies. "IMS data can probably be used for academic research to some extent, but the whole organization has been built around the business model, which is 'We sell data to pharma companies,'" said Stefan Larsson, a Boston Consulting Group senior partner who leads its Health Care Payers and Providers sector.

In many cases, government databases, such as a list of all prescriptions dispensed in Larsson's native Sweden, are more useful for researchers, he said. The same has often proved true in the United States. As noted earlier, academics studying state Medicare and Medicaid information from 2002 to 2004 observed that some patients taking the pain reliever Vioxx were more likely to experience serious and sometimes fatal heart problems than those not taking the drug. Another 2015 study, of noncommercial hospital data on 1,425 women at four institutions, including the Mayo Clinic, found that beta-blocker heart drugs can help women with ovarian cancer live longer.[7] Yet clinical trials had already shown evidence of dangerous side effects in Vioxx, and researchers plan a follow-up clinical trial to further investigate the ovarian cancer findings.[8]

Simply stated, randomized trials remain the gold standard in medical research and produce results superior to simply studying big medical data. IMS Health recognized the importance of such studies by merging in 2016 with Quintiles, which conducts clinical trials and helped develop or bring to market all of the world's top hundred best-selling drugs in 2013.[9] "You need large-scale, randomized evidence to answer a lot of questions, and I think the claim that database analysis will do so isn't justified," said Sir Richard Peto, a well-respected professor of medical statistics and epidemiology at the University of Oxford who has spent more than three decades studying the causes of cancer and the impact of smoking. "I am not saying that nothing is going to come out of analyzing lots and lots of medical records. But I think what is claimed is that you can often make lots of conclusions about which treatments work and which don't, and I think that is not true—that you can't sort that out reliably from medical records and who got which treatment."[10]

On the other end of the spectrum, privacy advocates have difficulty pointing to lives ruined by the sharing of their anonymized medical data. That does not mean the danger is not very real. Experts long ago warned of wider threats from hacking and credit card fraud—threats that only mushroomed later. The worst episodes of cyberterrorism and other risks in the Internet age are likely to still lie ahead. Overall, we can expect to see both health advances from the study of big data and real damage from privacy breaches—all the more reason to create conditions to harvest the good and create strong protections against the bad.

Honorable Intentions

Many of the active and retired data miners I have met are honorable and intelligent; many truly want to improve patient health and make money at the same time. They are not seeking to do any harm by selling such information. "I don't think there are any evil characters in all of this," said Kris Joshi, executive vice president at health-data company Emdeon. "IMS is not evil, pharmaceutical companies are not evil, and patients are definitely not evil, and neither are insurance companies evil."

Bob Merold, the former IMS official, summarized the difficulty in striking a proper balance and the need for caution when using longitudinal medical data: "There is a lot of goodness about it. There are huge amounts of potential evil about it."

The question thus becomes, How can society best harness the possibilities of big data in medicine and protect the interests of the individual at the same time? Corporations trading patient data say they help science, but they may not offer the best approach for society as a whole. However honorable the intentions of its protagonists, the big health-data bazaar has evolved in such a way that could put patients at risk. Such a worry exists for all personal data, as businesses across the economy seek increasingly more information to compete. But health issues are often our most intimate secrets; the downside potential is even greater.

"It depends on how you use it," said Stephen Schondelmeyer, head of the Department of Pharmaceutical Care and Health Systems at the University of Minnesota. "It's like any invention, you know. The atomic bomb had benefits and risks, and large data is sort of like that. If big data is used for internal proprietary, how-do-I-generate-money-off-the-health-care-market, I am not sure it is always a good thing. However, if it is used to identify individual and systematic health problems and to find ways to address and solve those problems while using resources more efficiently, it can be very valuable."

Paul Gertman, a pioneer in studying insurance claims data, is skeptical when data miners downplay the risks. "Once it is out loose and people have a right to pass it around, I don't see how it can be protected from determined access or misuse, because there is no control of it," he said. And just because big data are not misused most of the time today (although he says that more cases of abuse are being discovered) does not mean that the potential for abuse is not there, Gertman added.

Data miners respond that without the business motivation, the data aggregation might not occur, so the commerce helps pay for the scientific side. "I'm a cheerful capitalist about this stuff," said Bill Marder of Truven (now part of IBM Watson). "The making of money out of this is a good thing. It helps pay the bill" for medical research.

That's the tricky part. The same information that helps drug companies sell and market their products could enable researchers to gain new insights. "We need to figure out which patient subgroups are really going to benefit from this, and that is all driven off the same longitudinal piece of data that the Sanofi and Amgen guys are using to try to figure out who their market is, who to target," said Merold. "Increasingly, the commercial stuff is the same scientific insights. They are coming together on a more common footing because the business model is no longer 'push the pill out and charge whatever the hell.'"

Empowerment

Medicine is a business with its own twists and particularities, but one that caters to the real customer—the patient—far less than do many other sectors of the economy. As marketers developed more efficient ways to sell pharmaceutical products, individual patient needs were not always at the front of their minds. As the profession and business evolved, insurers, drug companies, and doctors had little incentive to share medical data with their patients. Rather, the opposite was true. The alignment between doctors, insurers, and drugmakers was dangerous anyway. It became much more so once the data were digitized, because along the way, doctors and insurers managed to lessen patients' privacy while still not giving them control of their own data. Thus, you may not have access to your complete personal medical records, but the underlying data, in anonymized form, are widely circulated to those who pay.

That's where we are today. We are poised on a precipice—moral and informational. We can create a world where medical data are treated securely on behalf of the individuals to whom it pertains and to whom it can represent literally a matter of life or death. Or we can let the market have its way.

What are the consequences of the choice? If the market takes charge—and right now, the outcome is not clear, because big pharma has huge political and financial leverage—outside businesses will know more and more about us and shape our futures accordingly. As outlined in chapter 12, marketers using a technique called propensity modeling are crunching data to target Internet advertising directly to groups according to their specific illnesses discerned from their anonymized medical information. If things turn out badly, the big health-data bazaar could lead to discrimination, exclusion from jobs and services, and humiliation.

In the alternate, more benign vision, patients will gain far greater say over their medical fates. Doctors and pharmaceutical companies will still do robust business—we will need their services and drugs as much as ever—but they will have to cede some of their control to patients. Individuals will be better informed about their illnesses and other issues, have control over their records, and determine how their intimate data are used to help medical science in the future. Data miners such as IMS can still prosper by providing valuable analysis and consulting services.

I wrote this book hoping to foster debate on how we can best balance the promise that big data offers to advance medicine and improve lives while also preserving the rights and interests of patients. To date, companies buying and selling patient information have often done all they can to obscure their activities from the public, the very source of these data. At times, they have treated us with condescension, suggesting they know better what to do with our data than we do. Yet unless companies such as IMS Health and its many data suppliers are more open, it is hard for citizens to engage in an informed discussion.

Not only is such a closed approach wrong, but it will not serve business interests in the long term. Many people will gladly share their health information if they know what is happening and if they have a reason to cooperate. Conversely, once they realize what is going on in the now hidden big health-data bazaar, the public may push for regulations to curtail data miners whose activities are opaque.

The US medical system must transform itself to put patients in control of their medical records. Before openly swapping our data—even if it's anonymized—marketers must obtain clear, knowing consent. It's a story drug companies, pharmacies, and data miners have prevented from being told to date. But it's a message we the patients deserve to hear. After all, it's our data.

ACKNOWLEDGMENTS

I OWE A DEBT of gratitude to Harvard University and its Institute for Quantitative Social Science for hosting me as a fellow through years of research and, in particular, Professor Latanya Sweeney for her continued support and insights.

The Rockefeller Foundation fueled the final stage of my work through a fellowship at its fantastic Bellagio Center in Italy; the center is run by Pilar Pilacia. A generous Abe Fellowship for Journalists from the Social Science Research Council enabled me to spend six weeks in Japan and Korea conducting research for chapter 10 and various other sections in this book. There, I thank Takuya Toda-Ozaki, Kevin Placek, and Nicole Restrick Levit. New York University's Arthur L. Carter Journalism Institute granted me its 2014 Reporting Award, which led to several medical-related articles on the path to writing this book.

I am grateful to everyone who took time to explain a complicated subject. In a field where many companies would rather give little or no public explanation about their gathering of patient data, I thank all of those who embraced transparency. Deborah Peel encouraged me to explore the themes in this book and provided many insights. Others who were especially generous with their time and knowledge are Jerry Avorn, Mark Degatano, Fritz Krieger (who shared his unpublished manuscript on pharmaceutical promotion), Per Lofberg, Warner Slack, and Larry Weed, who remains a vital force of energy and insights into his nineties.

Among the many who granted interviews and helped in my research are Swati Abbott, Julia Adler-Milstein, Shahram Ahari, Ross Anderson, Misha Angrist, Bridget Asay, Eric Avery, Linda Avey, Craig Barrett, Keith Batchelder, Brian Baum, Larry Belford, Marc Berger, Jason Bhan, Paul Black, Ernie Boyd, David Brailer, Denny Briley, Robin Brooks, Tim Burnell, Andy Burness, Steve Cantrill, Peter Castagna, Dick Cauchi, Robert Chernow, George Church, Norman Cohen, Ed Costello, Noah Craft, Stan Crosley, Peter Dietrich, the late Jim Donahue, Matthew Douglass,

Cynthia Dwork, Tina Egan, Greg Ellis, Yaniv Erlich, Barbara Evans, Judith Faulkner, Jay Flatley, Bob Gellman, Paul Gertman, Jennifer Barrett Glasgow, Janlori Goldman, Jack Gosselin, Adam Grossberg, Chris Harper, Bill Hamilton, Paul Harrington, Stephen Harrison, Zack Henderson, Doug Hoey, Paul Hooper, Ryan Howard, David Johnson, Kris Joshi, Arthur Kellermann, Aaron Kesselheim, Peter Klementowicz, Alfred Kuehn, Stefan Larsson, Bruce Laughrey, Warren Little, Richard Lubarsky, Thomas Ludlam, Laura Lyman Rodriguez, Jennifer Mallen, Richard Mannes, Gideon Mantel, Bill Marder, David McCallie Jr., Thomas McEnery, Deven McGraw, Tom Menighan, David Miller, Howard Miller, John Mizera, Keith Morgan, Ken Mortensen, Steve Munini, Faisal Mushtaq, Girish Navani, Peter Neupert, Sean Nolan, Ryan Olohan, Don Otterbein, Larry Parente, Neal Patterson, Greg Pelling, Max Petzold, Howard Pierce, Steven Pinker, Peter Pitts, Jacob Reider, Chesley Richards, Cindy Rosenwald, Marc Rotenberg, Steve Rusckowski, Stephen Schondelmeyer, Jan Schultz, Jodi Beth Segal, Lee Shapiro, Dermot Shorten, Suyash Shringarpure, Greta Lee Splansky, Jani Syed, Patsy Thomasson, Glen Tullman, Jonathan Wald, Jim Wanner, Jeff Wysong, David Yakimischak, Bill Yasnoff, and Yale Zhang. Some sources preferred to remain anonymous, and I have not mentioned everyone who has helped, but I thank them as well.

Several dozen people who worked at the L. W. Frohlich agency or IMS Health shared their past stories; the oldest of these interviewees, William Mandel, was ninety-eight. Veterans of the L. W. Frohlich agency in the 1950s and 1960s included Gerald Busby, William Castagnoli (who died in December 2015), Clyde Davis, Jack Fisher, Joseph Iozzi, Helen Itin-O'Malley (Marcel Itin's wife), Jerry McDaniel, Leonard Sirowitz, John Swift, and Gerald Weinstein; from the rival (and secret partner) McAdams agency, Win Gerson, John Kallir, and Rudi Wolff; and from Frohlich's radio station, David Dubal. Michael Sonnenreich, the lawyer for Arthur Sackler, offered key insights, as did Frohlich's lawyer Richard Leather.

From IMS's past, I single out and warmly thank Lars Ericson and Handel Evans, who patiently and repeatedly recounted stories about Frohlich and IMS, as well as Robert Merold, who comes from the company's more recent history. Other former IMS-ers to thank are Jeremy Allen, Tommy Boman, Tom Brogan, Alton Byrd, Dennis Calvanese, David Carlucci, Brenda Drinkwalter, Anita Fineberg, Maureen Gahan, Robert Hooper, Shunsuke Keimatsu, Tatsuya Kimura, Roger Korman, William Nelligan, Tohru Omoi, Mike Pierce, Tom Russell, Charlie Scott, Shel Silverberg, David Thomas, Dennis Turner, Robert Weissman, David West, Jeff Whittle, and Ana-Maria Zaugg. All of their help was especially valuable because the current leadership at IMS Health chose not to participate in my research, with the exception of Doug Long, who met for a short interview, and a few who preferred not to be named.

Many people helped in unearthing archival documents documenting the early life of Ludwig Wolfgang Frohlich, including Moriah Amit, Romain Collot, Laurence Davis, Karin Dengler, Kathleen Dow, Phil Goldfarb, Robert Greenwood, Wolfgang Hartmann, Jesper Hohmann, Ellen Jane Hollis, Karla Ingemann, Simone Langner, Monika Liebscher, Michael Maaser, Katrin Marx-Jaskulski, Elisabeth Straßer, and Silke Wagener-Fimpel.

In Japan, Ikuko Tomomatsu provided outstanding help as a translator and research partner throughout my time there. I also received help from Allison Alexy, Martin Nesirky, Marc Rodwin, Mayako Shibata, Akiko Sugaya, and Maria Toyoda. Many officials helped me understand Japan's "gray zone" of anonymized patient data: Shuroku Baba, John Campbell, Shunichi Fukuhara, Tsunehiro Fukushima, Jeffrey Gilbert, Norman Green, Rokuro Hama, Arisa Hasegawa, Junichi Hashimoto, Norio Higuchi, Masao Horibe, Ken Ikeda, Hiroyasu Iso, Manabu Ito, Kazuhito Kato, Bunji Kimura, Hiromichi Kimura, Hitoshi Kimura, Shinya Kimura, Akihiko Kitamura, Toyoyasu Kobatake, Kinya Kokubo, Hiraku Kumamaru, Yoshinori Kujirai, Emi Kuramae, Tomohiro Kuroda, Robert Leflar, Henry Marini, Reed Maurer, Yosuke Mitsuhara, Osamu Nagayama, Seishi Ohashi, Shigeru Ohta, Yoshinori Okiyama, Ron Queda, Charles Pomeroy, Bruno Rossi, Yoshiyuki Sankai, Taka-Aki Sato, Yasushi Shimizu, Roy Shore, Kiyoteru Suzuki, Soichiro Taguchi, Keiko Takahashi, Mataichirou Takasaka, Yusuke Tsugawa, Andreas Tsukada, Tetsuo Tsuji, Gen Uchida, Shusaku Uchiyama, Tomohiro Uebayashi, Atsushi Ugajin, Toshihiro Ukuda, Masayuki Yamamoto, Ryuichi Yamamoto, Yuji Yamamoto, Katsuya Yano, Yoshitake Yokokura, and Hiroyuki Yoshihira.

In South Korea, I thank Sung Hwan Chang, Dongcharn Cho, Lee Yong Jin, Minso Kim, Sung Bae Kim, Haksoo Ko, Chong Ae Lee, and my translator, Haeyon Chung.

Ambassador Fletcher Burton and Dr. David Kim both provided very valuable editing suggestions that helped improve the final manuscript.

Without the confidence and enthusiasm of my agent, Alice Martell, and Helene Atwan, director of Beacon Press, this book would not have come into being. And I am truly grateful for the support and encouragement of Celia, Adrian, and Clarissa, for their inspiration and support throughout this ambitious project.

NOTES

Introduction

1. Executive Office of the President, *Big Data*, 24. The report is archived at perma.cc/C2G5-VA6U (Perma.cc, a service developed by the Harvard Law School Library, records a permanent copy of a webpage and is used to archive webpages cited throughout this book).

2. Kris Joshi, interview with author. Because little has been written about the history of the commercial trade in patient data, this book draws principally on original research and several hundred interviews conducted in the United States and Canada, Europe, Asia, and Africa between 2012 and 2016, supplemented by a review of many thousands of pages of documents. Unless otherwise noted, quotes and recollections come directly from the participants involved in these episodes, crossed-referenced and checked as much as possible with others also present. Material from other sources is cited in endnotes.

3. Throughout this book, I use the term *data miner* to describe a commercial company that gathers medical data, typically to reassemble and summarize the information into commercial reports and analysis. Within the industry, such entities refer to themselves by different terms such as *health-care informatics* or *health-care analytics* companies.

4. Tanner, *What Stays in Vegas*.

Chapter 1: What the Pharmacy Knows

1. In this book, *patient data* refers to information such as the results of a doctor's examination, a blood test or an insurance claim and can either include the patient's name, or be anonymized. By contrast, many medical data buyers and sellers do not consider anonymized information to be patient data. Rather than embrace insider coded language, this book attempts to describe the business of medical data in terms a nonprofessional would understand.

2. Wells, *Wild Man*, 25. An audio file and transcription of Nixon's remark about Ellsberg, captured from the White House taping system, is at Miller Center, University of Virginia, "Richard M. Nixon Presidential Recordings," Nixon Conversation 006-021, archived at perma.cc/JU9X-4DZL.

3. Details for this section come from Gosselin, "Massachusetts Prescription Survey 1947" thesis.

4. See Gosselin, "The Statistical Analysis of the Distributions and Trends of Prescriptions Dispensed in Massachusetts in 1950"; and Gosselin, "History of the Determination of Market Share for Diethylstilbestrol in an Era Prior to the Development of Relative Denominator Values,"11. Other details are drawn

from Gosselin and Gosselin, "Gosselins in the Twentieth Century," and author interviews with Ray Gosselin's former colleagues and his children, March 4–5 and March 12, 2015.

Chapter 2: Data Bonanza for Pharmacies and Middlemen

1. ScriptLINE was known in the pharmacy business as a "pre/post adjudication agent." According to Fritz Krieger, pharmacies who used the service received an average of thirty-five cents more per prescription in compensation by cleaning up errors before sending the data to another middleman, called the pharmacy benefit manager.
2. Walgreens, "Walgreens Historical Highlights," archived at http://perma.cc /2HVY-6DJV.
3. Kyle Cromwell, e-mail to author, April 30, 2014.
4. Andrew Palmer, e-mail to author, August 29, 2014.
5. Jon Pybus, e-mail to author, April 28, 2014.
6. David Kirkus, e-mail to author, May 2, 2014.
7. Michael Polzin, e-mail to author, April 30, 2014. A year and a half later, on September 30, 2015, another spokesperson, Mailee Garcia, did provide a clearer answer about data gathered in the Walgreens loyalty program: "We also may sell, as do others, de-identified information to third parties such as health information service companies to help improve health care and control costs. All of this is done under the guidelines of our robust program to protect customer privacy."
8. Hired by large insurers or government entities paying prescription drug bills for covered patients, PBMs seek to manage costs by making deals with drug manufacturers and pharmacies. With their roots in the late 1960s, PBMs such as Express Scripts and CVS/Caremark grew in importance as more insurance plans covered prescription costs that Americans once paid out of pocket.
9. See *IMS 2002 Annual Report to Shareholders* (Fairfield, CT: IMS, 2003), 53; *IMS 2003 Annual Report* (Fairfield, CT: IMS, 2004), 51; and *IMS 2004 Annual Report* (Fairfield, CT: IMS, 2005), 54–55.
10. Some health-data middlemen openly advertise the possibility of sharing in data profits. QS/1, whose pharmacy software Menighan used in 1979, gives its drugstore clients the opportunity to sell prescription data to companies such as IMS, which "offers the stability of working with the world's largest aggregator of prescription data." QS/1, "IMS Rebate Program," form to be filled out on its webpage, http://www.qs1.com/index.php/services/ims-rebate-program, 2015, archived at http://perma.cc/75DM-SY6X.
11. Kolata, "When Patients' Records Are Commodities for Sale."
12. Almost all references to IMS and its history in this book use the premerger name of IMS or IMS Health.

Chapter 3: The Covert Alliance

1. The promotional video is at IMS Health, "IMS Health Overview," video, April 3, 2014, www.youtube.com/watch?v=FpNC7dqIc14.
2. An IMS spokesman responded to fact-checking questions for past magazine articles I have written, but not for this book. Another official sent a list of studies based on IMS data. Other current IMS officials quoted in this book spoke to me during brief encounters at conferences (and one via e-mail) or off the record.
3. IMS Health, "Company History," 2015, https://www.imshealth.com/en/about -us/our-company/company-history, archived at http://perma.cc/PG23-LLAH.

Frohlich is so little remembered at his company that for several years in the late 2000s, IMS even listed his middle name incorrectly.

4. In the original German, his surname is Fröhlich. Soon after arriving in the United States, he transliterated the German umlaut to *oe* and wrote *Froelich* on official documents, and used *Froehlich* on stationery in 1935. Then he used *Frohlich* as his Americanized surname for the rest of this life.

5. See Castagnoli, "There Were Giants in Those Days." Other former Frohlich associates tell a story that the two men met by chance on the street in New York City. The dates of Frohlich's businesses come from Julian Farren, the L. W. Frohlich agency's executive vice president, to the Senate Judiciary Subcommittee on Antitrust and Monopoly hearings, Part 6, Advertising Provisions, January 30, 1962, 3142.

6. Frohlich, "The Physician and the Pharmaceutical Industry in the United States," 582.

7. One former IMS official put specific numbers on the deal, saying Sackler owned 70 percent of L. W. Frohlich, but I was unable to confirm this number with others. In public, Sackler said that Frohlich was a friend but that he, Sackler, did not have an interest in Frohlich's agency. Glueck, "An Art Collector Sows Largesse and Controversy."

8. The words behind the initials *IMS* have changed over the years. In Germany, the firm's first home, the company's name was Institut für Medizinische Statistik. When it expanded to London in 1959, the first time IMS operated in an English-speaking country, its registration papers show the words "Intercontinental Marketing Services" crossed out and replaced by "Intercontinental Medical Statistics." In later years, "Intercontinental Marketing Services" became more common and the name eventually evolved to just "IMS."

9. Nielsen dabbled in many areas of market research, including radio and, eventually, television, and it is for those ratings that the company is best known today.

10. Kremers and Sonnedecker, *Kremers and Urdang's History of Pharmacy*, 85.

11. IMS today gives its founding date as 1954, but former IMS officials say the company did little or nothing in 1954 and 1955. Dubow was working in Germany from 1956, and he cited 1956 as the year of IMS' inception in Ellis, "Theme and Variation," 104.

12. The FBI investigated Frohlich as part of a review of his US citizenship application. A US government note from March 13, 1943, on the investigation reads: "Subj. has close relatives in Germany & was a member of the German ARBEITSDIENST a student working camp in Germany in 1933."

13. Kenneth Inman, letter to *British Medical Journal* 1, no. 5328 (February 16, 1963): 469.

14. Wiggins, "Tracking Drug Industry Sales."

15. *New York Times*, "Advertising: Getting Along with the FDA."

16. Revenue figures from the *New York Times*, "Advertising: B&B in New Health Field Bid," and *New York Times*, "Advertising: Biggest Health Agency Is for Sale."

17. *New York Times*, "L. W. Frohlich; Led Ad Agency." Some of the obituary's errors also appear in other reference books mentioning Frohlich, including *Who Was Who in America 1969–73*, vol. 5, 11th ed. (Berkeley Heights, NJ: Marquis Who's Who, January 1974), 253.

18. Frohlich's advertising operations continued in Europe and Asia under the name Intercon after his death.

19. Frohlich was also a half partner in the international editions of *Medical Tribune*, an advertising-supported free biweekly that Sacker founded in 1960.

When Handel Evans was in Japan from 1964 to 1969, he also oversaw its local edition of *Medical Tribune*. The details of the Sackler-Frohlich partnership were confirmed in several interviews, including with the two men's lawyers, who are still alive, and with former IMS and L. W. Frohlich agency employees, including Lars Ericson and Handel Evans.

20. The IPO prospectus said the executors of Frohlich's estate owned 1.85 million shares, and any proceeds from these shares above $6.25 million were to go to the two Sackler brothers. The IPO price per share was $25, of which $1.75 went to the underwriters as commission, so the Sackler brothers received nearly $37 million.

21. Former IMS staffers disagree as to who came up with the idea for IMS. Most say it was Frohlich; a few say Dubow. In any event, Dubow deserves credit for bringing the idea to life in Germany. No other surviving former McAdams, L. W. Frohlich, or IMS employee I interviewed knew that Dubow had earlier worked at McAdams. Michael Sonnenreich also said that after the company went public, Arthur Sackler regained a stake in IMS by buying shares on the stock market.

22. Ellis, "Theme and Variation," 104.

Chapter 4: Patient Power

1. This scene was reconstructed from author interviews with Lawrence Reed on November 3, 2014; November 14, 2014; December 17, 2014; and September 9, 2015.

2. In addition to Larry Weed and Warner Slack, whose stories are told here, a number of other researchers began experimenting with computerized patient records in the 1960s. See Sally Empey and Anne Summerfield, *Computer-Based Information Systems for Medicine: A Survey and Brief Discussion of Current Projects* (Santa Monica, CA: Systems Development Corporation, 1965).

3. Ledley and Lusted, "Reasoning Foundations of Medical Diagnosis," 9–21. Ledley later invented the first CT (computed tomography) scanner.

4. Warner Slack recounts this episode in his book *Cybermedicine*, 15–19.

5. National Educational Television Spectrum; the documentary is posted at Division of Clinical Informatics, "'LINC' with Tomorrow with Commentary from Warner Slack (1991)," accessed February 3, 2016, http://hmfpinformatics .org/history/video/Patient-computer-dialogue.

6. Slack, "The Patient's Right to Decide," 240.

7. In 2010, the US Department of Veterans Affairs introduced Blue Button, a service that enables military veterans to download their medical records, but this initiative did not assist Harper in this instance. At that time, Blue Button did not allow the transfer of records in a standard format to the patient's chosen provider. Officials at St. Francis Hospital did not respond to several requests for comment on Harper's case.

Chapter 5: The Dossier on Your Doctor

1. See Brody, *Hooked*, 141.

2. In 1986, Key Pharmaceuticals was bought by the Schering-Plough Corporation, which in turn was bought by Merck in 2009.

3. See, for example, R. Tamblyn, T. Eguale, A. Huang, N. Winslade, and P. Doran, "The Incidence and Determinants of Primary Nonadherence with Prescribed Medication in Primary Care: A Cohort Study," *Annals of Internal Medicine* 160 (2014): 441–50, doi:10.7326/M13-1705.

4. This account is based on author interviews with Handel Evans, Shel Silverberg, and Dennis Turner. Asked about the AMA's talks with Evans,

spokesman R. J. Mills said: "There is no record of this meeting, or any AMA backing of this service, in the AMA archives" (R. J. Mills, e-mail to author, October 13, 2015).

5. Shel Silverberg says that at its height, Source had about 450 employees in Phoenix and $140 million in annual revenue.

6. Kallukaran and Kagan, "Data Mining at IMS Health." The IMS reports also score a doctor's likeliness to switch medications they prescribe and their receptiveness to various sales rep strategies. "One practical application would be to predict a prescriber's reaction to a promotional event, such as a dinner meeting or a sales call," says Susan Neyhart, an IMS senior manager of strategic programs. See Neyhart, "Using Data Mining to Get Brand Switching," 80.

7. These numbers on detailers in the 1980s are cited in court documents in the *IMS Health v. Sorrell* case and come from Scott-Levin, a pharmaceutical research organization. They are cited in Tyler Chin, "Drug Firms Score by Paying Doctors for Time," Amednews.com, May 6, 2002.

8. Henry J. Kaiser Family Foundation, *Trends and Indicators in the Changing Health Care Marketplace 2002* (Menlo Park, CA: Henry J. Kaiser Family Foundation, April 30, 2002), 43.

9. See *IMS 2005 Annual Report* (Fairfield, CT: IMS, 2006), 21–23.

10. Edward Sagebiel, an Eli Lilly spokesman, responded: "We disagree with this statement. We have always been up front that we receive data from IMS and thus don't really understand why this statement was made." E-mail to author, December 9, 2015.

11. Ahari describes these personality types in Fugh-Berman and Ahari, "Following the Script," e150.

12. Institute for Motivational Research, *A Research Study on Pharmaceutical Advertising*, 22–23.

13. McQuillan, *Is the Doctor In?*, 61.

14. Elliott, *White Coat, Black Hat*, 52.

15. Institute for Motivational Research, *A Research Study on Pharmaceutical Advertising*, 22–23.

16. Senate Subcommittee on Antitrust and Monopoly, Administered Prices in the Drug Industry (Antibiotics): Hearings Before the Subcommittee on Antitrust and Monopoly, pt. 24, 86th Cong., 2d sess., 7–14 September 1960, 10368.

17. These figures provided by IMS CEO Ari Bousbib, remarks at J. P. Morgan 33rd Annual Healthcare Conference, San Francisco, January 13, 2015.

18. Ari Bousbib, remarks at J. P. Morgan Ultimate Services Conference, New York, November 10, 2015.

Chapter 6: Supreme Court Battle

1. As recounted in chapter 5, doctor-identified data started in the 1980s and became commonplace in the 1990s. One early national article on the topic was Stolberg and Gerth, "High-Tech Stealth Being Used to Sway Doctor Prescriptions."

2. Kowalczyk, "Drug Companies Secret Reports Outrage Doctors."

3. Kallukaran and Kagan, "Data Mining at IMS Health." IMS appears to have later sensed that the paper revealed too much: In 2007, it asked the organization that had originally published the article to remove it from the organization's website. An archived copy is available at https://is.gd/EeUHBn.

4. IMS Health background memo, "A Business Perspective on House Bill 1346: The Unintended Consequences of Bill Passage," January 26, 2006.

5. Frankel spoke to Vermont's House Committee on Health Care. The testimony is part of the documentation recorded in IMS Health v. Sorrell, Second

Circuit Court of Appeals, 09–2056-cv, Joint Appendix Volume II of VII, A-12430 through 1246. April 19, 2007, A-1280 through 81.

6. "All data products, including licensed data sales, credentialing products, and royalties, generated annual revenue of about $51 million in recent years," says AMA spokesman R. J. Mills. "It would be inaccurate to attribute the full amount of data product revenue to business agreements with aggregators. Data product revenue also includes the sale of credentialing products to physicians, hospitals, and managed care companies."

7. Tom Julin, testimony in IMS Health v. Sorrell, U.S. District Court, District of Vermont, July 28, 2008.

8. Ibid.

9. The testimony is part of the documentation recorded in ibid.

10. Jerry Avorn made this remark before the Vermont House of Representatives Health Committee on April 18, 2007. The testimony is part of the documentation recorded in ibid.

11. Before the case got to the Supreme Court, legal filings and related documentation typically refer to *IMS Health et al. v. Sorrell*. When the US Supreme Court reviewed it, the names were reversed to *Sorrell et al. v. IMS Health et al.*

12. Three Supreme Court justices dissented: Stephen Breyer, Ruth Bader Ginsburg, and Elena Kagan. Breyer wrote: "Shaping a detailing message based on an individual doctor's prior prescription habits may help sell more of a particular manufacturer's particular drugs. But it does so by diverting attention from scientific research about a drug's safety and effectiveness, as well as its cost. This diversion comes at the expense of public health and the State's fiscal interests." See https://perma.cc/VV2P-AY42.

13. Starr, *The Social Transformation of American Medicine*, 131.

14. Brody, *Hooked*, 145.

15. Reidy, *Hard Sell*, 70.

16. ZS Associates, "Even Traditionally Rep-Friendly Specialists Will See Fewer Pharmaceutical Sales Reps This Year," press release, July 22, 2014, archived at http://perma.cc/4HCQ-RBR6.

Chapter 7: Studying Patients over Time

1. Snow, *On the Mode of Communication of Cholera*.

2. Ibid. For Snow's discoveries, see David Vachon, "Doctor John Snow Blames Water Pollution for Cholera Epidemic," part 1, UCLA Department of Epidemiology, archived at http://perma.cc/K53E-EKZH. For a longer narrative account, see Johnson, *The Ghost Map*.

3. A good summary of the medical knowledge gained from the studies of atomic-blast survivors comes from J. D. Boice Jr., "Studies of Atomic Bomb Survivors Understanding Radiation Effects," *Journal of the American Medical Association* 264, no. 5 (1990): 622–23, doi:10.1001/jama.1990.03450050080033.

4. See Health Authority of Abu Dhabi, "Weqaya Disease Management Programme," *A Healthier Abu Dhabi* . . . webpage, archived at http://perma.cc/34K6-W2KM.

5. Datta and Dave, "Effects of Physician-Directed Pharmaceutical Promotion on Prescription Behaviors: Longitudinal Evidence."

6. Caremark, which later merged with CVS, bought Health Data Institute in 1985.

7. IBM, "IBM Watson Health Announces Plans to Acquire Truven Health Analytics for $2.6B, Extending Its Leadership in Value-Based Care Solutions," press release, February 18, 2016, archived at https://perma.cc/XM6G-63YK.

8. Jumping ahead in the story, IMS eventually acquired the Verispan business by taking over its successor company SDI in 2011. Then IMS merged with Quintiles in 2016.

9. Verispan, "Verispan Offers Breakthrough Market Research, Sales Targeting and Compensation Measures to Pharmaceutical Industry," press release, September 26, 2003, archived at http://perma.cc/K27S-3MXP.

10. See *IMS 2000 Annual Report to Shareholders*, 32.

11. Today, when doctors sign up for an Allscripts product such as ePrescribe, which electronically submits prescriptions, the fine print of its agreement allows the company to "de-identify PHI in accordance with HIPAA and use or disclose (and permit others to use or disclose) de-identified information on a perpetual, unrestricted basis." Allscripts, "Register for Allscripts ePrescribe (Step 1 of 3)," instruction page with agreement to be signed by subscriber, archived at https://perma.cc/6QT9-7Z47. Since doctors are the main customers, Allscripts does not share their names when selling data. "There was tons of resistance to electronic prescribing generally," former CEO Glen Tullman said. "We made sure it was never traceable back to a physician, because we didn't want the physicians getting hassled."

12. Revenue numbers were given for mid-2015 by Faisal Mushtaq, president of Allscript's payer/life sciences business, interview with author, August 7, 2015.

13. See IMS Health, "IMS to Combine Largest U.S. Health Plan Claims Database with IMS LifeLink, Enabling Innovative Patient Treatment Insights," press release, September 13, 2012, archived at http://perma.cc/3FFA-W9Y6.

14. Kaiser outlines some of the results of such studies at Kaiser Permanente, "Kaiser Permanente HealthConnect® Enables Care Improvement and Transformation," press release, March 6, 2013, archived at http://perma.cc/4LFM-GDRZ, and some of its history of research at Ginny McPartland, "Decades of Health Records Fuel Kaiser Permanente Research," March 6, 2013, *History of Total Health* (Kaiser Permanente blog), archived at http://perma.cc/524R-F5B6.

15. MedMining advertises its offerings in its MedMining newsletters (winter 2009 through January/February 2015), archived at http://perma.cc/U6GN-Z4U2, but prefers not to talk publicly about what it does. Julie Rockey, the chief operating officer, declined three years of requests to discuss her company's work.

16. See IBM, "IBM Watson Health Announces Plans to Acquire Truven Health Analytics," and IBM, "IBM Acquires Explorys to Accelerate Cognitive Insights for Health and Wellness," press release, April 13, 2015, archived at http://perma.cc/DBN5-VRM3.

17. LexisNexis advertises its medical data services at LexisNexis, "Medical Claims Data," *LexisNexis Solutions*, archived at http://perma.cc/D569-MT6P, and LexisNexis, "It's the Story in the Data That Matters," *LexisNexis MarketView*, archived at http://perma.cc/B8NF-GPXE. The number of covered patients comes from Zach Henderson, senior vice president, Healthcare Markets, interview with author, July 27, 2015. LexisNexis does not obtain claims directly from all of those companies. "The point is that claims data exists in many different areas, not just at the payer," Henderson explained. "The same claim form actually exists in at least three locations: in the system that created the claim (the provider), the clearinghouse that moved the claim and the entity that paid the claim (payer or PBM)." Zach Henderson, e-mail to author, November 11, 2015.

18. John Wilson and Adam Bock, "The Benefit of Using Both Claims Data and Electronic Medical Record Data in Health Care Analysis," white paper, Optum, April 30, 2014, archived at http://perma.cc/LPU5-GNXQ.

19. IMS, "IMS Announces Integration of Anonymized Patient-Level Data Across Global Portfolio of Offerings," press release, November 28, 2006, archived at http://perma.cc/5B67-2K3V.

20. List of countries available at IMS Health, "Patient-Level Data Assets," archived at http://perma.cc/PV5P-FPBN.

21. Ari Bousbib, remarks at J. P. Morgan Healthcare Conference, San Francisco, January 17, 2015.

22. IMS divides academic studies that have used its data into various categories: "Understanding Disease and Treatment Patterns," "Providing Content for Healthcare Costs," "Assessing Policy Levers," and "Advancing Real World Patient-Level Clinical Evidence." See IMS Institute for Health Informatics, "Advancing Academic Research; Bibliography of Published Papers and Presentations Using IMS Health Information," June 2015, archived at http://perma.cc/NT5N-JSSG. Truven says its MarketScan databases have been used in more than seven hundred peer-reviewed studies since 1990. Some of them are listed at https://perma.cc/CFS7-NUZT. There is a searchable online research bibliography at http://sites.truvenhealth.com/bibliography/. See also Optum, "Outcomes Informed Treatment Bibliography," October 2014, archived at http://perma.cc/GX9Q-7XUU.

Chapter 8: Fighting for Patients

1. Alina is an alias used to protect her privacy. Hers and that of a whistle-blower in South Korea are the only pseudonyms in this book.

2. The patient has shared copies of some of these files with the author.

3. Solomon et al., "Relationship Between Selective Cyclooxygenase-2 Inhibitors and Acute Myocardial Infarction in Older Adults," 2068–73. An earlier 2002 study, using data from the Tennessee Medicaid program, also identified a higher risk of heart disease for those using the drug. See Ray et al., "COX-2 Selective Non-Steroidal Anti-inflammatory Drugs and Risk of Serious Coronary Heart Disease,"1071–73. Wayne Ray told me his team did not pay for the data it received from Tennessee.

4. Federal Trade Commission, *Biennial Report to Congress: Under the Do Not Call Registry Fee Extension Act of 2007, FY 2014 and 2015* (Washington, DC: Federal Trade Commission, December 2015), 1. Although most companies abide by the Do Not Call Registry, some skirt the law by generating cheap Internet calls from abroad to numbers on the opt-out list. Such calls have fueled a surge of consumer complaints in recent years. If a similar list for medical data were created, such abuse would also be possible, but legitimate companies would be likely to follow patient preferences.

Chapter 9: How Safe Is "Anonymized"?

1. Kuehn, "Analysis of the Dynamics of Consumer Behavior."

2. On its Privacy Management webpage, IMS gives more details about the process: "Rendering information de-identified or anonymous takes a variety of skills and expertise, including statistical and cryptographic sciences, legal, privacy, information security & compliance expertise, as well as data processing skills—along with an understanding of how healthcare systems work within a country and related data flows. At IMS Health, we employ these skills and expertise together with decades of experience to perform this task millions of times each day." IMS Health, "Privacy Management," 2015, archived at http://perma.cc/F24M-SDK9.

3. In her filing, Sweeney takes issue with the conclusions of Khaled El Emam, the founder of a Canadian company called Privacy Analytics, which offers software to de-identify patient data. El Emam argues that there is a very small risk of re-identifying properly anonymized data. At a conference in 2012, I met a Privacy Analytics executive who boasted of the effectiveness of the company's software, but she declined several requests to provide access to the software for Harvard's Institute for Quantitative Social Science to test it for vulnerabilities.

IMS Health was impressed by the company's work and bought it in 2016 (see IMS Health, "IMS Health Acquires Privacy Analytics, Advancing Real-World Evidence Technology to Drive R&D and Commercial Performance," press release, May 25, 2016, archived at https://perma.cc/Y3PD-J87E). For Latanya Sweeney's filing, see "Patient Privacy Risks in U.S. Supreme Court Case Sorrell v. IMS Health Inc., Response to Amici Brief of El Emam and Yakowitz," working paper 1027-1015B, Data Privacy Lab, Harvard University, Cambridge, MA, 2011, archived at http://perma.cc/UR5K-JXZE.

4. Sweeney, "Uniqueness of Simple Demographics in the U.S. Population." A later study by a different author suggested that the number of people who can be identified from ZIP code, gender, and date of birth is somewhat less, at 63 percent. See Philippe Golle, "Revisiting the Uniqueness of Simple Demographics in the US Population," in *WPES '06 Proceedings of the 5th ACM Workshop on Privacy in Electronic Society* (New York: Association for Computing Machinery, 2006), 77–80. I've reached out to William Weld a number of times to ask about Sweeney's uncovering of his personal information, but he has never responded.

5. The ruling was made in Southern Illinoisan v. Dept. of Public Health, 349 Ill. App.3d 431 (Ill. App. Ct. 2004), and in an Illinois Supreme Court decision filed February 2, 2006. The latter decision is archived at http://perma.cc/6ZAB-9XVT.

6. Sweeney, "Patient Privacy Risks."

7. Sweeney et al., "Identifying Participants in the Personal Genome Project by Name."

8. I describe my modest experiment in re-identification in my 2014 book *What Stays in Vegas*, 106–7.

9. For example, a 2015 study re-identified nearly a quarter of a sample of users sequenced by 23andMe who had posted their information to the sharing site openSNP. "The matching risk will continuously increase with the progress of genomic knowledge, which raises serious questions about the genomic privacy of participants in genomic datasets," the paper concludes. "We should also recall that, once an individual's genomic data is identified, the genomic privacy of all his close family members is also potentially threatened." See Mathias Humbert, Kévin Huguenin, Joachim Hugonot, Erman Ayday, and Jean Pierre Hubaux, "De-anonymizing Genomic Databases Using Phenotypic Traits," *Proceedings on Privacy Enhancing Technologies* 2 (2015): 99–114, archived at https://perma.cc /GK5E-DC8G. After such re-identifications, researchers sought to strengthen privacy protections—only to see others find new holes. Even if outsiders can only ask yes-or-no questions about aspects of a genome, with enough questions, they can unmask someone's identity among a database of 1,000 people, a 2015 study found. See Suyash Shringarpure and Carlos Bustamante, "Privacy Risks from Genomic Data-Sharing Beacons," *American Journal of Human Genetics* 97 (November 5, 2015): 631–646, doi: 10.1016/j.ajhg.2015.09.010.

10. Sweeney, "Matching Known Patients to Health Records in Washington State Data."

11. The Hubway contest is at "Hubway Data Visualization Challenge," archived at http://perma.cc/64B3-V6EU. Sweeney explained her contest entry at "About My Ride," archived at http://perma.cc/Y3SM-4TA7.

12. An approach to improve the sharing of health data is outlined in Sweeney et al., "Sharing Sensitive Data with Confidence."

13. Barbaro and Zeller, "A Face Is Exposed for AOL Searcher No. 4417749."

14. Narayanan and Shmatikov, "Robust De-Anonymization of Large Sparse Datasets."

15. Arvind Narayanan, "About 33 Bits," *33 Bits of Entropy* (blog), archived at http://perma.cc/4N7H-GP4S. The site explains its name by saying one only

needs thirty-three bits of information about someone to identify him or her among the world's other 6.6 billion people.

16. Tanner, "Data Brokers Are Now Selling Your Car's Location For $10 Online."
17. Anthony Tockar, "Riding with the Stars: Passenger Privacy in the NYC Taxicab Dataset," *Neustar Research* (blog), archived at https://perma.cc/B9BT-7JQD.
18. Gymrek et al. "Identifying Personal Genomes by Surname Inference," 321.
19. Executive Office of the President, *Big Data*, 23.
20. Seventh Circuit in Northwestern Memorial Hospital v. Ashcroft, 362 F.3d 923 (7th Cir. 2004) 45 C.F.R. § 164.502(d)(2), decision archived at http://perma.cc /CC5R-PFVT.21. For latest health-data breaches, see US Department of Health and Human Services Office for Civil Rights, "Breaches Affecting 500 or More Individuals," in *Breach Portal: Notice to the Secretary of HHS Breach of Unsecured Protected Health Information*, accessed February 3, 2016, https://ocrportal.hhs.gov/ocr/breach/breach_report.jsf.
22. Anthem, Inc. Data Breach Litigation, U.S. District Court, Northern District of California, San Jose Division, case 15-md-02617 LHK.
23. For more details, see Camp and Johnson, *The Economics of Financial and Medical Identity Theft*, 64.
24. Ponemon Institute, *Fifth Annual Study on Medical Identity Theft*, 8.
25. Allen Stefanek, open letter, Hollywood Presbyterian Medical Center, Los Angeles, February 17, 2016, archived at https://perma.cc/C2V9-W72T.
26. Experian, "Data Industry Breach Forecast," Experian, 2015, archived at http://perma.cc/P3ZY-3LRF.
27. Tor Constantino, e-mail to author, September 12, 2014.
28. IMS Health, "Review of Directive 95/46/EC," IMS Health, July 2002, archived at http://perma.cc/W759-58KJ. The European Commission case against IMS was dropped in 2003. Emphasis in original.
29. See Wood et al., "Integrating Approaches to Privacy Across the Research Lifecycle."
30. See RelayHealth, "Expands Successful Patient Engagement Efforts Within Army, Navy and Air Force Medical Services," press release, October 15, 2012, archived at http://perma.cc/7F3E-GSL6. Overall, RelayHealth processes more than 2.3 billion financial transactions linked between 2,400 hospitals and 630,000 providers and operates an electronic records patient portal. See McKesson, "New ConnectCenter from RelayHealth Redefines Online Claims Management," press release, February 23, 2015, archived at http://perma.cc/ZC2S-J9J3.
31. For the outside sharing of aggregated information, see the "Aggregate Data" section in RelayHealth's privacy policy, archived at http://perma.cc/AF93 -VDV8. Regarding the military rules, US Military Health Systems, "Draft Business Associate Agreement," archived at perma.cc/SVD7-5P3H, notes: "The Business Associate is not permitted to de-identify PHI . . . nor is it permitted to use or disclose de-identified PHI."
32. IMS describes its work for the US military at IMS Health, "A 360° View of the Healthcare Marketplace," *Information Sources* (IMS Health blog), 2015, archived at https://perma.cc/932A-CERU?type=source. Wes Watkins is quoted from an e-mail to author, November 23, 2015.

Chapter 10: Korean War over Patient Data
1. IMS Health Form 10-K, filed on February 13, 2015, for year ending December 31, 2014, 27.
2. Although the practice is not common, many US states also allow doctors to prescribe and dispense drugs.

3. Tor Constantino, e-mail to author, May 28, 2015. He added: "We have been fully cooperating with the Korean authorities and will continue to do so through the resolution of this matter." Constantino declined to say whether IMS buys data from pharmacies that do not use the PM2000 software and would not say when IMS began buying data from pharmacies using PM2000.

4. Sweeney and Ji Su, "De-anonymizing South Korean Resident Registration Numbers Shared in Prescription Data."

Chapter 11: The Patient's Data Tower of Babel

1. Neal Patterson testimony before US Senate Committee on Health, Education, Labor, and Pensions, June 10, 2015.

2. Office of the National Coordinator for Health Information Technology, *Report on Health Information Blocking* (Washington, DC: ONC, Department of Health and Human Services, April 2015), archived at perma.cc/AU72-FLMU.

3. See, for example, Garber et al., "Redirecting Innovation in U.S. Health Care," 36–38.

4. Eric Schmidt, keynote speech, Healthcare Information and Management Systems Society Annual Conference, February 28, 2008, Orlando, archived at http://perma.cc/R4MW-P5HR.

5. Aaron Brown, "An Update on Google Health and Google PowerMeter," *Google Official Blog*, June 24, 2011, archived at http://perma.cc/3WSD-43EK.

6. When I asked Judy Faulkner, the founder of Epic, about this comment, she said, "We work with the vendors whom our customers want us to work with. Our customers didn't ask us to work with Microsoft."

7. This idea led to SOAP (subjective, objective, analytical, and planning) progress notes, an approach widely used today and Weed's contribution that is best known among medical professionals today.

8. Gordon Cook, "A Medical Revolution That Could . . . : The Work of the PROMIS Laboratory and Lawrence L. Weed, M.D.," Center for Occupational and Professional Assessment, Educational Testing Service, Princeton, NJ, September 29, 1978.

9. Lundsgaarde, Fischer, and Steele, *Human Problems in Computerized Medicine*, 18, wrote: "Some professional jealousies were generated by the competition for space and resources, which became limited, then actually scarce, in the early 1970s. Additionally, personal resentments grew at the perceived evangelistic attitudes of the PROMIS Laboratory staff."

10. Larry Weed's reading list, in addition to his own writings, includes Francis Bacon, *Novum Organum* (1620); Giovanni Battista Morgagni, *De Sedibus et Causis Morborum per Anatomen Indagatis* (Patavii: Sumptibus Remondinianis, 1765); Abraham Flexner, *Medical Education in the United States and Canada: A Report to the Carnegie Foundation for the Advancement of Teaching* (New York City, 1910); Graedon and Graedon, *Top Screwups Doctors Make and How to Avoid Them*; and Laura Snyder, *The Philosophical Breakfast Club: Four Remarkable Friends Who Transformed Science and Changed the World* (New York: Broadway Books, 2011).

Chapter 12: Twenty-First-Century Advances

1. IMS Health, "IMS Health and Quintiles to Merge; Quintiles IMS to Become Industry-Leading Information and Technology-Enabled Healthcare Service Provider," press release, May 3, 2016, archived at https://perma.cc/3D25-AG9S.

2. Quintiles and IMS Health, "Quintiles and IMS Health Announce Global Collaboration to Advance the Use of Next-Generation Real-World Evidence in

Late-Stage Clinical Research," joint press release, October 22, 2015, archived at https://perma.cc/746V-LRSR.

3. IMS Health, "IMS Health and Quintiles to Merge; Quintiles IMS to Become Industry-Leading Information and Technology-Enabled Healthcare Service Provider," press release, May 3, 2016, archived at https://perma.cc/3D25-AG9S.

4. The figure comes from former IMS CEO David Carlucci, interview with author, September 10, 2015.

5. Details of IMS data suppliers are in IMS Health, "A 360° View of the Healthcare Marketplace," *Information Sources* (IMS Health blog), 2015, archived at http://perma.cc/932A-CERU; and IMS Health, "Medical Claims," *Information Types*, IMS Health, accessed February 3, 2016, https://www.imshealth.com/en/about-us/core-strengths/information-types.

6. By mid-2016, IMS had collected more than 530 million anonymized patient dossiers. See Quintiles IMS Health Investor Briefing, May 3, 2016, archived at https://perma.cc/Y86Q-8QFG.

7. Symphony Health Solutions Corporation et al. v. IMS Health Incorporated, Pennsylvania Eastern District Court, Case No. 2:13-cv-04290.

8. IMS, "Media Statement Regarding IMS Health's Response to Symphony Health Solutions Complaint," press release, July 25, 2013, archived at http://perma.cc/FL48-7E24. For countersuit, see IMS Health Incorporated v. Symphony Health Solutions Corporation, Source Healthcare Analytics, LLC, and ImpactRx, Inc., U.S. District Court for Delaware, 1:13-cv-02071-GMS.

9. For an especially comprehensive list from a major data broker, see Epsilon's "Health and Ailment Database" list, archived at http://perma.cc/98W3-NX2G.

10. Veritas Genetics, "Terms of Use," Privacy and Legal section, effective date April 1, 2015, archived at https://perma.cc/4NDR-CXMK.

11. See NextMark, Inc., "STD.DATERS.COM: AIDS/HIV Members Postal & E-mail Mailing List," archived at http://perma.cc/6LPR-V6FH.

12. DataMasters.org website is archived at http://perma.cc/SAC3–4QBS.

13. Sharecare, the same company that bought Larry Weed's PKC Corporation, owns RealAge.

14. WebMD, "WebMD Privacy Policy Summary," effective date March 20, 2015, archived at http://perma.cc/D858-HZG3.

15. eMedicineHealth, "eMedicineHealth Privacy Policy Summary," effective date March 20, 2015, archived at http://perma.cc/93CE-Y5JM.

16. Your-life.com, "Privacy Statement," archived at http://perma.cc/P5A8-AL7X.

17. Korman also cites the huge fines, some in the billions of dollars, that many of the largest drug companies have paid in recent years for fraudulent or off-label marketing. The companies include Pfizer, Merck, GlaxoSmithKline, Sanofi-Aventis, Johnson & Johnson, AstraZeneca, Abbott, Amgen, and Endo.

18. Lexicon Pharmaceuticals Q3 2014 earnings call, November 4, 2014.

19. Hanson et al., "Tweaking and Tweeting," e62.

20. For an example of Dredze's work, see Dredze et al., "HealthTweets.org."

21. Among the major data brokers, Acxiom, Experian, and Epsilon all say they do not mine social media to append medical data in individual files.

22. IMS Institute for Healthcare Informatics, "IMS Institute Report Finds Nearly Half of Top 50 Manufacturers Have Active Social Media Engagement—Industry Standouts are Leading the Way," press release, January 21, 2014, archived at perma.cc/EEJ2-HCJZ.

23. Spokeswoman Sally Beatty at Pfizer, which makes Robitussin cough syrup, responds, "There is no evidence or indication to suggest its use will help women who are seeking to get pregnant."

24. Crossix webpage archived at http://perma.cc/B74Z-N2G9.

25. Kaye, "Sophisticated Health Data Industry Needs Self-Reflection."

26. Several companies, including Experian and Forbes, confirmed to me that they sold mailing lists that resulted in these solicitations.

Chapter 13: Intimate, Anonymized, and for Sale

1. eClinicalWorks, "Privacy Policy," archived at http://perma.cc/3FU8-SK27.

2. This statistic comes from IMS, "A Critical Connector in the Treatment Continuum," *Electronic Health Records*, 2015, archived at http://perma.cc/7W5X-EGLG. As mentioned in chapter 7, the middleman Allscripts, which also operates an electronic health record system, is one of IMS' many data partners.

3. Dwoskin, "The Next Marketing Frontier." Reader comments are accessible to *Wall Street Journal* subscribers at http://perma.cc/2CZG-UBU6.

4. Deborah Peel, e-mail to *Forbes* magazine, July 2011, shared with author, September 15, 2015.

5. Hong et al., "Chronic Recurrent Multifocal Osteomyelitis."

6. Other companies also forgo potentially lucrative anonymized patient data sales. Salesforce.com unveiled its Health Cloud in late 2015, promising to provide a "complete view of patient data" to health-care organizations. But the company says it can neither see nor sell anonymized data stored on its servers, nor does Surescripts, which processes prescriptions between doctors, pharmacies, and insurers.

7. LabCorp also shares data with Medivo, but declined to discuss the sales, which are hinted at in LabCorp, "Notice of Privacy Practices," effective date April 7, 2014, archived at http://perma.cc/C7DT-J7FX: "LabCorp may use and disclose health information that has been 'de-identified' by removing certain identifiers making it unlikely that you could be identified." The use of the vague word "unlikely" in describing the chance that someone would be identified is one of the less reassuring guarantees of anonymity that I have come across.

8. See IMS Health, "Diagnostic Reports from the Industry's Largest Anonymized Patient Set," *IMS Diagnostics* webpage, 2015, archived at http://perma.cc/B52U-STJU. Drugmakers have also combined Medivo and IMS longitudinal patient lab and prescription data for additional insights. See overview of one study done with AbbVie at Medivo, "Accelerating New Product Adoption Using Lab Results Linked to Treatment Dispensed: HCV, a Case Study," poster, Pharmaceutical Management Science Association Annual Conference, Arlington, VA, April 19–22, 2015, archived at http://perma.cc/3YAS-2ZKS.

9. ExamOne, "Prescription History Profiling Tool," *Our Solutions, ScriptCheck*, ExamOne website promotion, archived at perma.cc/XS3D-LLYD.

10. Ibid.

11. Milliman, "IntelliScript," webpage, archived at perma.cc/LLA8–238P. Milliman describes how it obtains its data, "IntelliScript: FAQ," archived at perma.cc/B8VF-KW2B.

12. IntelRx, "Underwriting Studies," 2004, archived at perma.cc/5GFW-KVDY.

13. Federal Trade Commission, "Providers of Consumers Medical Profiles Agree to Comply with Fair Credit Reporting Act," press release, September 17, 2007, archived at perma.cc/2BV4-DFC5.

14. Medical Information Bureau, "MIB's Secure & Confidential Codes," MIB website, archived at perma.cc/3EQG-XTAG.

15. This price range comes from Richard Jackson, a professor of pharmacy administration at Mercer University, e-mail to author, March 10, 2015. He added: "Certain aspects of the prescriptions are important such as the number that are one-time prescriptions, who the payer is and whether the purchaser has contract with them, the percentage generic, etc."

16. Walsh, "Pharmacies Can Sell, Transfer Prescription Files."
17. Richard Lubarsky, "Privacy of Pharmacy Prescription Files," post in *The Body: The Complete HIV/AIDS Resource*, April 6, 2000, archived at http://perma.cc/ESB5-RPDE. The legal case is Anonymous v. CVS Corp., 188 Misc.2d 616 (2001).

Chapter 14: At the Bottom of Niagara

1. Carenity, "Our Commitments," *About Carenity* webpage, archived at http://perma.cc/5LP8-4CG5.
2. IMS Health, "Privacy Commitment," archived at https://perma.cc/B3JL-HPNJ.
3. Apple describes its HealthKit policy at Apple, "HealthKit," in *Our Privacy Policy*, 2016, Apple webpage, archived at perma.cc/CT9R-2SK3.
4. Rhode Island Department of Health, "All Payer Claims Database Operations Guidance Memorandum," February 1, 2014, archived at http://perma.cc/7C3J-XZRQ.
5. For an example of an opt-out, see Framingham Heart Study, "Research Consent Form, Cohort Exam 29," archived at http://perma.cc/F6FK-VQBK. The second generation of participants opted out in the greatest numbers, at a rate of 8.5 percent; the third generation was considerably less, said Framingham's Greta Lee Splansky.
6. IMS cited the British National Health Service data in its 2014 IPO prospectus as a possible competitive threat. IMS Health IPO Prospectus, March 24, 2014, 25–26. Link to filing at https://is.gd/7GOwKH. An article discussing some of the controversies around the centralization of British medical data comes from Presser et al., "Care.Data and Access to UK Health Records."
7. Dormuth et al., "Higher Potency Statins and the Risk of New Diabetes."
8. B. Wettermark et al. "The Nordic Prescription Databases."
9. Centers for Medicare and Medicaid Services, "Medicare Provider Utilization and Payment Data: Part D Prescriber," last modified November 4, 2015, archived at http://perma.cc/W695-D28A. For more details on the 5 percent sample available to researchers, see Centers for Medicare and Medicaid Services, "Standard Analytical Files," last modified December 5, 2013, archived at http://perma.cc/GC2F-ASU3.
10. Maine was the first state to make patient health insurance and pharmacy claims data available for researchers in 2003. All-Payers Claims Database Council, "Interactive State Report Map," APCD Council, University of New Hampshire, archived at http://perma.cc/V3BF-EKEF, maintains a map showing how each state approaches such databases. One 2013 survey found that thirty-three states release some form of hospital discharge data. Hooley and Sweeney, "Survey of Publicly Available State Health Databases."
11. See, for example, Rodwin, "The Case for Public Ownership of Patient Data."
12. Drug companies still regularly contact the Health Care Cost Institute to try to get access to their 51 million patient files, and it is up to executive director David Newman to hold the line. "I got eight hundred calls from industry, and we explain that we don't license it to industry. We explain that it is only academics," he says. "And then they say, 'Oh, I need an academic to front for the company?'" Along these same lines, data miners are among the top purchasers of patient databases sold by individual US states.

Conclusion

1. One survey of privacy policies of companies covered by HIPAA found the policies to be either difficult or very difficult to understand, akin to professional medical literature or legal contracts. See Breese, "Readability of Notice of Privacy Forms Used by Major Health Care Institutions."

2. Office of the Press Secretary, the White House, "Remarks by the President in Precision Medicine Panel Discussion," transcript, February 25, 2016, archived at https://perma.cc/N4DH-KC4U.

3. Li et al., "Identification of Type 2 Diabetes Subgroups."

4. The fine print at 23andMe says the firm shares DNA information by default with third-party firms to improve its service. More than 80 percent of customers also consent to share more widely, allowing the firm to sell or share data to pharmaceutical companies such as Pfizer or Genentech or to nonprofits, said 23andMe privacy officer Kate Black. "We understand that people are worried about it and that there are inherent risks here, so we like to take all the legal, contractual, and administrative precautions that we can to limit the scope of those risks," she said. "We make sure all of our research partners and service providers are contractually obligated not to re-identify the information."

5. IMS lists academic papers that have used its data at IMS Institute for Healthcare Informatics, "Advancing Academic Research: Bibliography of Published Papers and Presentations Using IMS Health Information," IMS Institute for Healthcare Informatics, Parsippany, NJ, June 2015, archived at perma.cc/3GPJ-W56E.

6. For more background on value-based health care, see Michael Porter and Thomas Lee, "The Strategy That Will Fix Health Care," *Harvard Business Review*, October 2013; and Optum, "Can Value-Based Reimbursement Models Transform Health Care?" White Paper, August 2013, archived at https://perma.cc/4FGF-QW4N. Many others have written about the topic as well.

7. Watkins et al., "Clinical Impact of Selective and Nonselective Beta-Blockers on Survival in Patients with Ovarian Cancer."

8. Clinical trials had also earlier suggested safety issues with Vioxx. After getting regulatory approval from the Food and Drug Administration, Merck started selling Vioxx in 1999, and the drug became the company's most successful launch ever. Hoping to build on that success, Merck commissioned a second and even larger clinical study of the drug in 1999. This subsequent study of eight thousand patients indicated a heightened risk of heart problems. Documents revealed in later litigation showed that Merck downplayed the negative results of both that study and the original 1996–1997 clinical trial. For additional details on the Vioxx case, see Harlan Krumholz, Harold Hines, Joseph Ross, Amos H. Presler, and David S. Egilman, "What Have We Learnt from Vioxx?" *British Medical Journal* 334 (January 20, 2007): 120–123. doi: 10.1136/bmj.39024.487720.68.

9. From "Our Focus" section of Quintiles website, archived at https://perma.cc/YTK2-RXE5.

10. Manipulation of data can also slant medical outcomes and lead to needless expense, says Jacob Reider, the former deputy national coordinator at the Office of the National Coordinator for Health IT at the US Department of Health and Human Services. "Based on the data, one can cause patients and care providers to make different decisions," he says. "There are also things that would enhance the likelihood that a doc would make a certain diagnosis. Let's pick an easy one: low testosterone, a completely invented diagnosis. It is pretty well documented that it is an invented diagnosis. Who invented it? The companies that have the treatment for it. Doctors may be encouraged to order a testosterone-level test for men over fifty reporting fatigue and low libido, resulting in revenue for the company treating the supposed problem but offering little real help to the patient."

BIBLIOGRAPHY

Books

Altaras, Thea. *Stätten Der Juden in Giessen: Von Den Anfängen Bis Heute*, Die Blauen Bücher. Königstein im Taunus: K.R. Langewiesche, 1998.

Altenstetter, Christa. *Medical Technology Regulation in Japan: The Politics of Regulation*. New Brunswick, NJ: Transaction Publishers, 2015.

American Council on Education, Committee on the Pharmaceutical Survey. *Findings and Recommendations of the Pharmaceutical Survey, 1948*. Washington, DC: American Council on Education, 1948.

American Council on Education, Committee on the Pharmaceutical Survey, and Edward C. Elliott. *The General Report of the Pharmaceutical Survey, 1946–49*. Washington, DC: American Council on Education, 1950.

Angell, Marcia. *The Truth About the Drug Companies: How They Deceive Us and What to Do About It*. Rev. and updated ed. New York: Random House, 2005.

Avorn, Jerry. *Powerful Medicines: The Benefits, Risks, and Costs of Prescription Drugs*. Rev. and updated, 1st Vintage Books ed. New York: Vintage Books, 2005.

Brody, Howard. *Hooked: Ethics, the Medical Profession, and the Pharmaceutical Industry*. Explorations in Bioethics and the Medical Humanities. Lanham, MD: Rowman & Littlefield, 2007.

Burleson, Wayne, and Sandro Carrara. *Security and Privacy for Implantable Medical Devices*. New York: Springer, 2014.

Camp, L. Jean, and M. Eric Johnson. *The Economics of Financial and Medical Identity Theft*. New York: Springer, 2012.

Campbell, John Creighton, and Naoki Ikegami. *The Art of Balance in Health Policy: Maintaining Japan's Low-Cost, Egalitarian System*. Cambridge, UK: Cambridge University Press, 1998.

Carr, Nicholas G. *The Glass Cage: Automation and Us*. New York: W. W. Norton & Company, 2014.

Castagnoli, William G., and Medical Advertising Hall of Fame. *Medicine Ave.: The Story of Medical Advertising in America*. Huntington, NY: Medical Advertising Hall of Fame, 1999.

Christensen, Clayton M., Jerome H. Grossman, and Jason Hwang. *The Innovator's Prescription: A Disruptive Solution for Health Care*. New York: McGraw-Hill, 2009.

Dick, Richard S., Elaine B. Steen, and Don E. Detmer. *The Computer-Based Patient Record: An Essential Technology for Health Care*. Rev. ed. Washington, DC: National Academy Press, 1997.

Dilcher, Heinrich. *Buchenwald: 1937–1945: Ein SS-Konzentrationslager in Deutschland*. Hannover, Germany: Bund d. Antifaschisten Niedersachsen e.v. u. Heinrich Dilcher, 1981.

Ding, Min. *Innovation and Marketing in the Pharmaceutical Industry: Emerging Practices, Research, and Policies.* New York: Springer, 2013.

El Emam, Khaled, and Luk Arbuckle. *Anonymizing Health Data: Case Studies and Methods to Get You Started.* Beijing: O'Reilly, 2014.

El Emam, Khaled, editor. *Risky Business: Sharing Health Data While Protecting Privacy.* Bloomington, IN: Trafford, 2013.

Elliott, Carl. *White Coat, Black Hat: Adventures on the Dark Side of Medicine.* Boston: Beacon Press, 2010.

Ellsberg, Daniel. *Secrets: A Memoir of Vietnam and the Pentagon Papers.* New York: Viking, 2002.

Elston, Mary Ann, editor. *The Sociology of Medical Science and Technology.* Sociology of Health and Illness Monograph Series. Oxford, UK: Blackwell, 1997.

Farren, Julian. *The Train from Pittsburgh.* New York: A. A. Knopf, 1948.

Ferber, Robert, and Hugh C. Wales. *The Effectiveness of Pharmaceutical Promotion.* Illinois University Bureau of Economic and Business Research Bulletin Series. Urbana: University of Illinois, 1958.

Fishbein, Morris. *Tonics and Sedatives.* Philadelphia: J. B. Lippincott Co., 1949.

Fontenay, Charles L. *Estes Kefauver: A Biography.* Knoxville: University of Tennessee Press, 1980.

Gates, John J., and Bernard S. Arons. *Privacy and Confidentiality in Mental Health Care.* Baltimore: Paul H. Brookes Publishing, 2000.

Goetz, Thomas. *The Decision Tree: Taking Control of Your Health in the New Era of Personalized Medicine.* New York: Rodale, 2010.

Goldberg, Adele, and Association for Computing Machinery. *A History of Personal Workstations.* Reading, MA: Addison-Wesley, 1988.

Gorman, Joseph Bruce. *Kefauver: A Political Biography.* New York: Oxford University Press, 1971.

Gosselin, Chris, and Ray Gosselin. "Gosselins in the Twentieth Century." Unpublished manuscript, January 1999.

Gosselin, Ray. "History of the Determination of Market Share for Diethylstilbestrol in an Era Prior to the Development of Relative Denominator Values." PharmD thesis, University of South Carolina, 1995.

———. "Massachusetts Pharmacy Survey 1947." Master's thesis, Massachusetts College of Pharmacy, 1948.

———. "The Statistical Analysis of the Distributions and Trends of Prescriptions Dispensed in Massachusetts in 1950." MBA thesis, Boston University, 1951.

Graedon, Joe, and Teresa Graedon. *Top Screwups Doctors Make and How to Avoid Them.* New York: Crown Archetype, 2011.

Greene, Jeremy A., and Elizabeth Siegel Watkins. *Prescribed: Writing, Filling, Using, and Abusing the Prescription in Modern America.* Baltimore: Johns Hopkins University Press, 2012.

Greider, Katharine. *The Big Fix: How the Pharmaceutical Industry Rips Off American Consumers.* New York: Public Affairs, 2003.

Gross, Ken. *Ross Perot: The Man Behind the Myth.* New York: Random House, 1992.

Gunzert, Rudolf. *Konzentration, Markt Und Marktbeherrschung.* Frankfurt am Main: F. Knapp, 1961.

Haimowitz, Ira J. *Healthcare Relationship Marketing: Strategy, Design and Measurement.* Burlington, VT: Ashgate, 2010.

Hansert, Andreas. *Georg Hartmann (1870–1954): Biographie Eines Frankfurter Schriftgiessers, Bibliophilen Und Kunstmäzens.* Wien: Böhlau, 2009.

Harris, Richard. *The Real Voice.* New York: Macmillan, 1964.

Helmchen, H., and N. Sartorius. *Ethics in Psychiatry: European Contributions.* International Library of Ethics, Law and the New Medicine. Dordrecht: Springer, 2010.

Hu, Jun. *Privacy-Preserving Data Integration in Public Health Surveillance.* Ottawa: University of Ottawa, 2011.

Institute for Motivational Research. *A Research Study on Pharmaceutical Advertising.* Croton-on-Hudson, NY: Pharmaceutical Advertising Club, 1955

Jacquez, John A., and University of Michigan. *Computer Diagnosis and Diagnostic Methods: The Proceedings.* Springfield, IL: Thomas, 1972.

Johnson, Steven. *The Ghost Map: The Story of London's Most Terrifying Epidemic—and How It Changed Science, Cities, and the Modern World.* New York: Riverhead Books, 2006.

Kefauver, Estes, Irene Till, and Herbert Block. *In a Few Hands: Monopoly Power in America.* New York: Pantheon Books, 1965.

King, Patricia A., Judith C. Areen, and Lawrence O. Gostin. *Law, Medicine and Ethics.* New York: Foundation Press, 2006.

Klosek, Jacqueline. *Protecting Your Health Privacy: A Citizen's Guide to Safeguarding the Security of Your Medical Information.* Santa Barbara, CA: Praeger, 2011.

Knauss, Erwin. *Die Jüdische Bevölkerung Giessens, 1933–1945: E. Dokumentation.* Veröffentlichungen i.e. Schriften Der Kommission Für Die Geschichte Der Juden In Hessen. Wiesbaden: Kommission für die Geschichte der Juden in Hessen, 1974.

Kolassa, Eugene Mick, James Perkins, and Bruce Siecker. *Pharmaceutical Marketing: Principles, Environment, and Practice.* New York: Pharmaceutical Products Press, 2002.

Kremers, Edward, and Glenn Sonnedecker. *Kremers and Urdang's History of Pharmacy.* Philadelphia: American Institute of the History of Pharmacy, 1986.

Krieger, Fritz. "The Role of Pharmaceutical Marketing Research." Unpublished book manuscript, undated.

LaWall, Charles H. *Four Thousand Years of Pharmacy.* Philadelphia; London: J. B. Lippincott, 1927.

Lehmann, Harold P. *Aspects of Electronic Health Record Systems.* 2nd ed. Health Informatics Series. New York: Springer, 2006.

Lewis, Deborah. *Consumer Health Informatics: Informing Consumers and Improving Health Care.* Health Informatics. New York: Springer, 2005.

Lundsgaarde, Henry Peder, Pamela J. Fischer, and David J. Steele. *Human Problems in Computerized Medicine.* Publications in Anthropology. Lawrence: University of Kansas, 1981.

Maeder, Thomas. *Adverse Reactions.* New York: Morrow, 1994.

Mandel, William M. *Saying No to Power: Autobiography of a 20th Century Activist and Thinker.* Berkeley, CA: Creative Arts Book Co., 1999.

Maurer, P. Reed. *It's Worth Doing: Perspectives on the Japan Pharmaceutical Industry.* Bloomington, IN: Trafford, 2011.

McQuillan, Rufus L. *Is the Doctor In? The Story of a Drug Detail Man's Fifty Years of Public Relations with Doctors and Druggists.* New York: Exposition Press, 1963.

Meier, Barry. *Pain Killer: A "Wonder" Drug's Trail of Addiction and Death.* Emmaus, PA: Rodale, 2003.

Miller, Dinah, Annette Hanson, and Steven Roy Daviss. *Shrink Rap: Three Psychiatrists Explain Their Work.* Baltimore: Johns Hopkins University Press, 2011.

Mueller, Hanno. *Juden in Giessen 1788–1942.* Magistrat der Universitätsstadt Giessen, Stadtarchiv, 2012.

Neurath, Paul Martin, Christian Fleck, and Nico Stehr. *The Society of Terror: Inside the Dachau and Buchenwald Concentration Camps*. Boulder, CO: Paradigm Publishers, 2005.

Nielsen Company, A. C., John Karolefski, and Al Heller. *Consumer-Centric Category Management: How to Increase Profits by Managing Categories Based on Consumer Needs*. Hoboken, NJ: John Wiley & Sons, 2006.

Pathak, Dev S., Alan Escovitz, and Suzan Kucukarslan. *Promotion of Pharmaceuticals: Issues, Trends, Options*. New York: Pharmaceuticals Products Press, 1992.

Payton, Theresa, Ted Claypoole, and Howard A. Schmidt. *Privacy in the Age of Big Data: Recognizing Threats, Defending Your Rights, and Protecting Your Family*. Lanham, MD: Rowman & Littlefield, 2014.

Pentland, Alex. *Social Physics: How Good Ideas Spread—The Lessons from a New Science*. New York: Penguin, 2014.

Petersen, Melody. *Our Daily Meds: How the Pharmaceutical Companies Transformed Themselves into Slick Marketing Machines and Hooked the Nation on Prescription Drugs*. New York: Farrar, Straus and Giroux, 2008.

Pomeroy, Charles. *Pharma Delegates: Highlights from a Half-Century of Networking Within Japan's Pharmaceutical Industry*. Bloomington, IN: Trafford, 2013.

Reidy, Jamie. *Hard Sell: The Evolution of a Viagra Salesman*. Kansas City, MO: Andrews McMeel, 2005.

Rodwin, Marc A. *Conflicts of Interest and the Future of Medicine: The United States, France, and Japan*. Oxford, UK: Oxford University Press, 2011.

Rollins, Brent L., and Matthew Perri. *Pharmaceutical Marketing*. Burlington, MA: Jones & Bartlett Learning, 2014.

Rothstein, Mark A. *Genetic Secrets: Protecting Privacy and Confidentiality in the Genetic Era*. New Haven, CT: Yale University Press, 1997.

Shulman, Shelia R., Elaine M. Healy, and Louis Lasagna. *PBMs: Reshaping the Pharmaceutical Distribution Network*. New York: Pharmaceutical Products Press, 1998.

Slack, Warner. *Cybermedicine: How Computing Empowers Doctors and Patients for Better Care*. Rev. and updated ed. San Francisco: Jossey-Bass, 2001.

Smith, Mickey C. *Pharmaceutical Marketing: Principles, Environment, and Practice*. New York: Pharmaceutical Products Press, 2002.

———. *Principles of Pharmaceutical Marketing*. 3rd ed. Philadelphia: Lea & Febiger, 1983.

———. *Small Comfort: A History of the Minor Tranquilizers*. New York: Praeger, 1985.

Snow, John. *On the Mode of Communication of Cholera*. 2nd ed. London: J. Churchill, 1855.

Starr, Paul. *The Social Transformation of American Medicine*. New York: Basic Books, 1982.

Strom, Brian L. *Pharmacoepidemiology*. 4th ed. Hoboken, NJ: J. Wiley, 2005.

Tanner, Adam. *What Stays in Vegas: The World of Personal Data—Lifeblood of Big Business—and the End of Privacy as We Know It*. New York: PublicAffairs, 2014.

Taylor, Mark. *Genetic Data and the Law: A Critical Perspective on Privacy Protection*. Cambridge Bioethics and Law. Cambridge, UK: Cambridge University Press, 2012.

Technomic Publishing Company. *Marketing Guide to the Pharmaceuticals Industry*. Westport, CT: Technomic Publishing Company, 1973.

Tone, Andrea. *The Age of Anxiety: A History of America's Turbulent Affair with Tranquilizers*. New York: Basic Books, 2009.

Totten, Samuel, and William S. Parsons. *Centuries of Genocide: Essays and Eyewitness Accounts*. 4th ed. New York: Routledge, 2013.

Tzavaras, Kosta. *Pharmaceutical Sales Data 101, the Client Perspective*. Victoria, Canada: Phi Publications, 2004.

US Congress, Office of Technology Assessment. *Protecting Privacy in Computerized Medical Information*. Washington, DC: US Government Printing Office, 1993.

[US] Federal Committee on Statistical Methodology. *Report on Statistical Disclosure Limitation Methodology*. Edited by Statistical and Science Policy, Office of Information and Regulatory Affairs and Office of Management and Budget, 129, second version, December 2005.

US House, Select Committee on Small Business, Subcommittee on Environmental Problems Affecting Small Business. *Third Party Prepaid Prescription Programs*. Washington, DC: US Government Printing Office, 1971.

US Institute of Medicine, Committee on Improving the Patient Record. *The Computer-Based Patient Record: An Essential Technology for Health Care*. Washington, DC: National Academy Press, 1991.

Warrell, D. A., Timothy M. Cox, and John D. Firth. *Oxford Textbook of Medicine*. 5th ed. 3 vols. Oxford, UK: Oxford University Press, 2010.

Weed, Lawrence L. *Knowledge Coupling: New Premises and New Tools for Medical Care and Education*. Computers in Health Care. New York: Springer-Verlag, 1991.

———. *Medical Records, Medical Education, and Patient Care: The Problem-Oriented Record as a Basic Tool*. Cleveland: Press of Case Western Reserve University, 1969.

———. *Your Health Care and How to Manage It: Your Health, Your Problems, Your Plans, Your Progress*. Burlington, VT: PROMIS Laboratory, University of Vermont, 1975.

Weed, Lawrence L., Jay S. Wakefield, Stephen R. Yarnall, Washington State Medical Record Association, and Washington/Alaska Regional Medical Program. *Implementing the Problem-Oriented Medical Record*. Seattle: Medical Computer Services Association, 1973.

Weed, Lawrence L., and Lincoln Weed. *Medicine in Denial*. CreateSpace Independent Publishing Platform, 2011.

Wells, Tom. *Wild Man: The Life and Times of Daniel Ellsberg*. New York: Palgrave, 2001.

Westin, Alan F. *Information Technology in a Democracy*. Harvard Studies in Technology and Society. Cambridge, MA: Harvard University Press, 1971.

Articles and Reports

Abelson, Reed. "4 Insurers Will Supply Health Data." *New York Times*, September 19, 2011.

Adams, Chris. "Doctors 'Dine 'N' Dash' in Style, as Drug Firms Pick up the Tab." *Wall Street Journal*, May 14, 2001.

Aitken, Murray, Thomas Altmann, and Daniel Rosen. "Engaging Patients Through Social Media: Is Healthcare Ready for Empowered and Digitally Demanding Patients?" Parsippany, NJ: IMS Institute for Healthcare Informatics, January 2014.

Albert, Sherri. "Medical Privacy: The Data Wars." *Dissent* (2002): 8–11.

Alden, William, and Michael De La Merced. "Hurt in Crisis, TPG Pursues Smaller Deals." *New York Times*, March 24, 2014.

Allen, Anita. "Commercial Speech Bruises Health Privacy in the Supreme Court." *The Hastings Center Report* 41, no. 6:2 (November-December 2011).

Archives of Internal Medicine editorial. "The Challenge and the Opportunities of the Weed System." *Archives of Internal Medicine* 128, no. 5 (November 1, 1971): 832–34.

Avorn, Jerry. "Healing the Overwhelmed Physician." *New York Times*, June 1, 2013.

Avorn, Jerry, and S. B. Soumerai. "Improving Drug-Therapy Decisions Through Educational Outreach: A Randomized Controlled Trial of Academically Based 'Detailing.'" *New England Journal of Medicine* 308, no. 24 (1983): 1457–63.

Barbaro, Michael, and Tom Zeller Jr. "A Face Is Exposed for AOL Searcher No. 4417749." *New York Times*, August 9, 2006.

Barber, Grayson. "Electronic Health Records and the End of Anonymity." *New Jersey Law Journal* 198, no. 3 (October 19, 2009): 2.

Barrett, Tom. "Doctors Launch Attack on Drug Firms." *Edmonton Journal*, 2003.

Bayer, Ronald, and Amy Fairchild. "When Worlds Collide: Health Surveillance, Privacy, and Public Policy." *Social Research: An International Quarterly* 77, no. 3 (2014): 905–28.

Belopotosky, Danielle. "Partisan Rift over Patient Privacy." *National Journal*, July 1, 2006, 2.

Bhagwat, Ashutosh. "Sorrell v. IMS Health: Details, Detailing, and the Death of Privacy." *Vermont Law Review* 36, no. 4 (June 2012).

Blakenhorn, Kathy, and Lisa Stockwell-Morris. "Crossing the Great Divide." *Pharmaceutical Executive Supplement*, March 2004.

Bogdan, Herman A. "Felix Marti Ibanez—Iberian Daedalus: The Man Behind the Essays." *Journal of the Royal Society of Medicine* 86, no. 4 (October 1993).

Boumil, Marcia M., Kaitlyn Dunn, Nancy Ryan, and Katrina Clearwater. "Prescription Data Mining, Medical Privacy and the First Amendment: The U.S. Supreme Court in Sorrell v. IMS Health Inc." *Annals of Health Law* 21, no. 2 (Winter 2012).

Brand, Ron. "Detailing Gets Personal." *Pharmaceutical Executive*, August 1, 2003.

Breese, P., and W. Burman. "Readability of Notice of Privacy Forms Used by Major Health Care Institutions." *Journal of the American Medical Association* 293, no. 13 (2005): 1593–94.

Brooks, J. M., W. R. Doucette, S. Wan, and D. G. Klepser. "Retail Pharmacy Market Structure and Performance." *Inquiry* 45, no. 1 (2008): 75–88.

Brownlee, Shannon, and Jeanne Lenzer. "Spin Doctored." *Slate*, May 31, 2005.

Buckman, Rebecca. "Investing in Fixer-Uppers." *Forbes*, September 7, 2009, 42–44.

Caine, K., S. Kohn, C. Lawrence, R. Hanania, E. M. Meslin, and W. M. Tierney. "Designing a Patient-Centered User Interface for Access Decisions About EHR Data: Implications from Patient Interviews." *Journal of General Internal Medicine* 30, suppl. 1 (2015): S7–S16.

Caine, K., and W. M. Tierney. "Point and Counterpoint: Patient Control of Access to Data in Their Electronic Health Records." *Journal of General Internal Medicine* 30, suppl. 1 (2015): S38–S41.

Cantrill, Stephen. "Computers in Patient Care: The Promise and the Challenge." *Queue* (2010): 20–27.

Cardinale, V. "A Privacy Debate." *Drug Topics* (1998): 2.

Carlat, Daniel. "Dr. Drug Rep." *New York Times*, November 25, 2007.

Carter, Bill. "A. C. Nielsen Jr., Who Built Ratings Firm, Dies at 92." *New York Times*, October 4, 2011.

Cartwright-Smith, Lara, and Nancy Lopez. "Law and the Public's Health." *Public Health Reports* 128 (January–February 2013): 3.

Castagnoli, William. "Remembrance of Kings Past." *Medical Marketing & Media*, July 1996, 5.

———. "There Were Giants in Those Days." *Medical Marketing & Media*, March 1997, 26–42.

Cate, Fred H. "Protecting Privacy in Health Research: The Limits of Individual Choice." *California Law Review* 1765 (2010). http://scholarship.law.berkeley .edu/californialawreview/vol98/iss6/2 .

Chibber, Kabir. "VNU to Buy IMS Health for $7 Billion." Dow Jones, July 11, 2005.

Chithelen, Ignatius. "A Health Opportunity." *Forbes*, 1992, 46–47.

Cole, Agatha. "Internet Advertising After Sorrell v. IMS Health: A Discussion on Privacy and the First Amendment." *Cardozo Arts & Entertainment Law Journal* 30, no. 283 (2012).

Collins, Michael, and Deborah C. Peel. "Should Every Patient Have a Unique ID Number for All Medical Records?" *Wall Street Journal*, January 23, 2012.

Conn, Joseph. "A Flawed System." *Modern Healthcare*, January 26, 2013.

———. "Questions of Privacy." *Modern Healthcare*, January 28, 2013.

Cook, Gordon. "A Medical Revolution That Could . . . : The Work of the PROMIS Laboratory and Lawrence L. Weed, M.D." Center for Occupational and Professional Assessment, Educational Testing Service, Princeton, NJ, September 29, 1978.

Couzin-Frankel, Jennifer. "Trust Me, I'm a Medical Researcher." *Science*, January 30, 2015, 3.

Danciu, I., J. D. Cowan, M. Basford, X. Wang, A. Saip, S. Osgood, J. Shirey-Rice, J. Kirby, and P. A. Harris. "Secondary Use of Clinical Data: The Vanderbilt Approach." *Journal of Biomedical Informatics* 52 (2014): 28–35.

Datta, Anusua, and Dhaval M. Dave. "Effects of Physician-Directed Pharmaceutical Promotion on Prescription Behaviors: Longitudinal Evidence." Working paper 19592. National Bureau of Economic Research, Cambridge, MA, November 2013.

Demkovich, Linda E. "Controlling Health Care Costs at General Motors." *Health Affairs* 5, no. 3 (August 1986): 358–67.

Der Spiegel. "Kopfweh Wird Mitgeliefert." *Der Spiegel*, October 1963.

DeSalvo, K. B., and K. Mertz. "Broadening the View of Interoperability to Include Person-Centeredness." *Journal of General Internal Medicine* 30, suppl. 1 (2015): S1–S2.

Donohue, Julie. "A History of Drug Advertising: The Evolving Roles of Consumers and Consumer Protection." *Milbank Quarterly* 84, no. 4 (2006): 659–99.

Dormuth, Colin, et al. "Higher Potency Statins and the Risk of New Diabetes: Multicentre, Observational Study of Administrative Databases." *British Medical Journal* (2014): 348:g3244.

Dougherty, Philip. "Advertising: B&B in New Health Field Bid." *New York Times*, April 6, 1972.

———. "Advertising: Frohlich in General Practice." *New York Times*, March 3, 1970, 62.

———. "Advertising: Getting Along with the FDA." *New York Times*, December 11, 1966.

———. "Advertising: President of Frohlich Resigns." *New York Times*, January 25, 1972.

Douple, E. B., et al. "Long-Term Radiation-Related Health Effects in a Unique Human Population: Lessons Learned from the Atomic Bomb Survivors of Hiroshima and Nagasaki." *Disaster Medicine and Public Health Preparedness* 5, suppl. 1 (2011): S122–S133.

Doyle, James J. "Longitudinal Patient Data: Rx for Better Decisions." *Medical Marketing & Media*, September 1998.

Dredze, Mark, Renyuan Cheng, Michael J. Paul, and David Broniatowski. "Health tweets.org: A Platform for Public Health Surveillance Using Twitter." Association

for the Advancement of Artificial Intelligence, 2014. http://www.aaai.org
/ocs/index.php/WS/AAAIW14/paper/viewFile/8723/8218.

Dwoskin, Elizabeth. "The Next Marketing Frontier: Your Medical Records." *Wall Street Journal*, March 3, 2015.

Eisen, Marc. "Epic Systems: Epic Tale." *Isthmus*, June 20, 2008.

Elliott, Carl. "The Drug Pushers." *Atlantic*, April 2006.

Ellis, Barbara. "Theme and Variation." *Forbes*, February 4, 1980.

Emam, K. E., F. K. Dankar, R. Vaillancourt, T. Roffey, and M. Lysyk. "Evaluating the Risk of Re-Identification of Patients from Hospital Prescription Records." *Canadian Journal of Hospital Pharmacy* 62, no. 4 (2009): 307–19.

Etzioni, Amitai. "The New Enemy of Privacy: Big Bucks." *Challenge* 43, no. 3 (May–June 2000): 16.

Evans, Barbara J. "Much Ado About Data Ownership." *Harvard Journal of Law and Technology* 69 (Fall 2011): 69–130.

Executive Office of the President. *Big Data: Seizing Opportunities, Preserving Values*. The White House. Washington DC: Executive Office of the President, May 1, 2014.

Fabian, Gary. "What Does IMS Do with Your Rx Data?" *Pharmacy Post* 10, no. 10 (2002): 12.

Faughnder, Ryan. "Kravis Backs N.Y. Startups Using Apps to Cut Health Costs: Tech." *Bloomberg*, December 4, 2012.

Ferris, Andy, David Moore, Nathan Pohle, and Priyanka Srivastava. "Big Data: What Is It, How Is It Collected, and How Might Life Insurers Use It?" *Actuary Magazine*, December 2013/January 2014.

Fleming, N. S., S. D. Culler, R. McCorkle, E. R. Becker, and D. J. Ballard. "The Financial and Nonfinancial Costs of Implementing Electronic Health Records in Primary Care Practices." *Health Affairs (Millwood)* 30, no. 3 (2011): 481–89.

Flynn, Sean. "The Constitutionality of State Regulation of Prescription Data Mining." *Pharmaceutical Law and Industry* 5, no. 43 (2007).

Freudenheim, Milt. "Insurers vs. Doctors: A Software Battleground." *New York Times*, November 15, 1989.

———. "And You Thought a Prescription Was Private." *New York Times*, August 8, 2009.

———. "Business and Health; Why I.M.S. Lures Dun & Bradstreet." *New York Times*, February 9, 1988.

———. "Digitizing Health Records, Before It Was Cool." *New York Times*, January 14, 2012.

Frohlich, L. W. "The Physician and the Pharmaceutical Industry in the United States." *Proceedings of the Royal Society of Medicine* 53, no. 579 (1960): 1–8.

Fugh-Berman, Adriane. "Prescription Tracking and Public Health." *Journal of General Internal Medicine* 23, no. 8 (2008): 4.

Fugh-Berman, Adriane, and Shahram Ahari. "Following the Script: How Drug Reps Make Friends and Influence Doctors." *PLoS Medicine* 4, no. 4 (April 2007): 5, doi:10.1371/journal.pmed.0040150.

Furman, Bess. "U.S. Scientist Held Outside Jobs, Flemming Tells Drug Inquiry." *New York Times*, 1960.

Garber, Steven, Susan Gates, Emmett Keeler, Mary Vaiana, Andrew Mulcahy, Christopher Lau, and Arthur Kellermann, "Redirecting Innovation in U.S. Health Care: Options to Decrease Spending and Increase Value." *RAND Health*, 2014.

Geyelin, Milo. "Do Prescription Records Stay Private When Pharmacy Stores Are Sold?" *Wall Street Journal*, April 11, 2001.

Gibson, T. C., W. E. Thorton, W. P. Algary, and E. Craige. "Telecardiography and the Use of Simple Computers." *New England Journal of Medicine* 267 (1962): 1218–24.

Gillum, Richard F. "From Papyrus to the Electronic Tablet: A Brief History of the Clinical Medical Record with Lessons for the Digital Age." *American Journal of Medicine* 126, no. 10 (October 2013): 853–57.

Glazer, Kenneth. "The IMS Health Case: A U.S. Perspective." *George Mason Law Review* (July 2006).

Glenn, T., and S. Monteith. "Privacy in the Digital World: Medical and Health Data Outside of HIPAA Protections." *Current Psychiatry Reports* 16, no. 11 (2014): 494.

Glueck, Grace. "An Art Collector Sows Largesse and Controversy." *New York Times*, June 5, 1983.

———. "Dr. Arthur Sackler Dies at 73; Philanthropist and Art Patron." *New York Times*, May 27, 1987.

Goldman, J., and Z. Hudson. "Virtually Exposed: Privacy and E-Health." *Health Affairs (Millwood)* 19, no. 6 (2000): 140–48.

Goren, Ashley. "A Gold Mine of Information: Using Pharmaceutical Data Mining to Ensure Long-Term Safety and Effectiveness of Pharmaceuticals." LLM thesis, University of Toronto, 2013.

Gostin, Lawrence. "Marketing Pharmaceuticals: A Constitutional Right to Sell Prescriber-Identified Data?" *Journal of the American Medical Association* (February 22–29, 2012): 2.

Graham, Rosalyn. "The Symptom Sleuths." *Business People–Vermont*, 2006.

Grande, D. "A National Survey of Physician-Industry Relationships." *New England Journal of Medicine* 357, no. 5 (2007): 507–8 (author reply on p. 8).

Greene, Jeremy A. "Pharmaceutical Marketing Research and the Prescribing Physician." *Annals of Internal Medicine* 146, no. 10 (2007): 742–48.

Gunter, T. D., and N. P. Terry. "The Emergence of National Electronic Health Record Architectures in the United States and Australia: Models, Costs, and Questions." *Journal of Medical Internet Research* 7, no. 1 (2005): e3.

Gupta, Udayan. "Talking Strategy: Small Firms Aren't Waiting to Grow Up to Go Global." *Wall Street Journal*, December 5, 1989.

Gymrek, M., A. L. McGuire, D. Golan, E. Halperin, and Y. Erlich. "Identifying Personal Genomes by Surname Inference." *Science* 339, no. 6117 (2013): 321–24.

Halamka, J. D., K. D. Mandl, and P. C. Tang. "Early Experiences with Personal Health Records." *Journal of the American Medical Informatics Association* 15, no. 1 (2008): 1–7.

Hanson, C. L., S. H. Burton, C. Giraud-Carrier, J. H. West, M. D. Barnes, and B. Hansen. "Tweaking and Tweeting: Exploring Twitter for Nonmedical Use of a Psychostimulant Drug (Adderall) Among College Students." *Journal of Medical Internet Research* 15, no. 4 (2013).

Harris, Gardiner. "As Doctor Writes Prescription, Drug Company Writes a Check." *New York Times*, June 27, 2004.

Harrison, P. J., and Sam Ramanujan. "Electronic Medical Records: Great Idea or Great Threat to Privacy?" *Review of Business Information Systems*, first quarter 2011.

Hatzopoulos, Vassilis. "Case C-418/01, IMS Health GmbH v. NDC Health GmbH, Judgment of the Fifth Chamber of 29 April 2004, Nyr." *Common Market Law Review* 41, no. 6 (December 2004): 26.

Hawkins, Norman. "The Detailman and Preference Behavior." *Southwestern Social Science Quarterly* 40, no. 3 (December 1959): 12.

Healthcare Information and Management Systems Society. "Electronic Health Records: A Global Perspective." Edited by HIMSS Enterprise Systems

Steering Committee and the Global Enterprise Task Force: Healthcare Information and Management Systems Society, August, 2010.

Heesters, Michael. "An Assault on the Business of Pharmaceutical Data Mining." *University of Pennsylvania Journal of Business Law* 11, no. 3 (Spring 2009): 40.

Hensley, Scott. "Drug Industry Moves to Curb 'Dine and Dash' Marketing." *Wall Street Journal*, April 19, 2002.

Hersh, William R. "The Electronic Medical Record: Promises and Problems." *Journal of the American Society for Information Science*, no. 10 (1995).

Hogg, Jason. "Diagnosing MD Behavior." *Pharmaceutical Executive*, May 2005, 3.

Homer, Patrick, Craig Nestel, Mark Weadon, and Daniel Feldman. "A Revolution in Physician Targeting." SAS Institute, July 2009.

Hong, Cheng William, Edward C. Hsiao, Andrew E. Horvai, and Thomas M. Link. "Chronic Recurrent Multifocal Osteomyelitis with an Atypical Presentation in an Adult Man." *Journal of the International Skeletal Society* (March 17, 2015). Archived at http://perma.cc/EXE9-YBWC.

Hooley, Sean, and Latanya Sweeney. "Survey of Publicly Available State Health Databases." White paper 1075-1. Data Privacy Lab, Harvard University, Cambridge, MA, June 2013. Archived at http://perma.cc/FZ47-W8AE.

Horwitz, Nathan. "Arthur M. Sackler, M.D." *Medical Tribune*, June 10, 1987, front and back cover.

Hsiou, Melody Rene. "Pharmaceutical Company Data Mining in the Aftermath of Sorrell v. IMS Health: The Need for Comprehensive Federal Legislation to Protect Patient Privacy." *Student Scholarship, Seton Hall Law eRepository* 244 (May 1, 2013).

Hughes, Allen. "WNCN Will Drop Classical Music." *New York Times*, August 28, 1974.

IMS Health. "IMS Health Announces Integration of Anonymized Patient-Level Data Across Global Portfolio of Offerings." *Business Wire*, November 28, 2006.

Jacobs, L. "Interview with Lawrence Weed, MD—the Father of the Problem-Oriented Medical Record Looks Ahead." *Permanente Journal* 13, no. 3 (2009): 84–89.

Jaret, Peter. "Mining Electronic Records for Revealing Health Data." *New York Times*, January 14, 2015.

Jung, Sue. "This Doctor's Bag Holds a Computer." *Boston Globe*, August 3, 1987.

Kallukaran, Paul, and Jerry Kagan. "Data Mining at IMS Health: How We Turned a Mountain of Data into a Few Information-Rich Molehills." Paper 127. In *Proceedings of the 24th Annual SAS Users Group International*, 1999. Archived at https://is.gd/EeUHBn.

Kantrowitz, J. L. "Privacy and Disclosure in Psychoanalysis." *Journal of the American Psychoanalytic Association* 57, no. 4 (2009): 787–806.

Kaplan, B. "Selling Health Data: De-Identification, Privacy, and Speech." *Cambridge Quarterly of Healthcare Ethics* 24, no. 3 (2015): 256–71.

Kaplan, D. M. "Clear Writing, Clear Thinking and the Disappearing Art of the Problem List." *Journal of Hospital Medicine* 2, no. 4 (2007): 199–202.

Kaye, Kate. "Sophisticated Health Data Industry Needs Self-Reflection." *Advertising Age*, March 23, 2015.

Kayyali, Basel, David Knott, and Steve Van Kuiken. "The Big-Data Revolution in US Health Care: Accelerating Value and Innovation." McKinsey & Company, April 2013.

Kim, H. J., and J. P. Ruger. "Pharmaceutical Reform in South Korea and the Lessons It Provides." *Health Affairs (Millwood)* 27, no. 4 (2008): w260–w69.

Kohane, I. S., and R. B. Altman. "Health-Information Altruists: A Potentially Critical Resource." *New England Journal of Medicine* 353, no. 19 (2005): 2074–77.

Kohane, I. S., K. D. Mandl, P. L. Taylor, I. A. Holm, D. J. Nigrin, and L. M. Kunkel. "Medicine: Reestablishing the Researcher-Patient Compact." *Science* 316, no. 5826 (2007): 836–37.

Kolata, Gina. "The Health Care Debate: Finding What Works." *New York Times,* August 9, 1994.

———. "When Patients' Records Are Commodities for Sale." *New York Times,* November 15, 1995.

Kowalczyk, Liz. "Drug Companies Secret Reports Outrage Doctors." *Boston Globe,* May 25, 2003.

———. "As Records Go Online, Clash over Mental Care Privacy." *Boston Globe,* June 21, 2012.

Krogh, Egil. "The Break-in That History Forgot." *New York Times,* June 30, 2007.

Kuczynski, Kay, and Patty Gibbs-Wahlberg. "HIPAA the Health Care Hippo: Despite the Rhetoric, Is Privacy Still an Issue?" *Social Work,* 50, no. 3 (July 2005): 283–87.

Kuehn, Alfred. "Analysis of the Dynamics of Consumer Behavior and Its Implications for Marketing Management." PhD dissertation, Carnegie Institute of Technology, Pittsburgh, 1958.

Kuehn, B. M. "Growing Use of Genomic Data Reveals Need to Improve Consent and Privacy Standards." *Journal of the American Medical Association* 309, no. 20 (2013): 2083–84.

———. "More Than One-Third of US Individuals Use the Internet to Self-Diagnose." *Journal of the American Medical Association* 309, no. 8 (2013): 756–57.

Lamberg, Lynne. "Confidentiality and Privacy of Electronic Medical Records." *Journal of the American Medical Association* 285, no. 24 (June 27, 2001): 2.

Lancet. "Striking the Right Balance Between Privacy and Public Good." *Lancet* 367, no. 9507 (2006): 275.

Lawrence, Edward, Jane Qing Jiang Qu, and Ellen Briskin. "An Overview of Pharmacy Benefit Managers: Focus on the Consumer." Edited by College of Business Administration University of Missouri–St. Louis, June 1, 2012.

Lazarus, David. "CVS Thinks $50 Is Enough Reward for Giving Up Healthcare Privacy." *Los Angeles Times,* August 15, 2013.

Le, Net. "Intellectual Property Protection for Non-Innovative Markets: The Case of IMS Health." *Erasmus Law and Economics Review* 2, no. 1 (March 2006): 12.

Lear, John. "Scandal in the Drug Market." *New Scientist,* June 16, 1960, 1.

Ledley, Robert S., and Lee B. Lusted. "Reasoning Foundations of Medical Diagnosis." *Science,* New Series, 130, no. 3366 (July 3, 1959): 9–21.

Lee, Christopher. "Doctors, Legislators Resist Drugmakers' Prying Eyes." *Washington Post,* May 22, 2007.

Lee, L. M., and L. O. Gostin. "Ethical Collection, Storage, and Use of Public Health Data: A Proposal for a National Privacy Protection." *Journal of the American Medical Association* 302, no. 1 (2009): 82–84.

Lenzner, Robert. "A Financial Man and the Fogg." *Boston Globe,* February 16, 1982.

Leventhal, J. C., J. A. Cummins, P. H. Schwartz, D. K. Martin, and W. M. Tierney. "Designing a System for Patients Controlling Providers' Access to Their Electronic Health Records: Organizational and Technical Challenges." *Journal of General Internal Medicine* 30, suppl. 1 (2015): S17–S24.

Li, Li, et al. "Identification of Type 2 Diabetes Subgroups Through Topological Analysis of Patient Similarity." *Science Translational Medicine* 7, no. 311 (October 28, 2015): 311ra174.

Libert, Timothy. "Privacy Implications of Health Information Seeking on the Web." *Communications of the ACM* 58, no. 3 (March 2015): 10.

Liebman, Milton. "Solo Flight of IMS and Change for Market Research." *Medical Marketing & Media*, March 1998, 2.

Lohr, Steve. "The Healing Power of Your Own Medical Records." *New York Times*, March 31, 2015.

Lyles, A. "Direct Marketing of Pharmaceuticals to Consumers." *Annual Review of Public Health* 23 (2002): 73–91.

Mack, John. "Whose Data Is It Anyway?" *Pharma Marketing News* 5, no. 6 (June 2006).

Malin, Bradley, Latanya Sweeney, and Elaine Newton. "Trail Re-Identification: Learning Who You Are from Where You Have Been." No. LIDAP-WP12. Carnegie Mellon University, Laboratory for International Data Privacy, Pittsburgh, March 2003.

Martin, Douglas. "Robert Louis-Dreyfus, Turnaround Specialist, Dies at 63." *New York Times*, July 14, 2009.

May, Charles. "Selling Drugs By 'Educating' Physicians." *Journal of Medical Education* 36, no. 1 (January 1961): 36.

McFadyen, Richard E. "The FDA's Regulation and Control of Antibiotics in the 1950s: The Henry Welch Scandal, Félix Martí-Ibáñez, and Charles Pfizer & Co." *Bulletin of the History of Medicine* 53, no. 2 (1979): 11.

McGraw, D. "Building Public Trust in Uses of Health Insurance Portability and Accountability Act De-Identified Data." *Journal of the American Medical Informatics Association* 20, no. 1 (2013): 29–34.

Meslin, E. M., and P. H. Schwartz. "How Bioethics Principles Can Aid Design of Electronic Health Records to Accommodate Patient Granular Control." *Journal of General Internal Medicine* 30, suppl. 1 (2015): S3–S6.

Miller, Brad, Ling Huang, A. D. Joseph, and J. D. Tygar. "I Know Why You Went to the Clinic: Risks and Realization of HTTPS Traffic Analysis." In *Privacy Enhancing Technologies: 14th International Symposium*, PETS 2014, Amsterdam, The Netherlands, July 16–18, 2014, Proceedings, edited by Emiliano De Cristofaro and Steven J. Murdoch, 143–163. Cham, Switzerland: Springer, 2014.

Miller, Kristina. "Shrinking Drug Costs Without Silencing Pharmaceutical Detailers: Maryland's Options After Sorrell v. IMS Health." *Journal of Health Care Law and Policy* 16, no. 215 (2013).

Milne, Celia. "Following the Script." *Medical Post* 38, no. 45 (2002): 32–33.

Mitka, Mike. "New HIPAA Rule Aims to Improve Privacy and Security of Patient Records." *Journal of the American Medical Association* 309, no. 9 (March 6, 2013): 861–62.

Morris, Lisa. "Same Market, New Opportunities." IMS Health, 2006.

Moukheiber, Zina. "An Interview with the Most Powerful Woman in Health Care." *Forbes*, May 15, 2013.

———. "Epic Systems' Tough Billionaire." *Forbes*, April 18, 2012.

Mullin, Joe. "States Consider Limits on Medical Data-Mining." Associated Press, April 7, 2007.

Mushlin, Alvin, et al. "Anonymous Linking of Distributed Databases." In *Mini-Sentinel:* Sentinel Initiative, August 30, 2013. Archived at https://perma.cc /GYL7-NCZT. Mini-Sentinel is an FDA-sponsored pilot project to monitor the safety of the agency's regulated medical products.

Nakashima, Ellen. "Prescription Data Used to Assess Consumers." *Washington Post*, August 4, 2008.

Narayanan, Arvind, and Vitaly Shmatikov. "Robust De-Anonymization of Large Sparse Datasets." *29 Proceedings of the 2008 IEEE Symposium on Security and Privacy* 111 (2008).

National Health Policy Forum. "The ABCs of PBMs." Washington, DC: George Washington University, October 27, 1999.

New York Civil Liberties Union. "Protecting Patient Privacy: Strategies for Regulating Electronic Health Records Exchange." New York Civil Liberties Union, New York, March 2012.

New York Times. "Biggest Health Agency Is for Sale." *New York Times*, January 1972.

———. "Dr. Felix Marti-Ibanez Is Dead; Psychiatrist and Publisher, 60." *New York Times*, May 25, 1972.

———. "L. W. Frohlich; Led Ad Agency." *New York Times*, September 29, 1971.

———. "W. D. M'adams, 68, Advertising Man." *New York Times*, August 16, 1954.

Neyhart, Susan. "Using Data Mining to Get Brand Switching." *Medical Marketing & Media* 33, no. 4 (1998): 3.

Nielsen, A. C. "Greater Prosperity Through Marketing Research: The First 40 Years of A. C. Nielsen Company," Newcomen Address, Newcomen Society in North America, New York, 1964.

Nunley, Ryan, and the Washington Health Policy Fellows. "Habit-Forming: Access to Physician Prescribing Patterns." American Academy of Orthopaedic Surgeons (November 2007). Archived at https://perma.cc/CYW9-V6XZ.

Office of the National Coordinator for Health Information Technology. "Report on Health Information Blocking." ONC, Department of Health and Human Services, Washington, DC, April 2015.

Onishi, Norimitsu. "Japan, Seeking Trim Waists, Measures Millions." *New York Times*, June 13, 2008.

O'Reilly, Kevin. "Doctors Increasingly Close Doors to Drug Reps, While Pharma Cuts Ranks." *American Medical News*, March 23, 2009.

Ornstein, Charles. "Big Data + Big Pharma = Big Money." *Pro Publica*, January 10, 2014.

Palad, Isabelle. "'Physician Privacy' Unabridged: How Prescription Data-Mining Catalyzed a Debate on Competing Visions of the Medical Profession." Master's thesis, Carleton University, Ottawa, May 2011.

Pear, Robert. "Privacy Issue Complicates Push to Link Medical Data." *New York Times*, January 17, 2009.

———. "Tech Rivalries Impede Digital Medical Record Sharing." *New York Times*, May 26, 2015.

Pines, W. L. "A History and Perspective on Direct-to-Consumer Promotion." *Food and Drug Law Journal* 54, no. 4 (1999): 489–518.

Ponemon Institute. *Fifth Annual Study on Medical Identity Theft.* Traverse City, MI: Ponemon Institute, February 2015.

Porter, C. Christine. "De-Identified Data and Third Party Data Mining: The Risk of Re-Identification of Personal Information." *Washington Journal of Law, Technology & Arts* no. 1 (September 23, 2008).

Presser, L., M. Hruskova, H. Rowbottom, and J. Kancir. "Care.Data and Access to UK Health Records: Patient Privacy and Public Trust." *Technology Science* (August 11, 2015), http://techscience.org/a/2015081103.

PricewaterhouseCoopers. "Transforming Healthcare Through Secondary Use of Health Data." PricewaterhouseCoopers, New York, 2009.

Puris, Martin. "Bringing Back Adidas." *Advertising Age*, March 8, 1999.

Ray, Wayne, Michael Stein, James Daugherty, Kathi Hall, Patrick Arbogast, and Marie Griffin. "COX-2 Selective Non-Steroidal Anti-inflammatory Drugs and Risk of Serious Coronary Heart Disease." *Lancet* 360, no. 9339 (2002): 1071–73.

Richards, T. "Court Sanctions Use of Anonymised Patient Data." *British Medical Journal* 320, no. 7227 (2000): 77B.

Robertson, Jordan. "The Big Business of Selling Prescription-Drug Records." *Bloomberg*, December 11, 2014.

Robertson, Jordan, and Shannon Pettypiece. "They Know You Buy Viagra and They Want to Sell You More." *Bloomberg*, December 10, 2014.

Rodwin, Marc A. "Patient Data: Property, Privacy & the Public Interest." *American Journal of Law Medicine* 36, no. 4 (2010): 586–618.

———. "The Case for Public Ownership of Patient Data." *Journal of the American Medical Association* 302, no. 1 (July 1, 2009): 86–88.

Rosenbloom, S. T., P. Harris, J. Pulley, M. Basford, J. Grant, A. DuBuisson, and R. L. Rothman. "The Mid-South Clinical Data Research Network." *Journal of the American Medical Informatics Association* 21, no. 4 (2014): 627–32.

Rothstein, Mark A., and M. K. Talbott. "Compelled Disclosure of Health Information: Protecting Against the Greatest Potential Threat to Privacy." *Journal of the American Medical Association* 295, no. 24 (2006): 2882–85.

Ruge, Richard. "Regulation of Prescription Drug Advertising: Medical Progress and Private Enterprise." *Law and Contemporary Problems* 32 (Fall 1967): 24.

Sanchez, Jesus. "Dun Agrees to Buy Health Care Database Firm: IMS to Get $1.7 Billion in Stock, Remain Separate." *Los Angeles Times*, February 8, 1988.

Saul, Stephanie. "Court Strikes Law Barring Sale of Drug Data." *New York Times*, May 1, 2007.

———. "Doctors Object as Drug Makers Learn Who's Prescribing What." *New York Times*, May 4, 2006.

Scarf, Maggie. "Secrets for Sale." *Social Research* (Spring 2001): 333–38.

Schisgall, Oscar. "International House: Bulwark Against War." *Rotarian*, September 1968, 24.

Schultz, Jan, Stephen Cantrill, and Keith Morgan. "An Initial Operational Problem Oriented Medical Record System—for Storage, Manipulation and Retrieval of Medical Data." In *Proceedings of the May 18–20, 1971, Spring Joint Computer Conference, Atlantic City, N.J.*, edited by Nathaniel Macon, 239–64. Montvale, NJ: AFIPS Press, 1971.

Schwartz, P. H., K. Caine, S. A. Alpert, E. M. Meslin, A. E. Carroll, and W. M. Tierney. "Patient Preferences in Controlling Access to Their Electronic Health Records: A Prospective Cohort Study in Primary Care." *Journal of General Internal Medicine* 30, suppl. 1 (2015): S25–S30.

Shalo, Sibyl, and Joanna Breitstein. "Getting Hip to HIPAA." *Pharmaceutical Executive* 21, no. 10 (2001): 88–90.

Shapiro, S., and S. H. Baron. "Prescriptions for Psychotropic Drugs in a Noninstitutional Population." *Public Health Reports* 76, no. 6 (1961): 481–88.

Sheikh, A., A. Jha, K. Cresswell, F. Greaves, and D. W. Bates. "Adoption of Electronic Health Records in UK Hospitals: Lessons from the USA." *Lancet* 384, no. 9937 (2014): 8–9.

Sherry, Mike. "Cerner Finds a Treasure in Data Mining." *Kansas City Star*, May 31, 2009.

Shima, D., Y. Ii, Y. Yamamoto, S. Nagayasu, Y. Ikeda, and Y. Fujimoto. "A Retrospective, Cross-Sectional Study of Real-World Values of Cardiovascular Risk Factors Using a Healthcare Database in Japan." *BMC Cardiovascular Disorders* 14 (2014): 120.

Shimizu, Eiko, and Kazuo Kawahara. "Assessment of Medical Information Databases to Estimate Patient Numbers." *Japan Journal of Pharmacoepidemiology* 19, no. 1 (June 2014).

Shin, Laura. "Medical Identity Theft: How the Health Care Industry Is Failing Us." *Fortune*, August 31, 2014.

Slack, Warner. "The Patient's Right to Decide." *Lancet* 2, no. 8031 (July 30, 1977): 240.

Slack, Warner, et al. "Evaluation of Computer-Based Medical Histories Taken by Patients at Home." *Journal of the American Medical Informatics Association* 19, no. 4 (2012): 545–48.

———. "Test–Retest Reliability in a Computer-Based Medical History." *Journal of the American Medical Informatics Association* 18 (November 27, 2010): 4.

Sloane, Leonard. "Business People: A New Chief for I.M.S." *New York Times*, October 12, 1981.

Smith, Christopher R. "Somebody's Watching Me: Protecting Patient Privacy in De-Identified Prescription Health Information." *Vermont Law Review* 36 (2011).

Smith, Mickey. "Some Historical Perspectives on the Marketing of Medicines in the Twentieth Century." *Journal of Pharmaceutical Marketing & Management* 18, no. 1 (2006): 13.

———. "The Legislative Environment of Pharmaceutical Marketing." *Journal of Pharmaceutical Marketing & Management* 18, no. 1 (2006): 73.

Solomon, D. H., S. Schneeweiss, R. J. Glynn, Y. Kiyota, R. Levin, H. Mogun, and J. Avorn. "Relationship Between Selective Cyclooxygenase-2 Inhibitors and Acute Myocardial Infarction in Older Adults." *Circulation* 109, no. 17 (May 4, 2004): 2068–73.

Soumerai, S. B., and J. Avorn. "Principles of Educational Outreach ('Academic Detailing') to Improve Clinical Decision Making." *Journal of the American Medical Association* 263, no. 4 (1990): 549–56.

Southern, Walter. "Sources of Drug Market Data." *Pharmacy in History* 44, no. 2 (2002): 5.

Stark, Karl. "Clued In to Who's Prescribing What." *Philadelphia Inquirer*, September 16, 2007.

Steinbrook, R. "For Sale: Physicians' Prescribing Data." *New England Journal of Medicine* 354, no. 26 (2006): 2745–47.

Stolberg, Sheryl Gay, and Jeff Gerth. "High-Tech Stealth Being Used to Sway Doctor Prescriptions." *New York Times*, November 16, 2000.

Suka, M., K. Yoshida, and S. Matsuda. "Effect of Annual Health Checkups on Medical Expenditures in Japanese Middle-Aged Workers." *Journal of Occupational and Environmental Medicine* 51, no. 4 (2009): 456–61.

Sullivan, June M. "HIPAA: A Practical Guide to the Privacy and Security of Health Data." Health Law Section, American Bar Association, 2004.

Sweeney, Latanya. "Matching Known Patients to Health Records in Washington State Data." Paper 1089-1. Data Privacy Lab, Harvard University, Cambridge, MA, June 2013, http://perma.cc/S5CK-J9D9.

———. "Patient Identifiability in Pharmaceutical Marketing Data." Working paper 1015. Data Privacy Lab, Harvard University, Cambridge, MA, 2011.

———. "Patient Privacy Risks in U.S. Supreme Court Case Sorrell v. IMS Health Inc.: Response to Amici Brief of El Emam and Yakowitz." Working paper 1027-1015B. Data Privacy Lab, Harvard University, Cambridge, MA, 2011.

———. "Uniqueness of Simple Demographics in the U.S. Population." Technical report LIDAP-WP4, Data Privacy Laboratory, School of Computer Science, Carnegie Mellon University, Pittsburgh, 2000.

Sweeney, Latanya, Akua Abu, and Julia Winn. "Identifying Participants in the Personal Genome Project by Name." White paper 1021-1. Data Privacy Lab, Harvard University, Cambridge, MA, April 29, 2013, http://perma.cc/3B3P-CJN6.

Sweeney, Latanya, Mercè Crosas, and Michael Bar-Sinai. "Sharing Sensitive Data with Confidence: The Datatags System." *Technology Science* (October 16, 2015). Archived at http://perma.cc/35YY-H7Z5.

Sweeney, Latanya, and Yoo Ji Su. "De-anonymizing South Korean Resident Registration Numbers Shared in Prescription Data." *Journal of Technology Science* (September 29, 2015).

Swire, Peter. "Application of IBM Anonymous Resolution to the Health Care Sector." On Demand Business, IBM, Las Vegas, February 2006, 30.

Takabayashi, K., S. Doi, and T. Suzuki. "Japanese EMRs and IT in Medicine: Expansion, Integration, and Reuse of Data." *Healthcare Informatics Research* 17, no. 3 (2011): 178–83.

Tamersoy, Acar, Grigorios Loukides, Mehmet Ercan Nergiz, Yucel Saygin, and Bradley Malin. "Anonymization of Longitudinal Electronic Medical Records." *IEEE Transactions on Information Technology in Biomedicine* 16, no. 3 (May 2012).

Tanaka, Hiroshi. "Current Status of Electronic Health Record Dissemination in Japan." *Japan Medical Association Journal* 50, no. 5 (2007): 5.

Tanner, Adam. "Data Brokers Are Now Selling Your Car's Location For $10 Online." *Forbes*, July 10, 2013.

Taylor, Lynne. "Restrictions on IMS Rx Data Sales Still Needed, Says UK Watchdog." *Pharma Times*, December 24, 2013.

TechNavio Insights. "Global Big Data Market in the Healthcare Sector 2011–15." *TechNavio Insights* 38.

Terhune, Chad. "They Know What's in Your Medicine Cabinet." *Bloomberg*, July 22, 2008.

Tierney, W. M., S. A. Alpert, A. Byrket, K. Caine, J. C. Leventhal, E. M. Meslin, and P. H. Schwartz. "Provider Responses to Patients Controlling Access to Their Electronic Health Records: A Prospective Cohort Study in Primary Care." *Journal of General Internal Medicine* 30, suppl. 1 (2015): S31–S37.

Tripathi, M. "EHR Evolution: Policy and Legislation Forces Changing the EHR." *Journal of the American Health Information Management Association* 83, no. 10 (2012): 24–29; quiz 30.

Tu, K., T. Mitiku, D. S. Lee, H. Guo, and J. V. Tu. "Validation of Physician Billing and Hospitalization Data to Identify Patients with Ischemic Heart Disease Using Data from the Electronic Medical Record Administrative Data Linked Database (EMRALD)." *Canadian Journal of Cardiology* 26, no. 7 (2010): e225–e28.

Tuck, Lon. "Convictions of the Collector." *Washington Post*, September 21, 1986.

Ullyot, Glenn E., Barbara Hodsdon Ullyot, and Leo B. Slater. "The Metamorphosis of Smith-Kline & French to Smith Kline Beecham: 1925–1998." *Bulletin for the History of Chemistry* 25, no. 1 (2000): 16–20.

US Department of Veterans Affairs. "Blueprint for Excellence." Veterans Health Administration, September 21, 2014.

Ventola, C. L. "Direct-to-Consumer Pharmaceutical Advertising: Therapeutic or Toxic?" *Pharmacy and Therapeutics* 36, no. 10 (2011): 669–84.

Vivian, Jesse. "Pharmacists Beware: Data Mining Unlawful." *U.S. Pharmacist*, June 18, 2009, 2.

Walsh, Lawrence. "Pharmacies Can Sell, Transfer Prescription Files." *Pittsburgh Post-Gazette*, February 20, 2002.

Walton, J., R. Doll, W. Asscher, R. Hurley, M. Langman, R. Gillon, D. Strachan, N. Wald, and P. Fletcher. "Consequences for Research If Use of Anonymised Patient Data Breaches Confidentiality." *British Medical Journal* 319, no. 7221 (1999): 1366.

Watkins, J. L., et al. "Clinical Impact of Selective and Nonselective Beta-Blockers on Survival in Patients with Ovarian Cancer." *Cancer* 121 (2015): 3444–51, doi: 10.1002/cncr.29392.

Weber, Bruce. "Mortimer D. Sackler, Arts Patron, Dies at 93." *New York Times*, March 31, 2010.

Weed, Lawrence L. "Medical Records That Guide and Teach." *New England Journal of Medicine* 278, no. 11 (March 14, 1968): 593–600.

Weed, Lawrence L., and Lincoln Weed. "Diagnosing Diagnostic Failure." *Diagnosis* 1, no. 1 (January 8, 2014): 4.

Wentz, Laurel. "Robert Louis-Dreyfus, Former Saatchi CEO, Dies at 63." *Advertising Age*, July 6, 2009.

Wettermark, B., et al. "The Nordic Prescription Databases as a Resource for Pharmacoepidemiological Research: A Literature Review." *Pharmacoepidemiology and Drug Safety* 22, no. 7 (2013): 691–99.

Whalen, Jeanne. "Drug Makers Replace Reps with Digital Tools." *Wall Street Journal*, May 10, 2011.

Whitney, Jake. "Big (Brother) Pharma." *New Republic*, August 29, 2006.

Wiggins, Phillip. "Tracking Industry Drug Sales." *New York Times*, March 23, 1979.

Williams, David F., Nicholas G. Anderson, and John S. Pollack. "Making the Most of EHR Data." *New Retina MD* (Fall 2013): 3.

Wilson, John, and Adam Bock. "The Benefit of Using Both Claims Data and Electronic Medical Record Data in Health Care Analysis." White paper. Optum, 2012.

Wolf, Asher. "Thanks to Care.Data, Your Secrets Are No Longer Safe with Your GP." *Wired*, February 7, 2014.

Wood, Alexandra, et al. "Integrating Approaches to Privacy Across the Research Lifecycle: Long-Term Longitudinal Studies." Berkman Center Research Publication 2014-12 Harvard University, Cambridge, MA, July 22, 2014. Archived at https://perma.cc/S9EK-SXM3.

Wright, A. "You, Me, and the Computer Makes Three: Navigating the Doctor-Patient Relationship in the Age of Electronic Health Records." *Journal of General Internal Medicine* 30, no. 1 (2015): 1–2.

Yakowitz, Jane, and Daniel Barth-Jones. "The Illusory Privacy Problem in Sorrell v. IMS Health." Edited by Tech Policy Institute, May 2011.

Yasnoff, W. A., L. Sweeney, and E. H. Shortliffe. "Putting Health IT on the Path to Success." *Journal of the American Medical Association* 309, no. 10 (2013): 989–90.

Yasunaga, H., T. Imamura, S. Yamaki, and H. Endo. "Computerizing Medical Records in Japan." *International Journal of Medical Informatics* 77, no. 10 (2008): 708–13.

Zigomitros, Athanasios, Agusti Solanas, and Constantinos Patsakis. "The Role of Inference in the Anonymization of Medical Records." In *2014 IEEE 27th International Symposium on Computer-Based Medical Systems*. Washington, DC: IEEE Computer Society, 2014.

Zoutman, D. E., B. D. Ford, and A. R. Bassili. "The Confidentiality of Patient and Physician Information in Pharmacy Prescription Records." *Canadian Medical Association Journal* 170, no. 5 (2004): 815–16.

INDEX